27|6|08

Thinking Through the Skin

This exciting new collection engages with and extends the growing feminist literature on lived and imagined embodiment. It argues for consideration of the skin as a site where bodies take form, suggesting that skin is already written upon, as well as being open to re-inscription. Divided into parts on skin encounters, skin surfaces and skin sites, the contributions in the book are informed by psychoanalytical, phenomenological and post-colonial approaches to embodiment, as well as by feminist theory.

Individual contributors consider issues such as: the significance of piercing, tattooing and tanning; the assault of self-harm upon the skin; skin as the site of memory and forgetting; the relationship between human and robotic skins; skin colour; the relation between body painting and the land among the indigenous people of Australia; and the cultural economy of fur in Canada.

Whether the skin is mortified or glorified, marked or scarred by ageing or disease, or stretched in enveloping the skin of another in pregnancy, it is lived as both a boundary and a point of connection. The skin is the place where one touches and is touched by others; it is both the most intimate of experiences and the most public marker of raced, sexed and national histories.

This book will be essential reading for students and academics specialising in feminist and body theory. Contributors include Jennifer Biddle, Claudia Castañeda, Steven Connor, Penelope Deutscher, Jane Kilby, Chantal Nadeau, Elspeth Probyn, Jay Prosser, Renata Salecl, Margrit Shildrick, Tina Takemoto, Shirley Tate and Imogen Tyler.

Sara Ahmed is Senior Lecturer in the Institute for Women's Studies at Lancaster University. **Jackie Stacey** is Reader in Sociology and Women's Studies in the Department of Sociology, Lancaster University. They are currently Co-Directors of the Institute for Women's Studies at Lancaster University.

Transformations: Thinking Through Feminism
Edited by: Maureen McNeil
Institute of Women's Studies, Lancaster University
Lynne Pearce
Department of English, Lancaster University
Beverley Skeggs
Department of Sociology, Manchester University

Advisory editorial board:

Sara Ahmed, Lancaster University, UK; Linda Anderson, University of Newcastle upon Tyne, UK; Lauren Berlant, University of Chicago, USA; Rosemary Betterton, Lancaster University, UK; Christine Bold, Guelph University, Canada; Avtar Brah, University of London, UK; Tess Cosslett, Lancaster University, UK; Barbara Creed, University of Melbourne, Australia; Laura Doan, State University of New York at Geneseo, USA; Mary Evans, University of Canterbury at Kent, UK; Sneja Gunew, University of British Columbia, Canada; Donna Haraway, University of California at Santa Cruz, USA; Joanna Hodge, Manchester Metropolitan University, UK; Christina Hughes, University of Warwick, UK; Grace Jantzen, Manchester University, UK; Maria Jarvela, Oulu University, Finland; Annette Kuhn, Lancaster University, UK; Celia Lury, Goldsmiths College, London, UK; Gail Low, Dundee University, Scotland; Marcia Pointon, Manchester University, UK; Jenny Popay, University of Salford, UK; Elspeth Probyn, University of Sydney, Australia; Kay Schaffer, Adelaide University, Australia; Jackie Stacey, Lancaster University, UK; Penny Summerfield, Manchester University, UK; Jane Sunderland, Lancaster University, UK; Carol Thomas, Lancaster University, UK; Gill Valentine, University of Sheffield, UK; Lorna Weir, York University, Canada; Sue Wise, Lancaster University, UK; Alison Young, University of Melbourne, Australia.

Other books in the series include:

Transformations: Thinking Through Feminism
Edited by Sara Ahmed, Jane Kilby, Celia Lury, Maureen McNeil and Beverley Skeggs

Strange Encounters: Embodied Others in Post-Coloniality
Sara Ahmed

Feminism and Autobiography: Texts, Theories, Methods
Edited by Tess Cosslett, Celia Lury and Penny Summerfield

Advertising and Consumer Citizenship: Gender, Images and Rights
Anne M. Cronin

Mothering the Self: Mothers, Daughters, Subjects
Stephanie Lawler

Thinking Through the Skin

**Edited by Sara Ahmed and
Jackie Stacey**

London and New York

First published 2001
by Routledge
2 Park Square, Milton Park, Abingdon, Oxon, OX14 4RN

Simultaneously published in the USA and Canada
by Routledge
270 Madison Ave, New York NY 10016

Routledge is an imprint of the Taylor & Francis Group

Transferred to Digital Printing 2005

Typeset in Baskerville by RefineCatch Limited, Bungay, Suffolk

British Library Cataloguing in Publication Data
A catalogue record for this book is available from the British Library

Library of Congress Cataloging in Publication Data
Thinking through the skin/edited by Sara Ahmed and Jackie Stacey.
        p. cm. – (Transformations)
    Includes bibliographical references and index.
    1. Skin – Social aspects. 2. Body, Human – Social aspects. 3. Feminist
theory. I. Ahmed, Sara. II. Stacey, Jackie. III. Series.
GT498.S56 T55 2000
    306.4 – dc21   2001019140

ISBN 0–415–22355–5 (hbk)
ISBN 0–415–22356–3 (pbk)

Printed and bound by Antony Rowe Ltd, Eastbourne

Contents

Plates

Notes on contributors

Sara Ahmed is Senior Lecturer in Women's Studies at Lancaster University. She is currently co-director, with Jackie Stacey, of the Institute for Women's Studies. Her first book, *Differences that Matter: Feminist Theory and Postmodernism*, was published in 1998. She has since published two books in the Routledge Transformations series, *Strange Encounters: Embodied Others and Postcoloniality* (2000) and (co-edited with Jane Kilby, Celia Lury, Maureen McNeil and Beverley Skeggs) *Transformations: Thinking Through Feminism* (2000).

Jennifer Biddle lectures in Anthropology at Macquarie University in Sydney, Australia. She has worked with Warlpiri Aboriginal Women since 1989, and writes on art, literacy, affect and embodiment in relation to cultural difference.

Claudia Castañeda is Lecturer in the Centre for Science Studies and Institute for Women's Studies at Lancaster University. Her work lies in the area of the cultural and feminist studies of science and technology. Her publications include *Figurations: Child, Bodies, Worlds* (2002, forthcoming) and 'Child Organ Stealing Stories: Risk, Rumour and Reproductive Technologies' in Barbara Adam and Joost van Loon (eds) *Risks, Technologies, Futures* (2000).

Steven Connor is Professor of Modern Literature and Theory at Birkbeck College, London. He is the author of numerous works on literature and cultural theory, including books on Dickens, Beckett, Joyce and contemporary fiction, as well as *Postmodernist Culture: An Introduction to Theories of the Contemporary* (1989, 1996), *Theory and Cultural Value* (1992) and *A Cultural History of Ventriloquism* (2000). Other essays, including work in progress can be found on his website at www.bbk.ac.uk/eh/skc/

Penelope Deutscher is Senior Lecturer in the Department of Philosophy, Australian National University. She is the author of *Yielding Gender: Feminism, Deconstruction and the History of Philosophy* (1997) and co-editor (with Kelly Oliver) of *Enigmas: Essays on Sarah Kofman* (1999).

Jane Kilby has recently completed her doctoral thesis in the Institute for Women's Studies at Lancaster University on the contemporary conditions of possibility for childhood sexual trauma testimony. She is co-editor of

Transformations: Thinking Through Feminism, with Sara Ahmed, Celia Lury, Maureen McNeil and Beverley Skeggs (2000) and is currently working on editing her thesis into a book. She has begun a new research project on self-harm as a traumatic form of embodied testimony.

Chantal Nadeau is Assistant Professor in the Department of Communication Studies, Concordia University, Montreal, where she teaches film criticism, cultural studies and feminist theory. She has published and given lectures on women's cinema, popular culture and lesbian representation. Her book on the sexual and colonial economy of fur in Canada and Québec entitled *Fur Nation: From the 'Beaver' to Brigitte Bardot* is to be published in 2001.

Elspeth Probyn is Associate Professor of Gender Studies at University of Sydney, Australia. She is the author of numerous publications on feminism and queer theory including *Sexing the Self* (1993), *Outside Belongings* (1996) and *Carnal Appetites: FoodSexIdentities* (2000).

Jay Prosser is Lecturer in American Literature at the University of Leeds. He is the author of *Second Skins: The Body Narratives of Transsexuality* (1998), and is currently writing a book on autobiography and skin disorders.

Renata Salecl is a philosopher and sociologist. She is Senior Researcher at the Institute of Criminology at the Faculty of Law, University of Ljubljana and Centennial Professor at the London School of Economics. She is the author of *The Spoils of Freedom* (1994), and *(Per)versions of Love and Hate* (1998) and the editor of *Sexuation* (2000).

Margrit Shildrick is Senior Research Fellow in Humanities and Social Sciences at Staffordshire University. She has published extensively in the area of feminist philosophy and bioethics, and has recently completed a book about encounters with the vulnerable self. She is the author of *Leaky Bodies and Boundaries: Feminism, Postmodernism and (Bio)ethics* (1997) and co-editor, with Janet Price, of both *Vital Signs: Feminist Reconfigurations of the Bio/logical Body* (1998) and *Feminist Theory and the Body: A Reader* (1999).

Jackie Stacey is Reader in Sociology and Women's Studies in the Department of Sociology at Lancaster University. She is currently co-director, with Sara Ahmed, of the Institute for Women's Studies. Her publications include *Star Gazing: Female Spectatorship* (1994), *Teratologies: A Cultural Study of Cancer* (1997) and (with Sarah Franklin and Celia Lury) *Global Nature, Global Culture* (2000). She is also an editor of the film and television studies journal *Screen*.

Tina Takemoto is Assistant Professor in Art History at Loyola Marymount University and is currently completing her doctoral research on illness, race and collaborative performance art in Visual and Cultural Studies at the University of Rochester.

Shirley Tate is Lecturer in Sociology in the Sociology Department at Lancaster University. She has a Ph.D. from Lancaster University based on research on

Black British identities and hybridity. Her research interests are 'race', ethnicity and identity and the body. Her other recent and forthcoming publications are 'Making your Body your Signature: Weight-training and Transgressive Femininities' in S. Roseneil and J. Seymour (eds) *Practising Identities: Power, Resistance* (1999), 'Is it possible to find hybridity in Black people's narratives?' in J. Helsloot and C. Wijers *Roots and Rituals: Managing Ethnicity* (2000) and 'Colour Matters, "Race" Matters: African Caribbean Identity in the 20th Century', forthcoming in Christian M. *et al.* (eds) *African Caribbean Identity in the Twentieth Century*.

Imogen Tyler is Lecturer in the Institute for Cultural Research at Lancaster University and is currently working on a book on gender and narcissism. Her publications include 'Re-framing Pregnant Embodiment' in Sara Ahmed, Jane Kilby, Celia Lury, Maureen McNeil and Beverley Skeggs (eds) *Transformations: Thinking Through Feminism* (Routledge 2000).

Series editors' preface

Modern feminism has been a body politics. From the women's suffrage hunger strikers that figured at the beginning of the twentieth century to the cyborgs and nomads that gained prominence at the end of that century, feminists have registered their political protests and aspirations in and through their bodies. But bodies also trouble feminism and have troubled feminists: physically, psychically, intellectually, politically. Such troubling has animated feminist thinking, including Simone de Beauvoir's regret that women were, for the most part, 'shut up in immanence', and Shulamith Firestone's claim that 'women's reproductive biology . . . accounted for [their] original and continued oppression'. In contrast, celebration of female anatomy and functioning has also recurringly inspired feminist theory in forms as diverse as Luce Irigaray's philosophy of 'two lips', or Sara Ruddick's 'maternal thinking'. Moreover, the most widely circulated text of second-wave feminism is, in fact, *Our Bodies Ourselves*.

The editors of *Thinking Through the Skin* are mindful of this genealogy, situating this collection in relation to 'the feminist project of taking bodies seriously as both the subject and object of thinking' (p. 3). Nevertheless, the collection also acknowledges that, despite the genealogy of feminist body politics, feminists have no priority within this domain. Genealogical awareness and critical openness make this volume an appropriate and important contribution to the Transformations Series which shows that, far from being exhausted, there is new life in, and new forms of, feminist body politics.

As editors it is our hope that the Transformation Series will blend empirical and theoretical research that registers current concerns, whilst taking them in challenging, new directions. *Thinking Through the Skin* embodies these expectations. The specification of corporeal focus – skin – facilitates a textured exploration of legacies, encounters and new trajectories in body politics. The result is a fresh and invigorating set of investigations of the meaning and significance of skin. Readers are invited to feel their way into contemporary skin politics in its diverse manifestations – bodily self-harm, fur trading, racist markings, robotics, and so on – through a rich tapestry of empirical analysis and theoretical development.

Maureen McNeil
Lynne Pearce

Acknowledgements

We would like to thank past and present members of the Institute for Women's Studies for all their support, in particular those who contributed to the *Thinking Through the Skin* seminar series that took place in 1997–1998 at Lancaster University. We are particularly grateful to Maureen McNeil for her detailed and insightful reading of the manuscript and to Hilary Hinds for her generous help at the proof stage.

The authors and publishers would also like to thank the following for granting permission to reproduce material in this work:

Jennifer Biddle would like to thank the *Kirda* and *Kurdungurlu* of *Purlapa Wiri Jukurrpa* in Lajamanu, NT, for their permission to reproduce the photo on p. 181.

Angela Ellsworth and Tina Takemoto for their 'Her/She Senses Imag(in)ed Malady' images.

Annie Leibovitz and *Vanity Fair* for the Demi Moore *Vanity Fair* cover, August 1991.

McGill University Archives for the *My Fur Lady* poster.

Susan McKenna and Elizabeth Hynes for 'Instructions of the Body', 'The Re-integration of Self' and 'Book of Skin'.

Louise Roxanne Pembroke for her 'Professional Thought Disorder' series of illustrations.

A shorter version of Renata Salecl's chapter 'Cut in the body: from clitoridectomy to body art' appeared in *New Formations*, 1998, 35: 28–42.

Introduction

Dermographies

Sara Ahmed and Jackie Stacey

> Why should our bodies end at the skin, or include at best other beings encapsulated by skin?
>
> (Donna Haraway 1991: 178)

This book takes the 'skin' not only as its object, but as a point of departure for a different way of thinking. We seek to think *about* the skin, but also to think *with* or *through* the skin. Such an approach engenders a way of thinking that attends to the forms and folds of living skin at the same time as it takes the shape of such skin, as it forms and re-forms, unfolds and refolds. Whilst this collection stages an intimate dialogue with the growing feminist literature on lived and imagined embodiment, it avoids taking 'the body' as its privileged figure. Instead, it focuses on 'the skin', as the outer covering of the body that both 'protects us from others and exposes us to them' (Cataldi 1993: 145). In making this shift, we call for a skin-tight politics, a politics that takes as its orientation not the body as such, but the fleshy interface between bodies and worlds. 'Thinking through the skin' is a thinking that reflects, not on the body as the lost object of thought, but on inter-embodiment, on the mode of being-with and being-for, where one touches and is touched by others.

Thinking Through the Skin poses the question of how skin becomes, rather than simply is, meaningful. To ask such a question is to suggest that the skin is always open to being read. If the skin is always open to being read (and being read differently), we can also consider the ways in which these various techniques for reading produce skins in specific and determinate ways. For example, in consumer culture we are encouraged to read skin, especially feminine skin, as something that needs to be worked upon in order to be protected from the passage of time or the severity of the external world, and in order to retain its marker of gender difference in the softness of its feel. We may be encouraged to fear 'skin conditions' and to use creams to prevent the signs of ageing from appearing on our skins. We may worry about the stretch marks that tear (through) the skin, both an affect and sign of the expansion and contraction of our bodily forms, as Imogen Tyler discusses in her chapter on pregnant embodiment. Or, as Tina Takemoto suggests in her chapter, we may feel pressured to cover the traces of illness and surgery, succumbing to or resisting the shame of their bodily evidence. Or, indeed, as Jay Prosser explores in his chapter on skin autobiographies, we may dread the diseases in which the skin falls away, revealing the subject's vulnerability to external scrutiny.

Despite this apparently ubiquitous desire for smooth skin, the skin is also subject to many forms of assault in contemporary culture, as Steven Connor suggests in his chapter. The skin surface, as the 'bearer or scene of meaning', is pierced, cut and tattooed. Indeed, skin surfaces will always fail to be smooth, whether that failure is dependent upon the deliberate markings of skin or upon the unwanted traces of bodily changes or medical intervention, or upon the impossible desires produced by consumer culture. As Anne McClintock has demonstrated, the imperative of consumption is to work towards smooth and shiny surfaces that conceal the signs of labour as well as time (McClintock 1995: 219). Importantly, the desire for smooth skin requires that skin surfaces are not smooth in the present.

The marking of the skin is linked to both its temporal and spatial dimensions. Skin is temporal in the sense that it is affected by the passing of time or, to put it differently, it materialises that passing in the accumulation of marks, of wrinkles, lines and creases, as well as in the literal disintegration of skin. As Penelope Deutscher's chapter suggests, we are invited to 'see' the marks on the body as signs of ageing, as the tear of time. Furthermore, as Jay Prosser argues in his contribution, skin remembers: skin surfaces record our personal biographies, however imperfectly. The skin is also spatial in the sense that it expands and contracts. Indeed, the skin, as bodyscape, is inhabited by, as well as inhabiting, the space of the nation and the landscape, as Chantal Nadeau and Jennifer Biddle suggest in their chapters. As a result, the skin is not simply in the present (in the here or the now); in so far as it has multiple histories and unimaginable futures, it is worked upon, and indeed, it is worked towards.

As a way of 'thinking through the skin', we ask: How does the skin come to be written and narrated? How is the skin managed by subjects, others and nations? We examine the different technologies of the skin and how particular discourses – medical, scientific, aesthetic – intersect to produce the intelligible skin, even when the skin cannot be held in place by such knowledges. This book hence draws on multiple theoretical and disciplinary paradigms to consider how the skin is lived, read, written, narrated, seen, touched, managed, worked, cut, remembered, produced and known. These diverse approaches to thinking about the skin as a boundary-object, and as the site of exposure or connectedness, invite the reader to consider how the borders between bodies are unstable and how such borders are already crossed by differences that refuse to be contained on the 'inside' or the 'outside' of bodies.

Thinking bodies

Our title clearly references Jane Gallop's book *Thinking Through the Body* (1988), which represents one of the many important feminist contributions to theorising embodiment. As her title indicates, Gallop's intervention demonstrated that the body, which has been read by traditional philosophy as mere and brute matter, remains to be thought. Here, bodies are no longer assumed simply to be given in and to the world but are rather understood as both the locus of thinking – the site from which thinking takes place – and as the object of thought – as being already subject to interpretation and conceptualisation. As Elaine Scarry has shown in *The Body in Pain*, the interfaces between bodies and their worlds are made and unmade through social practices, the pain of which may shatter language and defy its representational potential (1985: 5). Thus the practices of thinking are not separated from the realm of the body but are implicated in the passion, emotions and materiality that are associated with lived embodiment. The task of *Thinking Through the Skin* is, at one level, to continue the feminist project of taking bodies seriously as both the subject and object of thinking.

Certainly, within recent feminist theory, 'bodies' have become a privileged focus of attention. This can partly be explained by the feminist recognition that women's marginalisation from philosophical discourses and the public sphere has been produced through the association between masculinity and reason and femininity and the body. The feminist concern with revaluing the body, and undermining such mind/body dualism, has led to an acknowledgement that bodies are not simply given (as 'nature'), that bodies are differentiated and that subjectivity and identity cannot be separated from specific forms of embodiment (Bordo 1993). An approach which refuses to privilege mind over body, and which assumes that the body cannot be transcended, is one which thus emphasises contingency, locatedness, the irreducibility of difference, the passage of emotions and desire, and the worldliness of being.

Although *Thinking Through the Skin* will be read as a contribution to feminist theories of embodiment, it also seeks to provide a critique of how 'the body' can become a privileged object within feminist theory.[1] For in some sense, the very argument that 'the body' has been elided, negated and devalued in masculinist thought can fetishise the body, can allow it to appear as if it is an object that could be simply missing. In *Thinking Through the Skin*, we do not assume that we can find difference simply through evoking the lost object of the body. What is required, we suggest, is a recognition of the function of social differences in establishing the very boundaries which appear to mark out 'the body'. Otherwise, we are in danger of fetishising 'the body' by assuming that it contains these differences within the singularity of its figure.

In order to address the question of embodiment without fetishising the body as the lost object, this book calls for us to think, instead, through the skin. This is not to replace one fetish with another (the body with the skin), but rather we seek to interrogate how 'the skin' is attributed a meaning and logic of its own. The task of the book is thus in part to think through how 'the skin' acquires the status of a 'fetish', that is, how the skin is assumed to contain either the body, identity, well-being or value. It is the fetishising of the skin as boundary-object that allows the contours of the body to appear as a given. In Shirley Tate's chapter, for example, there is an analysis of how racial differences are read on or even off the surface of the skin (skin colour). Tate examines how processes of abjection – the expulsion of what is undesirable from the body (see Kristeva 1982) – serve to constitute and transgress the skin as a boundary in the encounters with Black others who are already associated with 'skin' and seen as the 'cause' of abjection. Furthermore, as Takemoto suggests in her contribution, we often (wrongly) assume we can know an other through the sight of the skin and through its marking. In other words, not only is skin assumed to be a sign of the subject's interiority (for example, what it means to be white or Black, ill or well), but the skin is also assumed to reflect the truth of the other and to give us access to the other's being. As these contributions suggest, the skin is fetishised as a boundary-object by a variety of different and overlapping discourses which measure the truth, health or nature of bodies through the skin. It is one of the tasks of this book to account for the cultural function of this skin fetishism.

In so far as we frame this book around the social and cultural production of the skin, we follow the work of Elizabeth Grosz, Rosi Braidotti and Judith Butler. In Grosz's *Volatile Bodies*, the challenge to mind/body dualism also challenges the surface/depth model of subjectivity (1994: 218). For Grosz, following from Gilles Deleuze and Felix Guattari (1992), embodiment involves the intensity of desires and flows which themselves produce the effect of 'depth' or interiority. In Rosi Braidotti's work, also in dialogue with Deleuze and Guattari, the body is understood in terms of folding: 'it is a folding-in of external influences and a simultaneous unfolding outwards of affects' (2000: 159). For Judith Butler, taking a different route through Foucault and Lacan, the 'materialisation' of the body is defined as an 'effect of boundary, surface and fixity' (1993: 9). Grosz, Braidotti and Butler have shown that challenging the mind/body dualism also requires a rethinking of the relationship between depth and surface, between inside and outside and between self and other. To this extent, these writers all refuse to take the contours or boundaries of the body for granted: they refuse to simply inhabit the skin or to assume that the skin cloaks the body. Hence we can read their work as contributing to a feminist philosophy of skin. This is not to suggest that skin is their object, but rather that we can understand their work on embodiment as a rethinking of how skin comes to materialise in the forms that it does, at the same time as they show how skins, as well as other bodily surfaces and folds, expose bodies to other bodies, rather than simply containing 'the body' as such.

Inter-embodiment

As well as seeking to challenge the long-standing traditions of thinking that have denigrated the body in favour of the mind, feminist and other critical work on embodiment has also emerged as a response to the 'disembodying' models of power and subjectivity brought centre-stage by the impact of dominant models of structuralism and poststructuralism, which placed language both literally and metonymically at the centre of theories of culture. Whilst welcoming the ways in which these models dislodged some of the problematic economic and technological determinism of many Marxist understandings of culture, some feminist writers have remained highly critical of the 'subjects without bodies' so many of these theories posited.[2] Whilst much feminist work on embodiment continues numerous dialogues with these theoretical frameworks, the proliferation of writing on the body nevertheless testifies to a frustration with their refusal to address how subjectivities are necessarily embodied.

Two recent turns are indicative of the desire for an increasingly located and, indeed, fleshy body. First, feminists have turned to Maurice Merleau-Ponty for a phenomenological account of inter-embodiment. For example, Gail Weiss (1999) has offered an exploration of the relationships between body images, imaginary morphologies and materialisations. Her approach stresses the significance of Merleau-Ponty's notion of 'intercorporeality': 'to describe embodiment as intercorporeality is to emphasize that the experience of being embodied is never a private affair, but is always already mediated by our continual interactions with other human and non-human bodies' (Weiss 1999: 5). In Merleau-Ponty's (1968) work, there is an emphasis on embodiment, not only as fleshy and material but also as 'wordly', as being in an intimate and living relationship to the world, which is a world made up of other bodies. Given his focus on the experiential, Merleau-Ponty's work attends to the multiplicity of sense perceptions: bodies can be touched as well as seen. Following from Merleau-Ponty and Cathryn Vasseleu (1998), Claudia Castañeda's contribution to this collection attends to the relationship between touch and the sociality of embodiment: one is always touched by others, not all of whom are necessarily human.

Merleau-Ponty theorises the fleshiness of such intercorporeality through considering the concept of the reversibility of touch:

> While each monocular vision, each touching with one sole hand has its own visible, its tactile, each is bound to every other vision, to every other touch; it is bound in such a way as to make up with them the experience of one sole body before one sole world, through a possibility for reversion, reconversion of its language into theirs, transfer and reversal. . . . Now why would this generality, which constitutes the unity of my body, not open it to other bodies? The handshake too is reversible; I can feel myself touched as well and at the same time as touching.
>
> (Merleau-Ponty 1968: 142)

For Merleau-Ponty the very experiences which make the body 'my body', as if it were a 'sole body before a sole world', are the very same experiences which open 'my body' to 'other bodies', in the simultaneous mutuality of touch and being touched, and seeing and being seen. In this sense, 'my body' does not 'belong to me': embodiment is what opens out the intimacy of 'myself' with others. The relationship between bodies is characterised by a 'with' that precedes, or is the condition of possibility for, the apartness of 'my body'. This 'with' is the fleshiness of the world which inhabits us and is inhabited by us – flesh, not understood simply as matter, but as the very sensibility of the seen, and the very sight of the sensible. Indeed, in Penelope Deutscher's contribution to this volume, it is the erotics of tactile encounters that open up a different way of thinking the body.

Skin opens our bodies to other bodies: through touch, the separation of self and other is undermined in the very intimacy or proximity of the encounter.

However, for feminist, queer and post-colonial critics there remain the troubling questions: If one is always with other bodies in a fleshy sociality, then how are we 'with' others differently? How does this inter-embodiment involve the social differentiation between bodily others? For example, in her recent book *The Skin of the Film: Intercultural Cinema, Embodiment and the Senses*, Laura Marks draws on phenomenology and Deleuzian theory to explore an embodied model of cinematic spectatorship (see also Sobchack 1992) that places cultural difference centre-stage. The image that evokes a sensual memory of lost loved ones (people, places, homes) operates through a distinctive visual register of touch: what Marks calls a 'haptic visuality'. Marks uses this notion of haptic visuality to explore the relationships of present, absent and remembered bodies and places in the category of 'intercultural cinema', a group of films and videos which interrogate the political issues of displacement and hybridity (Marks 2000: 2). For Marks, whereas the dominant mode of optic visuality 'sees things from enough distance to perceive them as distinct forms in deep space . . . [and] depends on a separation between the viewing subject and the object', in contrast haptic visuality refers to the way in which 'the eyes themselves function like organs of touch'. Rather than plunging the depth of the object, haptic looking moves over the surface, according to Marks, 'not to distinguish form so much as to discern texture' (Marks 2000: 162). Thus, the tactility of the image, the ways that spectators might touch the film with their eyes, is intimately bound up with the differential effects of diasporic culture in which the 'sometimes traumatic interrogation of personal and family memories, only . . . create[s] an empty space where no history is certain' (Marks 2000: 5).

Similarly, forms and processes of cultural differentiation are central to the way this book explores how bodies are 'with' other bodies. Feminists and other theorists have criticised the universalism of Merleau-Ponty's phenomenology of the body, and have tried to examine how bodies may be lived differently. For example, in her chapter in this volume, Jennifer Biddle considers how bodies are differentiated from each other, but not simply through the marking of the skin. And Margrit Shildrick's contribution seeks to think through the specificity of the embodiment of conjoined twins without assuming we can access the truth of their lived embodiment. As she suggests, to say that there are bodies that are marked as different from the normalised body is not to assume that we can know what that body is, or how it feels to inhabit it. So, while many of these chapters follow from the phenomenological emphasis on lived, felt inter-corporeality, they also suggest that such inter-corporeality is subject to forms of social differentiation, although such differences cannot simply be found on the bodies of those who are marked.

Several chapters in this book think of skin as a border, but as a border that feels. And yet the skin is not like a mirror, it does not reflect the truth of the inner self. Despite our desires to the contrary, skin 'lacks the depth, the interiority, we want it to give us' (Phelan 1997: 41). So although skin may have a testimonial function, the act of bearing witness to trauma, injustice, violence and the pain of others cannot involve simply the transformation of skin into voice, as Jane Kilby demonstrates in her chapter. While the nearness of others is always 'felt' on the skin, that nearness also involves distance, or the impossibility of getting inside the other's skin. As Tina Takemoto's chapter also suggests, skin encounters may only partially fulfil the needs and desires of the testifier and the witness, bringing them up against the limits of embodied empathy. Inter-embodiment is hence a way of thinking through the nearness of other others, but a nearness which involves distanciation and difference. Elspeth Probyn explores in her chapter how the nearness of others can be thought of in terms of the proximity and sensuality of eating, of breaking the skin or the seal, and of the moisture that drips from one body to another. Thinking through the skin is a thinking that attends not only to the sensuality of being-with-others, but also to the ethical implications of the impossibility of inhabiting the other's skin.

Materialising skin

Another significant way in which feminists and other critical theorists have sought to rethink lived embodiment, though with rather different outcomes from the phenomenological turn, is through the work of Freudian psychoanalyst Didier Anzieu (1989) in *The Skin Ego*. For Anzieu, the 'skin ego' refers to the 'mental image of which the Ego of the child makes use during the early phases of its development to represent itself as an Ego containing psychic contents, on the basis of its experience of the surface of the body' (1989: 40). Basing his model of subjectivity on the body rather than on language, Anzieu seeks to challenge the Lacanian wisdom encapsulated in the claim that 'the unconscious is structured like a language', arguing instead that 'the unconscious seems to me to be structured like a body' (cited in Prosser 1998: 66).

Like other writers keen to emphasise the fleshy refusals of the body to simply be 'an effect of language', Jay Prosser has turned to Anzieu's reworking of psycho-analysis in search of a fully embodied understanding of the subject. Indeed, in his book *Second Skins*, Prosser offers an account of the body narratives of transsexuality using Anzieu's theory of the way the subject develops a sense of a bounded ego through the touch of the surface of the body, the skin. Joining Anzieu in his challenge to the tendency towards 'desomatisation' since the rise of structuralism, in which the body's referentiality has been recast as 'psychic and cultural signified', Prosser advocates instead a model which 'works to reconstitute and sustain the material body as discrete, generative, or productive referent' (Prosser 1998: 66).

Like other psychoanalytic models, however, Anzieu's theory is premised on a number of problematic assumptions about embodiment and, most specifically, about the maternal body. Prosser is indeed aware of the need to think questions of sexual and racial difference more fully through the skin ego, and there remains much scope for extending these critiques of some of the basic categories in Anzieu's work. Indeed, Imogen Tyler's chapter in this collection challenges Anzieu's failure to attend to how the skin ego might itself be the site of social differentiation; in his conflation of the maternal body and the pregant body, she argues, Anzieu makes it impossible to conceptualise pregant embodiment as anything other than a generative environment. Tyler's intervention argues for an understanding of the differentiation *between* bodily others (who are not necessarily separated as beings, but who are also not as one).

One example from Prosser's account illustrates the broader demand for a theorisation of the fleshiness of bodies that reccurs throughout this book. Prosser raises a number of crucial questions about the transformability of the relationship between the self, the body and the skin in this narration of his own public exchange with the surgical performance artist Orlan. The perfomance, 'Orlan: Omnipresence', involved the surgical reconstruction of Orlan's face to 'resemble a computer composite of five canonical representations of beautiful women (the Mona Lisa and Botticelli's Venus among them)' (Prosser 1998: 61). The video of the surgery (originally relayed live to a number of international art galleries) was shown at a New York exhibition in 1993, where there was also a televised discussion with the artist. Contrary to many who celebrate Orlan's surgical performance as exemplifying 'an image trapped in a woman's body', and demonstrating 'that there is nothing behind the mask' (cited in Prosser 1998: 64), Prosser reads her performance of the 'literalisation of the body as costume' as providing 'an insane personification of the post-structuralist insistence on the absolute constructedness of the body' (Prosser 1998: 62). Posing the problem of how one's sense of identity might be transformed by the surgical changes to the body, Prosser raises the issue of transsexuality. Whilst intrigued by Orlan's claim to feel like 'une transsexuelle femme-a-femme', Prosser nevertheless concludes that Orlan's surgical performance showed much evidence of precisely 'the body's materiality (its fleshiness, its nonplasticity, and its nonperformativity)', not least in the puffy and bruised face of Orlan herself hidden behind enormous dark glasses (Prosser 1998: 62). For Prosser, then, a number of questions remain: 'If skin is a mask, where is the self in relation to the body's surface? Deeper than the skin (underneath the mask?) Or not "in" the flesh at all?'. In relation to transsexuality, he asks: Is our corporeal outside simply a 'mask', so detachable from, so insubstantial for, the self? (Prosser 1998: 62, 65).

We take from Prosser's work in *Second Skins* an imperative to rethink 'where' and 'how' materiality comes to be lived, as well as to figure as a limit and constraint to embodied lives. This imperative to attend to corporeal materiality has thus in part been related to the need to attend to the limits of transgression, to what resists being transformed. Bodies might resist the very reading of bodies as transformable; they may return, in this way, like the repressed, with symptoms that confound our reading. Our skin might sweat at the most unlikely of times, and betray feelings that we have not even admitted to ourselves. As Prosser suggests in his contribution to this volume, the skin's memories may not be conscious. And the skin might not be as straightforwardly transparent as it at first appears: it is not simply a voice that speaks to us through the changes in its colour or its contours. In a very different reading of Orlan in this collection, Renata Salecl suggests that the attempt to 'mark' the surface of the body is also an attempt to make the body 'permanent' and individual. In others words, she suggests that the desire to mark the body might also be read as a reaction against the postmodern discourse that the body is changeable. These conflicting readings of Orlan's performance exemplify how the skin becomes a site of contest over identity – over what it means to be a subject – but a contest that is very much specific to a particular time and place. While many of the contributors to this collection draw on the work of Anzieu in the *Skin Ego* alongside Merleau-Ponty's phenomenology, they also seek to complicate the apparent universalism of both models by asking what the specific historical conditions are in which skin comes to matter. The turn to Merleau-Ponty and to Anzieu (whatever reservations we might have about their apparent universalisms) is symptomatic of a more general move towards a model of embodiment that facilitates understanding of the processes through which bodies are lived and imagined in more visceral and substantial ways.

What we are calling for in this book is an understanding of how 'skins' have been inhabited, lived and indeed (re)produced very differently in historically specific situations. For example, in Chantal Nadeau's reflection on the relationship between skin, women and fur, she shows how histories of skin involve the transformation of skin into a sexualised and racialised commodity. At the same time, attending to such histories does not mean holding the skin in place: the skin can be re-imagined and relived, but the possibilities for this re-imagining and reliving are not endless, or a matter of choice.

The skin of the book

The first part of the book is entitled 'Skin surfaces'. Chapters in this section all offer accounts of the transformation of the skin's surface: the cutting of the skin (Salecl), the assault on the skin (Connor), the writing of the skin (Prosser), and the production of skin as surface (Tyler). But in each case the skin is considered as a surface in such a way as to challenge the idea that skin pre-exists inscription and is simply there as a blank outer covering awaiting the mark of culture. Each chapter explores the complexities of how the skin signifies in culture and the multiplicity of its figurations of the self, the body and of difference. The multiplication of skin surfaces in different cultural spaces suggests that the skin marks difference, as well as being marked by differences.

In Chapter 1, Renata Salecl begins by asking how we can explain how skins have become the object of forms of mutilation (including body piercing and clitoridectomy) without assuming the equivalance of these practices. Using a Lacanian framework, she suggests that such practices, which cut the skin, are different answers to the same question: 'What is the place of the subject in contemporary society?' Mapping the divisions of traditional, modern and postmodern as overlapping, and by no means mutually exclusive, modes of cultural formation, Salecl reads the cutting of the body as the enactment of the meaning of sexual difference in relation to the changing authority of 'the big Other', or the symbolic structure. Clitoridectomy is hence a forced choice that guarantees the subject's relationship to the big Other. Examining other skin practices, including tattooing, Salecl argues that 'making a cut in the body does not mean that the subject is simply playing with his or her identity; by irreversibly marking the body, the subject also protests against the ideology that makes everything changeable.' With a final analysis of such body artists as Orlan and Stelarc, Salecl shows how the inscriptions on postmodern skins are an attempt to make the skin the locus of the real, given the failure of the big Other to guarantee the Real in Lacanian terms in contemporary culture.

The contradictions at stake in contemporary skin inscriptions are also the subject of Steven Connor's chapter. Connor suggests that, on the one hand, the skin is the visible object of forms of imaginary and actual assault; but on the other, there is an anxiety and perceived need to care for the skin, a sense of its vulnerability and exposure. This chapter explores these tensions by complicating our understanding of what is at stake in assaults on the skin. In the first instance, we are asked to consider how the skin figures, how it is always written, or bears the marks of time. And yet, at the same time, Connor questions what is figured in skin, and what we can see in the skin surfaces that are multiplied in contemporary culture. As a result, Connor suggests that skin-assaults are not simply assaults on an already marked surface, but that they are assaults upon the skin as the bearer of meaning which is always yet to be inscribed; it is not simply about leaving marks, but also about the possibility of their erasure.

In his analysis of autobiographical narratives of skin (in particular, of skin disorders) in Chapter 3, Jay Prosser suggests that we become aware of skin as a visible surface through memory, and that skin remembers, both literally in its material surface and metaphorically in the signification given to the surface. Skin memories are phantasmatic, and burdened with the unconscious. This notion of skin memory draws on the work of Didier Anzieu (1989), who argues that the ego is first and foremost a skin ego: 'the projection in the psychic of the body'. Prosser examines how skin disorders affect this skin ego, alongside skins which are 'seen to be' damaged, such as Black skins. Both autobiography and skin disorders involve, as Updike puts it, 'scab picking'. Prosser shows how these 'skin autobiographies' are cathartic; they recover a skin ego that is damaged in the original skin memory. Skin memories are hence re-memories; they are as layered as skin itself.

In the final chapter in this section, Imogen Tyler explores ways of thinking through the skin of the pregnant subject in order to challenge the individualistic notions of 'the body' and 'the skin' which permeate so much philosophical and psychoanalytic theory, including, she argues, Anzieu's suggestive but deeply flawed model of the skin ego. In this context, Tyler offers a detailed reading of the photograph of the heavily pregnant Demi Moore that appeared on the front cover of *Vanity Fair* in 1991. Tyler stages this taboo-breaking moment in the history of the invisibility of pregnant bodies as an encounter between the structuring conventions of imaging the female body and the discursive limits of theoretical debates about embodiment and subjectivity. Tyler suggests this new visibility of pregnant celebrities might be read as a symptom of the intensification of technological intrusions into the pregnant body which have accompanied the emergence of foetal personhood. By examining how Anzieu's *The Skin Ego* remains premised on the negation of the mother's body, despite its emphasis on the contracting and expanding boundaries of the skin surface, Tyler suggests we need to think of the bodily specificity of pregnant skin, as a skin which envelops the skin of others.

The second part of the book is entitled 'Skin encounters'. Chapters in this section are concerned with how the skin involves encounters with others that challenge the separation of self and other. They examine the fluidity between bodies and do not take the boundary line of the skin for granted. Rather than thinking of the skin as holding the subject apart, they consider how skin opens bodies to other bodies, in the sense that skin registers how bodies are touched by other bodies. Refusing a model of either separation or merger, these chapters call for a theoretical reconsideration of the demarcation between self and other. The chapters examine different skin encounters: Elspeth Probyn considers proximity through her notion of eating skin; Tina Takemoto considers empathy as a response to others; Jane Kilby considers the closeness or intimacy of reading skin testimonies; Penelope Deutscher considers tactile encounters in relation to ageing skin; and Margrit Shildrick considers the ethics of relationship and connectedness.

Combining autobiography, family history and critical theory, Elspeth Probyn is concerned with the ethical significance of skin in Chapter 5. Probyn reflects on the desire for the skin of others, considering skin as both metaphor and metonym, as well as that which allows the self to 'eat' its way into the cultural present. Although she recognises the problematic history of that desire (where desire for the other often translates into the desire to inhabit the skin of the other), she also suggests we can understand its history differently. Rather than just thinking of the other as eaten and appropriated, Probyn invites us to think of eating skin as the transformation of the very border between self and other: eating skin transforms the one who eats and the one who is eaten in the very intimacy of the encounter. By telling the story of how her white grandmother masqueraded as a native Canadian woman, Probyn tries to rethink that history as itself opening up a different relationship between self and other, where the intensity of eating, as a desire that rips bodies apart and open, undermines the possibility of any assimilation. The sheer intensity of eating, as an eating of skin (rather than an eating of one by the other), is for Probyn an ethical imperative. Ethics here becomes the prickly, porous and sticky site of skin itself, rather than the abstract duties or demands which keep others at a distance.

In a very different context, the ethics of responding to the skin of the other is explored by Tina Takemoto in Chapter 6. Posing the problem of the limits of empathy in relation to illness, Takemoto reflects on a collaborative project that she began with Angela Ellsworth when Ellsworth was diagnosed with lymphoma. Asking whether there can be a melancholia of illness, Takemoto reflects on how cancer leaves its mark on the skin; how the skin becomes an open wound. Responding to the illness of a loved one is therefore also responding to the language of skin. The project involved visual rhymes on the skin: Takemoto mimes the effects of cancer on her friend's skin. The skin becomes the site in which the desire for identification and the impossibility of identity is played out. By rereading Derrida's work on mourning and Freud's work on mourning and melancholia,

Takemoto suggests that the melancholy of illness is a form of suspended grief that resists and anticipates the possibility of the loss of a loved one. Within the collaboration, the body's surface became a literal and corporal register of difference and identification which wounds the skin, which itself is already marked by illness, race and gender.

In Jane Kilby's analysis of how sexual trauma is 'an unethical transgression of a skin boundary', she offers an understanding of skin as testimony. However, rather than suggesting that skin speaks, that it simply has a voice that can be heard by others, she suggests that the skin must be read, and that it is the reader who must embody the possibility of skin as testimony. In a close analysis of Louise Pembroke's drawings about self-harm, Kilby shows how the self-harm testimony appears to deny any form of communication and dialogue. By thinking through how the boundary between life and death is itself animated by skin in self-harm testimony, Kilby calls for a different ethics of reading. The skin appeals to us, in the immediacy of exposure, an appeal that refuses to allow the reader to absent herself from the relationship to the other's skin. But at the same time that the reader is brought closer, so too the reader is kept at a distance, 'at arm's length'. Although communication takes place, what occurs is not disclosure. The reader thereby becomes responsible for precisely that which resists reading, for a harm that cannot be translated into truth. Thus Kilby reverses the conventional wisdom that reads self-harm as the masochistic inversion of the previous violence of sexual abuse, suggesting that the skin is not responsible for the truth of testimony but rather that this is a responsibility to be borne by others.

In Chapter 8 Penelope Deutscher considers the ethics of touching skin by revisiting the encounter between Jean-Paul Sartre and Simone de Beauvoir. While Beauvoir is often understood as applying Sartre's existential phenomenology to women, Deutscher suggests a different way of understanding their exchange. In Sartre, touch is a constant drive to appropriate the other. But for de Beauvoir, to touch the skin of the other is 'to experience one's own and the other's desire'. Indeed, unlike Sartre, de Beauvoir valorises the troubling nature of the alterity of (the flesh of) objects. The touch of the skin does not remain on the surface: 'the touch represents a making oneself body, with the aim of being surprised by, rather than possessing, objects and others'. Reading the ambivalence of de Beauvoir's analysis of ageing skin in her autobiographical work, Deutscher shows how 'the erotic' is the means by which de Beauvoir rethinks what is valuable in self–other relations, despite the horror she expresses at the 'sight' of her own ageing body. Indeed, by showing how de Beauvoir's emphasis on touch undermines the association of the other with sight, Deutscher suggests that it is through tactile pleasures that ageing skin might come to be lived differently.

In the final chapter in this section, Margrit Shildrick problematises the model of the normative subject as the one who is bound by the skin, by thinking through monstrous corporeality. As she argues, the skin, as the most visible boundary of all, is both 'the limit of the embodied self and the site of potentially transgressive psychic investments'. By examining how monstrous bodies, in particular conjoined twins, disturb the assumption that the skin separates one body from another, Shildrick calls for an ethics of relationship. Rather than being simply an instance of otherness, monstrous bodies remind us of what must be abjected from the self's clean and proper body in order to define the borders of the skin. Shildrick suggests that the skin is not simply about separation, but also about the intimate relationship between self and other as indicated in, for example, the reversibility of touch. In the case of conjoined twins, it is the assumption that separation (and with it, singularity and autonomy) is the proper way of being, that makes the surgical intervention, or cut, seem necessary. Shildrick examines the case of Katie and Eilish Holton (through the documentaries made of their lives), to show how, in the act of separation, the twin that is left behind after the cut, still carries the memory of the presence of the other, who is hence both there, and not there, suggesting the relationship between self and other, and between bodies, is chiasmatic.

In the final part of the book, entitled 'Skin sites', we consider the skin and its relationship to spaces and places, asking how and where skin is produced and reproduced. Such a concern with skin sites allows us to pose the question of how skin is marked by cultural differences, including race, class, gender and sexuality. Throughout this section there is an emphasis on skin as cultural and national economy, as the site of labour, as well as differentiation, in the circulation of spaces, bodies and subjectivities. Each chapter poses the problem of the location of skin: Jennifer Biddle considers the relationship between skin and land in indigenous cultures; Chantal Nadeau places fur at the heart of the national and sexual economy; Shirley Tate situates the production of racialised skin in talk; and Claudia Castañeda stretches the skin question to consider bodies that are beyond the human.

In the opening chapter to this final section, Jennifer Biddle suggests that the skin is very much the 'stuff' of culture, and that it is involved in the production of the very distinction we call 'human'. Her analysis of skin as the stuff of culture, and also of difference, involves an investigation of the inscriptive practices of a group of Indigenous Australians, the Warlpiri. In her reading of these practices, she shows how skin becomes the same 'substance' as country; both carry the traces of an ancestral past. Unlike the pencil or pen, Warlpiri styluses literally drag the mark behind them, creating a friction between stylus and surface. Furthermore, in such practices one becomes ancestor, or country; or at least there is an intercorporeal exchange between bodies and land that involves proximity, if not merger. The differences of such bodily practices are not then simply about different modes of inscription. As Biddle suggests, the *Yapa* are demanding, in their inscriptions in which land (almost) becomes skin and skin (almost) becomes land, a recognition of a difference that is not simply 'skin deep'.

Chantal Nadeau is also concerned with 'where' skin takes shape. In Chapter 11, she examines the gendering and sexualisation of national space by looking at the 'beaver economy' or the fur trade in Canada. As she suggests, the beaver economy, drawing on the interfaces of skin, flesh and fur, is what keeps the 'business' of the nation going. Given the cultural and economic links between women and fur, women's bodies are fundamental to the production of the national skin. Indeed, the furladies (a term that derives from a 1950s Canadian fur musical review, *My Fur Lady*) embody the sensational value of the female skin in the economy of the nation. Against the model of the female body as static matter, Nadeau's analysis of the fur economy introduces movement and displacement in the constitution of women as national agents.

Similarly emphasising the dynamic processes of the cultural reproduction of identities, Shirley Tate offers an analysis of Black skin as a marker of difference in dominant discourses of race in Britain. In this chapter, Tate examines the relation between place, skin and community by addressing the dialogical production of hybridised Black identities in diasporic space. With reference to Frantz Fanon's work (1975), she points to how Black skin becomes a prison of flesh, and yet at the same time she argues that Black subjects continually contest the meanings of skin through everyday conversations or talk. Extending Paul Gilroy's notion of 'double consciousness' (1993), Tate explores the conversational strategies through which Black subjects negotiate their relationship to, and forge new meanings beyond, the stereotyped meanings attributed to Black skin. Relocating the concept of abjection within the social processes of dialogic exchange, Tate explores the instability of the sites of otherness of speech. As a result, Tate suggests that Blackness is both 'already there' (the skin is not blank, and then coloured) and open to being reinterpreted and negotiated. Skin itself is hence located in the third space; the skin is both a marker of racial otherness and the site of hybridity.

The final chapter pushes the question of the skin to explore the limits of the human-ness of the body. Claudia Castañeda begins with the provocative question: 'Can robots have skin?' Such a question disturbs any assumption that the skin is organic, and that it belongs to humans and guarantees human form. The fact that, through technology, skin is made on bodies that are other than human demonstrates how skin interrupts the human/non-human divide. Indeed, Castañeda extends her analysis by rethinking what it means to touch if skin can be robotic: 'Rather than being grounded in the stuff of human embodiment, this touch is generated through the combination of materials and qualities: leaf fingers, myriad joint sensors, exquisite sensitivity, piezo-electric membranes, changeability'. As a result, Castañeda suggests, touch can be understood as a form of encounter between bodies that do not necessarily take a human form.

The chapters in this collection invite the reader to consider different ways in which feminism can think through the skin. They examine how bodies 'take form', rather than assuming that bodies are already formed. While some papers take the 'skin' as itself a fleshy, and yet imagined, substance that needs to be thought, other papers 'touch on' the meanings of skin, only ever sliding across it. Although they think the skin very differently (some thinking 'on' it, others 'through' it, and some even 'as' it), the contributors seek to contest bodily boundaries by exploring the skin as surface, encounter and site, in which more than one body is always implicated. Thus, throughout the book, the skin does not simply contain the body, nor is skin simply there, already formed, in its place; rather, the skin is both already inscribed, or marked, and is always yet to be inscribed. In this collection, we aim to give life to bodies that, as Donna Haraway suggests so provocatively, have no necessary ends or endings (1991: 178). In the same way that Haraway argues that bodies do not necessarily end at their skins, we suggest that skins do not necessarily end at their bodies.

Dermographia

We invite readers to approach this collection as a form of *dermographia*, that is, as a form of skin writing (from the Greek 'derma', skin, and 'graphesis', writing) (see Stacey 1997: 84). The word 'dermographia' is a medical term that means writing on, or marking, the skin. But here we use it to suggest that skin is itself also an effect of such marking. This is not to say that skin can be reduced to writing, for the skin matters as matter: it is a substantial, tactile covering that bears the weight of the body. But the substance of the skin is itself dependent on regimes of writing that mark the skin in different ways or that produce the skin as marked. The skin is a writerly effect. We could also suggest that writing is an effect of skin: the touch of the technologies that produce the words; the skin that is shed in the endless processes of composition and decomposition. Here, more provocatively, we could consider the materiality of the signifier as produced by skin, by the weight of the bodies that are formed as they are marked, cut or written into the world. Writing can be thought of as skin, in the sense that what we write causes ripples and flows that 'skin us' into being: we write, we skin. The varied contributions in this collection, which think through the skin, can be read as rewriting the skin, or re-skinning the writing. In linking writing to skin in this way, we suggest that both are processes that involve materiality and signification, limits and possibilities, thought and affect, difference and identity.

Indeed, part of the work of this introduction has been to show how skin has multiple histories and multiple contexts in which it has formed or taken shape. But it is a necessary characteristic of writing, as Jacques Derrida (1988) has argued, to be repeatable, to be able to be 'cut off' from its context of utterance. Skin, like writing, can be 'cut off' and made to signify anew. It can acquire new meanings, new forms, new shapes. But this potential does not render irrelevant the historical contexts in which skin has already been marked or which skin has already marked. For, like writing, skin carries traces of those other contexts in the very living materiality of its forms, even if it cannot be reduced to them. Indeed, as Freud's model of the mystic writing pad suggests, the process of 'cutting off' or 'erasure' also leaves its mark (1964: 230). This relationship to the past, which is neither simply absent nor present on the surface of the skin, is hence also an opening up of a different future. It is precisely by paying attention to the already written, to what has already taken shape (for example, the colonial, racialised and sexed histories of touch as ownership and possession) that one can open up that which has yet to be written, and even touch the skin that has yet to be lived.

Notes

1 We can note then the huge number of books on bodies written by feminists in the 1990s. Titles include: *Spectacular Bodies* (Tasker 1993), *Bodies that Matter* (Butler 1993), *Volatile Bodies* (Grosz 1994), *Sexy Bodies* (Grosz and Probyn 1994), *Bodies of Women* (Diprose 1994), *Deviant Bodies* (Terry and Urla 1995), *Flexible Bodies* (Martin 1995) and *Imaginary Bodies* (Gatens 1996). Although as individual texts many of the books on 'the body' in feminist theory during this period did not seek to fetishise bodies or extract them from their contexts of production and consumption, one effect of their combined impact has arguably been for courses and readings in this area to designate 'the body' an object of study. Thus we are suggesting that the use of 'bodies' as an object of study (that which the work is 'on') can have the problematic effect of constituting bodies as objects as such, even when the studies themselves call into question the very discreteness of bodies. These books are of course indebted to an earlier tradition of feminist scholarship on embodiment such as: *Our Bodies Ourselves* (Boston Women's Health Collective 1973); *Seizing Our Bodies: The Politics of Women's Health* (Dreifus 1978); *Biological Women: The Convenient Myth* (Hubbard *et al* 1982); *Women, Feminism and Biology: The Feminist Challenge* (Birke 1986).

2 So, for example, although both Rosi Braidotti's (1994) and Elizabeth Grosz's (1994) work have been very much influenced by Deleuze and Guattari's model of becoming (1992), they have also provided strong critiques of how their work effaces the specificity of sexual difference. Braidotti also questions Deleuze and Guattari's notion of 'bodies without organs' by considering the exchange of 'organs without bodies' (1994). Indeed, given that the skin is usually represented in bio-medical discourses as the largest organ of the body (see Ahmed 1998), then it is interesting to think of our project, not as presupposing the existence of bodies with organs, or bodies without organs, but as investigating how bodies come to be identified as having organs in the first place.

References

Ahmed, S. (1998) 'Animated Borders: Skin, Colour and Tanning' in M. Shildrick and J. Price (eds) *Vital Signs: Feminist Reconfigurations of the (Bio)Logical Body*, Edinburgh: Edinburgh University Press.

Anzieu, D. (1989) *The Skin Ego: A Psychoanalytic Approach to the Self*, New Haven: Yale University Press.

Birke, L. (1986) *Women, Feminism and Biology: The Feminist Challenge*, Brighton: Harvester Wheatsheaf.

Bordo, S. (1993) *Unbearable Weight: Feminism, Western Culture and the Body*, Berkeley: University of California Press.

Boston Women's Health Collective (1973) *Our Bodies Ourselves*, New York: Simon and Schuster.

Braidotti, R. (1994) *Nomadic Subjects: Embodiment and Sexual Difference in Contemporary Feminist Theory*, New York: Columbia University Press.

—— (2000) 'Teratologies' in I. Buchanan and C. Colebrook (eds) *Deleuze and Feminist Theory*, Edinburgh: Edinburgh University Press.

Butler, J. (1993) *Bodies that Matter: On the Discursive Limits of 'Sex'*, New York: Routledge.

Cataldi, S. (1993) *Emotion, Depth and the Flesh: A Study of Sensitive Space*, New York: State University of New York Press.

Deleuze, G. and Guattari, F. (1992) *A Thousand Plateaus: Capitalism and Schizophrenia*, trans. B. Massumi, London: The Athlone Press.

Derrida, J. (1988) *Limited Inc*, trans. Samuel Weber and Jeffrey Mehlman, Evanston: North Western University Press.

Diprose, R. (1994) *The Bodies of Women*, London: Routledge.

Dreifus, C. (1978) *Seizing our Bodies: The Politics of Women's Health*, New York: Vintage.

Fanon, F. (1975) *Black Skin, White Masks*, London: Paladin.

Freud, S. (1964) *The Standard Edition of the Complete Psychological Works of Sigmund Freud*, Vol. 19, trans. J. Strachey, London: The Hogarth Press.

Gallop, J. (1988) *Thinking Through the Body*, New York: Columbia University Press.

Gatens, M. (1996) *Imaginary Bodies: Ethics, Power and Corporeality*, London: Routledge.

Gilroy, P. (1993) *The Black Atlantic: Modernity and Double Consciousness*, London: Verso.

Grosz, E. (1994) *Volatile Bodies: Toward a Corporeal Feminism*, St Leonards, NSW: Allen and Unwin.

Grosz, E. and Probyn, E. (1994) (eds) *Sexy Bodies: The Strange Carnalities of Feminism*, London: Routledge.

Haraway, D. (1991) *Simians, Cyborgs and Women: The Reinvention of Nature*, London: Free Association Books.

Hubbard, R., Henifin, M. S. and Fried, B. (eds) (1982) *Biological Woman: The Convenient Myth*, Cambridge, MA: Schenkman.

Kristeva, J. (1982) *Powers of Horror: An Essay on Abjection*, trans. L. S. Roudiez, New York: Columbia University Press.

Lacan, J. (1982) 'God and the Jouissance of the Woman' in J. Mitchell and J. Rose (eds) *Feminine Sexuality: Jacques Lacan and the Ecole Freudienne*, New York: Norton.

McClintock, A. (1995) *Imperial Leather: Race, Gender and Sexuality in the Colonial Context*, New York: Routledge.

Marks, L. U. (2000) *The Skin of the Film: Intercultural Cinema, Embodiment and the Senses*, Durham, NJ: Duke University Press.

Martin, E. (1995) *Flexible Bodies: Tracking Immunity in American Culture from the Days of Polio to the Days of Aids*, Boston: Beacon Press.

Merleau-Ponty, M. (1968) *The Visible and the Invisible*, trans. A. Lingis, Illinois: Northwestern University Press.

Phelan, P. (1997) *Mourning Sex: Performing Public Memories*, London and New York: Routledge.

Prosser, J. (1998) *Second Skins: The Body Narratives of Transsexuality*, New York: Columbia University Press.

Scarry, Elaine (1985) *The Body in Pain: The Making and Unmaking of the World*, Oxford: Oxford University Press.

Sobchack, Vivian (1992) *The Address of the Eye: Phenomenology and Film Experience*, Princeton: Princeton University Press.

Stacey, J. (1997) *Teratologies: A Cultural Study of Cancer*, London: Routledge.

Tasker, Y. (1993) *Spectactular Bodies: Gender, Genre and the Action Cinema*, London: Routledge.

Terry, J. and Urla, J. (eds) (1995) *Deviant Bodies: Critical Perspectives on Difference in Science and Popular Culture*, Bloomington: Indiana University Press.

Vasseleu, C. (1998) *Textures of Light: Vision and Touch in Irigaray, Levinas and Merleau-Ponty*, London: Routledge.

Weiss, G. (1999) *Body Images: Embodiment as Intercorporeality*, London: Routledge.

Part I

Skin surfaces

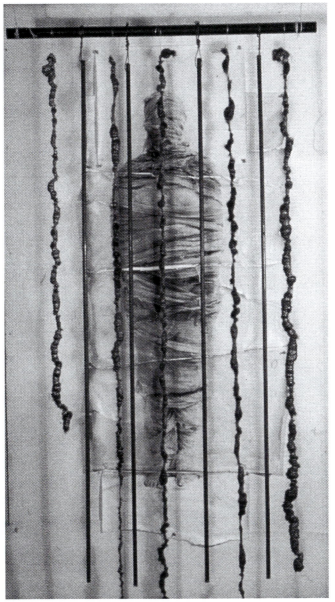

Frontispiece 1 'Instructions of the Body'
Toned photographic mural print with oil, steel bar and braided hair, from installation *Writ(e) of Habeus Corpus*, 5 ft × 5 ft

Susan McKenna and Elizabeth Hynes

1 Cut in the body

From clitoridectomy to body art

Renata Salecl

How can one explain the fact that today in the same quarter of New York one finds youngsters who decorate their skin with body piercing, artists who use body mutilation as a form of art and African immigrants who practice clitoridectomy? The latter are usually fully integrated into Western society, that is, they work or go to school, they participate in public life and so on while still practising traditional initiation rituals. In such forms of body mutilations as clitoridectomy, one does not find simply the repetition of premodern forms of initiation; the return to these forms of initiation should rather be understood as a way in which the contemporary subject deals with the deadlocks or antagonisms of so-called post-modern society. And some practices of body art, as well as the fashion for body-piercing and tattooing can be seen as another way of dealing with these deadlocks.

I will analyze the practice of clitoridectomy in comparison with the masochistic turn in body art. I am not saying, however, that these forms of body transformation are in any way equivalent. What makes them comparable is the fact that they are two ways of dealing with the same question: What is the place of the subject in contemporary society?

Before making connections between these two practices, one needs to analyze different ways in which the subject identifies with the symbolic order in premodern, modern and post-modern societies. My intention, however, is not to trace the genealogy of these forms of society, but to take them as representing three different types of the subject's relation to the so-called big Other, that is, the symbolic structure. If people today are returning to body painting or even to old forms of initiation, they are not simply copying some old cultural forms, they are reinterpreting these old forms in a new way. To understand this reinterpretation one first needs to analyze the original meaning of such initiation rituals as clitoridectomy.

Initiation and individualization

The ritual of clitoridectomy in the developing world is a topic that from time to time attracts the attention of the Western media and provokes almost universal admonishment from the public.[1] There tend to be two types of reaction to clitoridectomy. First, those who defend universal human rights are for strict prohibition of this ritual; and second, those who insist on the right to cultural differences usually still oppose clitoridectomy while stating that, however appalling they may find the practice, Westerners have no right to impose their standards on non-Western cultures. Things get even more complicated when the Westerners realize that the rituals of clitoridectomy are performed not only in Africa or Asia, but also among the immigrants in the middle of New York, London, Paris. Here the legal prohibition of the ritual has no real effect, since clitoridectomy is never performed as a public act, but as a secret ritual. From the Western point of view, it is shocking that something like this happens in democratic societies.[2] And it is also surprising that the development of global capitalism has not contributed to the extinction of clitoridectomy; on the contrary, in some countries the practice has become even more widespread in recent years. How can we explain this fact?

Women from the ethnic groups that support such initiation rites usually claim that this practice is part of their ethnic identity and has been performed by their ancestors, and that by carrying on with the initiation rituals they are essentially contributing to the survival of their tradition. When the members of such ethnic groups migrate to the West, they insist on their right to protect their identity through the performance of clitoridectomies. Women also claim that if they have not been initiated via clitoridectomy they cannot get married; and mothers who submit their daughters to this ritual usually state: 'If it was good for me, it will also be good for my daughter.'

While Westerners fear that the habits of immigrant non-Westerners will shatter the Western way of life, the immigrants complain that the Western states' prohibition of certain initiation rituals endangers their ethnic identity. It is thus not only Westerners who see the danger of the erosion of their culture in others (that is, the immigrant cultures); the immigrant groups also perceive themselves as endangered by the dominant Western cultures.

The case of clitoridectomy creates many dilemmas that go far beyond a simple decision as to whether one is against or in favour of this ritual. The question is: What role does clitoridectomy play in the formation of women's sexual identity and how essential is this ritual for transmission of sexual norms from generation to generation? A further implicit question is: How does sexual difference inscribe itself in pre-modern and in modern societies, and how is one to understand a return to the body mutilation that occurs in post-modern society, for example in the case of some practices of body art?

Let me first summarize the explanations given by the supporters of clitoridectomy as to why this ritual needs to be preserved. Although different ethnic groups usually justify clitoridectomy with different mythologies, one can make some basic comparisons. A widespread belief is that clitoridectomy assures women's fertility. Various mythologies take the clitoris as something impure and dangerous for the future child. The clitoris is also taken as a rival to a man's phallus. In Ethiopia, for example, one finds a belief that the uncut clitoris grows to the size of a man's penis and thus prevents insemination. And the Bambara from Mali claim that a man who has intercourse with an uncircumcised woman might die, since the clitoris produces poisonous liquid. They also believe that at the time of birth one finds in the child both female and male traces. The clitoris is the trace of the male in the female and the prepuce is the trace of the female in the male. In order to clearly define the child's sex, one therefore needs to extinguish the trace of the opposite sex via male and female circumcision.

Other justifications for clitoridectomy stress the importance of group identity. A woman who is submitted to this ritual becomes the equal of other women in her ethnic group – she is thus accepted in her community. The circumcised woman finds 'the feeling of pride in being like everyone else, in being "made clean", in having suffered without screaming'.[3] For women, to be different, i.e., unexcised or noninfibulated, produces anxiety: such a woman may be ridiculed and despised by the others, and she will also be unable to marry in her community.

Some ethnic groups also claim that clitoridectomy protects women from their excessive sexuality. This ritual thus makes women faithful. Since excised women are supposed to be less sexually demanding, men can have many wives and keep them all satisfied. Others argue the opposite: the excised woman is supposed to be more inclined to have extramarital affairs, since she is always sexually unsatisfied. But, a very common position is that clitoridectomy helps to retain a woman's virginity, which is especially important in the communities that make virginity the absolute prerequisite of marriage and in which women's extramarital affairs are strongly condemned.

Some defenders of clitoridectomy also claim that this ritual needs to be understood as an aesthetic practice: the infibulated woman's sexual organ is supposed to be much more attractive than the noninfibulated one. And the most beautiful organ is the one that, after the scar is healed, feels smooth like a palm.[4]

Why do women who are submitted to the torturous practice of clitoridectomy not rebel against it, why do they calmly accept mutilation of their genitals, and why do they force their daughters to do the same? The problem is not simply that women live in patriarchal societies in which they have no power to express their disagreement with the rituals. Many cultures that perform clitoridectomy are not classical patriarchies – in some cultures men are even perceived as quite powerless (see Heald 1994; Bloch 1986) – and often much authority is in the hands of the older women, who are cherished as authority figures and as guardians of tradition, which is why these women are entrusted with the task of performing the ritual of clitoridectomy. The dilemma of why women support clitoridectomy thus primarily concerns the position the subject has in his or her culture, that is, the way the subject is entangled in his or her community.

Max Horkheimer (1972) pointed out how, with the advent of the Enlightenment type of patriarchal family, one can discern a process of individualization that does not exist in the pre-modern family. The modern subject is, of course, linked to his or her tradition, family, national community, but this tradition is no longer something that fully determines the subject and gives him or her stability and security. The modern subject is expelled from his or her community – this subject is an individual who has to find and reestablish his or her place in the community again and again. That modern society no longer stages the ritual of initiation means that the subject must 'freely' choose his or her place in the community, although this choice always remains in some way a forced choice. As we know from psychoanalysis, the subject who does not 'choose' his or her place in the community becomes a psychotic – a subject who feels themselves external to the community yet is not barred by language.

But this forced choice to become a member of the community also enables the subject to experience some actual freedom, for example, to reject the rituals of his or her community. Only when the subject is no longer perceived as someone who essentially contributes to the continuation of his or her tradition and is completely rooted in his or her community does the moment emerge when the subject can distance himself or herself from this community, for example, by criticizing its rituals. Western feminists justly take clitoridectomy to be a horribly painful practice. However, one can arrive at such position only after going through the process of individualization, that is, only when the subject has already made a break with his or her tradition.

When we say that in pre-modern society subjects are not yet individualized and are thus unable to distance themselves from the tradition, this does not mean that when people support clitoridectomy today they are falling back to the level of pre-modern family organization. On the contrary, the return to old traditions needs to be understood as a way subjects deal with the deadlocks of the highly individualized contemporary society. Thus, when people propagate old initiation rituals they are not simply nostalgic for the past or unable to oppose their tradition (usually they are quite willing to give up many other rituals and prohibitions), but rather they are trying to find some stability in today's disintegrating social universe.

There are various ways subjects deal with individualization in contemporary society. A young punk, for example, seems to respond to individualization by taking it to the extreme: he or she adopts an ultra-individualized stance and constantly searches for new decorations for his or her body to create a unique image. Such a punk makes an effort to dress differently from the dominant fashion trends, but then he or she also strongly identifies with some peer group. The punk's response to individualization is thus finally a formation of another group ideology. Although this ideology encourages people to look different from each other, it none the less quickly forms new fashion codes. In contrast, an African immigrant might respond to radical individualization by strongly identifying with his or her ethnic tradition. In this case, too, group identity, paradoxically, appears as a solution to the difficulties of individualization. If individualization first happens when the subject makes a break with tradition, the deadlocks that accompanies individualization incites either a return to tradition or a formation of some new group identity.

The impotence of authority

It is well known that both types of initiation – male circumcision and clitoridectomy – are ways in which pre-modern societies mark sexual difference. In these societies, biological sex is deemed not enough to ensure their reproduction.

It is the symbolic cut made by the law, that is, by language, that enables the continuation of tradition. The pre-modern society imposes all kinds of prohibitions and rituals that make a social being out of the human being. But in this society the symbolic cut in the body, the inscription of the subject's identity, occurs as something real. In the act of initiation, the subject receives a physical mark on his or her body, in most cases through circumcision but in some cases also through paint on the body or a tattoo. Anthropologists stress that initiation is an extremely traumatic event, especially if it happens in adolescence, since before being initiated the subject has no clear identity but after initiation the subject becomes heavily burdened by his or her sexual function and is thus expected to perform in accordance to it.

The pre-modern subject may have doubts about his or her sexual identity, but the gesture of initiation is supposed to alleviate these doubts and, through the cut in the body, confirm the subject's sexual identity. This mark on the body is therefore the answer of the big Other, of the symbolic structure, to the subject's dilemma. In the case of the modern subject, we no longer have the inscription of sexual identity on the body, since it is enough that the subject is marked by symbolic castration in his or her inner self. (St Paul, for example, explains that Christians do not prescribe circumcision, because the subject is already cut in his or her soul.) In modern society, the big Other still has power, since socialization usually proceeds via submission to the symbolic law represented by the paternal authority. By contrast, in contemporary post-modern society, there has been a radical change in the organization of the family, which also entails a different relation of the subject towards the symbolic order: the return to the ritual of clitoridectomy as well as other forms of inscription on the body (even genital mutilation) in some practices of body art is not the answer to the big Other, but rather the subject's answer to the nonexistence of the big Other.

Before dealing with this return to the cut in the body, let me first try to give a psychoanalytic account of clitoridectomy. The ethnic groups that support this practice usually claim that by cutting the female genitals they protect the woman's honor and thus show respect for her. The cultures that perform clitoridectomy perceive Western cultures as degenerate, since they do not honor women. Here, we have two totally different points of view about what women's honor is: for the Westerners, clitoridectomy is an act that mutilates women and violates human rights, and thus also dishonors women; while for people who embrace clitoridectomy, the absence of this ritual devalues women.

How would psychoanalysis explain this logic of honor and respect for women? Freud dealt with the problem of female shyness, which he linked to the lack or the absence of a phallus. By being shy, the woman tries to cover the lack and to avert the gaze from it. However, this shyness has in itself a phallic character. So it can be said that the very lack of the phallic organ in woman results in the phallicization of her whole body or a special part of the body; and covering up this part of the body has a special seductive effect.

There is no significant difference between women's shyness and their honor: 'The respect for women means that there is something that should not be seen or touched' (Miller 1997: 8). Both, shyness and respect, concern the problem of castration, the lack that marks the subject. The insistence on respect is a demand for distance, which also means a special relation that the subject needs to have towards the lack in the other.

Freud thought of woman as the subject who actually lacks something, which means that in her case castration was effective. As a result of this, the woman has *Penisneid* (penis envy). In psychoanalytic practice, women's 'deprivation' appears in many forms: as a fantasy of some essential injustice, as an inferiority complex, as a feeling of nonlegitimacy, as a lack of consistency or a lack of control, or even as a feeling of body-fragmentation. The Freudian solution for this 'deprivation' was maternity. But for Lacan, women's relation to the lack is much more complicated: the problem of femininity is not linked simply to having or not having a penis. The lack concerns the subject's very being – both a man and a woman are marked by lack, but they relate differently to this lack. Woman does not cover up the lack by becoming a mother, since for Lacan the problem of the lack cannot be solved on the level of having but only on the level of being. Motherhood is not a solution to woman's lack, since there is no particular object (not even a child) that can ever fill this lack.

Respect, therefore, has to do with the subject's relation to the lack in the other, which also means that respect is just another name for the anxiety that the subject feels in regard to this lack. The respect for the father, for example, needs to be understood as a way in which the subject tries to avoid the recognition that the father is actually impotent and powerless – that there is nothing behind his authority. Here, we come again to the problem of castration. Lacan understands castration as something that is linked to the radical emptiness of the subject. The subject is nothing by him or herself; he or she gets all authority and power from outside – from symbolic insignias. When we respect the father, we believe that the insignias have real power and thus we cover up the fact that the father is castrated, which means that he is himself an empty and powerless subject.

Respect is therefore an imaginary relationship that the subject has towards another subject or, better, towards the symbolic status that this other subject temporarily assumes. (Of course, respect does not concern only our relationship with another subject, but also with the big Other, the symbolic structure itself. Paying respect to our homeland, the flag, the law, and so on, are all a subject's imaginary means of accepting the big Other as consistent order.)

The modern idea of human rights is based on the Kantian subject. And, especially in the case of human rights, we usually invoke the idea of respect. Human rights concern some part of the subject's inner freedom, which the community or other people have no right to violate. (And here freedom is also meant as protection of the subject's bodily integrity. From this perspective, those who criticize clitoridectomy rightly point out that this practice contradicts the idea of human rights.) If we take into account the aforementioned thesis that respect means the need for a distance toward the lack that marks the subject, the idea of respect that human rights invoke also assumes another meaning. The inner freedom of the subject that human rights protect concerns the lack that marks the subject when he or she becomes a speaking being. And when we respect the bodily integrity of the subject, this actually means that we avert our gaze from the fact that the subject, in truth, does not have a naturally given bodily integrity, since this integrity comes into being only when the subject undergoes symbolic castration. Then the subject will be temporarily endowed with a certain symbolic power, but the lack that pertains to his or her subjectivity will none the less remain.

It is well known that human rights were invented at the time of Enlightenment when the subject lost his or her roots in nature as well as in tradition (Salecl 1994). From the Enlightenment, many political struggles have conceived of human rights in a nondiscriminatory way. Today, the very principle of human rights is that the subject should be respected regardless of gender, age, race, and so on. Here, then, we have an understanding of respect that differs greatly from the idea of respect embraced by the defenders of clitoridectomy. The latter can respect only a women who has been initiated and not just any woman. Similarly, some cultures respect women only when they are covered by a veil.

Contemporary understanding of human rights also includes the idea of the freedom of choice. A widespread liberal stand in regard to clitoridectomy, for example, is that women need to be educated about the violent nature of this practice; but if an educated woman still insists on being circumcised, then the educators can only conclude powerlessly conclude: 'What can we do, this is her choice.' But education does not simply establish a neutral terrain on which the subject can make a free choice, it also imposes a certain dominant ideology on the subject. Similarly, at another level, the subject's ethnic community imposes its ideology on him or her.

Let us now turn to self-torture in body art. Such practices are usually understood as an individual's choice to use his or her body as he or she pleases. However, it is only quite recently that the practices of bodily-mutilation have become perceived as art. What a specific culture perceives as art always depends on a certain social consensus and not simply on the idea of a personal choice (Lacan 1993). People have always mutilated and tortured themselves, but self-mutilation came to be understood as an artistic practice and not simply as the private indulgence of a masochist when a change occurred in the social symbolic organization.

So what happened in contemporary society to allow the cut in the body to be perceived as art? A generally accepted thesis is that in today's society the way the subject identifies with the law or, better, with the symbolic order, has changed. The dissolution of the traditional family structure has changed the subject's relation to authority, which means that the subject now appears as someone who is in a position to choose freely his or her own identity, including even sexual orientation. In pre-modern society, initiation ritual situated the subject in the social structure and assigned to him or her a special place as well as a sexual role. In modern, Enlightenment society, we no longer have initiation rituals, but the authority of the law is still at work. The law is linked to the role of the father; and in taking a position against this law, that is, by distancing him or herself from this law, the modern subject acquires his or her 'freedom'. In contrast, in post-modern society we have a total disbelief in authority and in the power of the symbolic order, the so-called big Other. But this disbelief has not resulted simply in the subject's liberation from the law or other forms of social coercion. The post-modern subject no longer accepts the power of the institutions or society's power to fashion his or her identity, and sometimes believes in the possibility of self-creation, maybe in the form of playing with his or her sexual identity or making out of him or herself a work of art. However, in this process of freeing the subject from the big Other, one can also observe the subject's anger and disappointment in regard to the very authority of the big Other. It thus appears, not as if it the subject has recognized that the big Other does not exist and that the authority is just a fraud, but rather that the big Other has somehow 'betrayed' the subject: the father's authority, for example, has revealed itself only as a mask of his impotence, the social rituals in institutions appear more and more as farce. However, this apparent liberation of the subject from authority can also be understood as a 'forced' choice that the subject has to make when he or she acknowledges the impotence of the authority.

What does this disbelief in the big Other mean? We have always known that the big Other was just a fiction and that people somehow pretend when they follow state, religious, or family rituals. Most of the time we believe only that someone else believes in these rituals, which is why we follow them: in order to avoid offending the others. This belief in the belief of the others is well exemplified in the parents' pretense that they are playing Santa Claus because children believe in it. But when children find out that Santa Claus is just a fiction, they go on pretend-ing to believe in it, so that they will not offend their parents, who still think the children believe in Santa Claus. What we have today is precisely the disbelief in the fiction of the big Other. The logic of this disbelief is exemplified in the well-known anecdote from the Marx brothers. When Groucho Marx was once caught out in an obvious lie, his response was: 'Whom do you believe – my words or your eyes?' The belief in the big Other is the belief in words, even when they contradict one's own eyes. What we have now is therefore precisely a mistrust in mere words (that is, in the symbolic fiction). People want to see what is behind the fiction.

But the encounter with what is behind the fiction can be most traumatic for the subject. The rules of politeness in speech are one example of the fictional char-acter of the big Other. When we meet someone we usually say, 'How nice to see you', even if we actually think, 'Drop dead, I really hate you.' If we stop using the polite words, we do not achieve a simple liberation from the fictional character of politeness, but instead encounter violence, which radically disrupts the social bonds.

Lacan famously said that what is excluded from the symbolic returns as real. As an example of this return of the real, Lacan takes psychotics. They are the ones who do not identify with the fiction of the symbolic order, but deal with the real. A psychotic, for example, does not believe in the fictional character of God, but has direct contact with God: he hears the voice of God, God's eyes are constantly pursuing him and so on.

On another level, today's disbelief in the fictional character of the father's authority has brought about a return of the father as real – the father who is a harasser, abuses children, has insatiable sexual desires, that is, a father who very much resembles the character of the Freudian father of the primal horde, who was the possessor of all women and denied his sons access to *jouissance*.

The disbelief in the symbolic fiction and the search for the real thing was also obvious at the time of the tragic death of Princess Diana. In opinion polls, the majority of the British people state that the monarchy is a relic of the past – an archaic institution that needs to be either abolished or radically changed. So people no longer believe in the fictional character of the kingdom. However, at the time of Diana's funeral, people were terribly upset that the Queen did not show enough emotion. People wanted the Queen to show physical signs of sorrow, to address the nation and hang the flag in front of the Royal Palace at half-mast. On the one hand, therefore we disbelieve in the fiction of monarchy but, on the other hand, we have a desperate need for the fiction to cease to be a fiction so that people see what is behind it – for the Queen to cry, for centuries-old rituals concerning the flag to be changed, and so on.

The public identification with Diana also shows the changes that have come about in the way the public identifies with its idols. In the past, the idols were supposed to be active for the ordinary people. People endowed the idols with outstanding abilities – bravery, intelligence, and so on. But Diana was a passive idol for the people. Her attitude greatly resembled the usual attitude of an ordinary person who complains about the institution but is actually part of it, who likes to help others, but does not sacrifice his or her own well-being. If, in the past, people tended to identify with an idol who was not like them, in the case of Diana they identified with someone who was exactly like them.

One of the ways in which the subject today deals with the absence of the big Other is to turn to narcissistic self-admiration. The lack of identification with some ego-ideal (a symbolic role or authority-ideal) results in the subject's identification with some imaginary role (the ideal-ego) in which the subject finds himself or herself likeable. This narcissistic search for the perfect image results in the subject's obsession with changing his or her body with the help of excessive dieting, exercise and plastic surgery. Another aspect of the subject's concern with the nonexistence of the big Other is discernible in the contemporary phenomena of the so-called 'culture of complaint'. Western societies nowadays are brimming with complaints about all kinds of injustices people feel are being done to them in their private and public lives: people search for the culprits who deprived them of their enjoyment, wealth, respect, and so on. The disbelief in the power of the big Other has resulted in the belief that there are various small others (institutions and authorities in the subject's immediate environment) who are guilty of causing the trouble in the people's lives. And the legal as well as financial compensation that the subjects seek is supposed to reinstall the lost equilibrium, at least for a moment.

Still another reflection of today's disbelief in the big Other is displayed in the practices of body art. Isn't this inscription on the body an attempt by the subject to deal with the absence of the big Other? Has the contemporary subject taken initiation into his or her own hands?

A documentary entitled *Sick: The Life and Death of Bob Flanagan, Supermasochist* (Kirby Dick, 1996) deals with the theme of masochism and art. The film depicts the performance artist Bob Flanagan, who enjoyed masochistic rituals in which, with the help of his mistress – his wife, cuts his skin, mutilates his genitals, and so on. It is crucial that the artist suffers an incurable illness, cystic fibrosis, which makes him unable to breathe without an iron lung. The film is a collage of the artist's performances, most of which were presented in art galleries. The end of the film also records the artist's death and his corpse being photographed by his devoted wife. The most shocking scene includes an act of a genital self-mutilation, when the artist nails his penis onto a wooden board. While he removes the nails, the blood squirts onto the camera. (This scene is hard to watch – many of the male observers identify so strongly with the painful ritual that they scream in panic, some even have to leave the room.)

Now, how can one understand the artistic enjoyment in masochistic practices? First, it must be pointed out that masochism and sadism never go hand in hand. As Gilles Deleuze (1991) said, a masochist and a sadist do not form a couple. A sadist takes himself to be the executor of some higher will, an ideal – in effect he becomes a mere object through which this ideal fulfills itself. And the sadist tortures victims because he is executing the desire of this higher will. The masochist, in contrast, searches for a torturer whom the masochist himself will educate and instruct. In the masochistic situation, the victim speaks through the torturer: here, it is therefore not the torturer who invents the forms of punishment; the inventor is the victim himself.

The torturer is usually a woman who takes on the role of the severe, cold mother. It is essential for the masochist to establish a contract with the torturer that describes in detail the conditions of the torture. The masochist is thus not simply tied by chains, but by the power of the contract through which he invests in the torturer the symbolic power of the law. The torturer acts like a cruel mother who humiliates the father figure, who is incarnated in the victim himself. The masochist therefore invests the law in his mother – in the very object of incestuous enjoyment – and by doing so excludes the father from the symbolic. Here, one again needs to invoke the familiar Lacanian thesis that what is excluded from the symbolic returns in the real. In the case of the masochist, the excluded father returns in the guise of the masochist himself, since the masochist takes on the role of the weak, humiliated father who needs to be punished.

For the masochist, castration has not been completed, which means that the symbolic law did not become fully operative. This is why the masochist, in his torturous ritual, caricatures castration and tries to make the law operative through the contract with his mistress. The subject (that is, the hysteric or the obsessional) for whom the castration was effective is always unsatisfied with the ways he or she tries to fill up the lack: the subject thus complains about the law that supposedly prevents his or her enjoyment. However, the subject finds a special enjoyment in this very dissatisfaction. The masochist finds enjoyment in punishment imposed by the law that he himself establishes. Since he lacks the symbolic prohibition, the masochist becomes an executioner for himself.

How can one therefore understand the turn to perversion in contemporary art? My point is not that the use of the body in art presents some kind of generalized perversion of our society. If a masochist castrating himself on the stage might be clinically a pervert, this is not the case for the majority of artists who use their bodies in art work. Similarly, one cannot universally take body piercing and tattooing as clinical forms of perversion. Most of the people who in one way or another mark their bodies are more likely to fall into the clinical category of neurosis rather than perversion; their acts are an imitation of perversion and not an actual perversion. But what is the difference between the perverts and the neurotics who just imitate perversion? Both of them stage some kind of drama when they paint or mutilate their bodies. The perverts stage this drama in order to deny castration: via their masochistic ritual, they mock castration. At the same time this very staging is also an attempt to find a law which would complete castration. In the case of the perverts, castration is thus first denied, then it is mockingly staged as an outside event, which does not touch the subject's inner beings. Behind this is a failed attempt to make castration operative again. The neurotics, in contrast, stage perverse rituals in order to come to terms with the lack that has been introduced by castration. Since, for the neurotics, castration was effective, they create a fantasy scenario to cover up the lack which is the result of castration: that is, they try to show how they are not essentially marked by the law, since they can openly play with the castration rituals on the stage.

What is behind the imaginary simulacra?

The fact that subjects face a radical change in the belief in the big Other or that they know very well that the big Other actually does not exist, does not mean that the symbolic structure is not operative. Subjects are still very much marked by the symbolic prohibition, although they might no longer identify with the authorities who are supposed to be bearers of this prohibition.

The symbolic structure today appears increasingly replaced by imaginary simulacra with which the subjects identify. Life seems like a computer game in which the subject can play with his or her identity, can randomly follow fashion rituals and can have no strong national or religious beliefs. But the fact that life appears as a screen on which everything is changeable has resulted in a desperate search for the real behind the fiction. The cuts in the body thus appear as an escape from the imaginary simulacra that dominate our society.

Young people usually explain their obsession with tattooing and body-piercing as ways to escape the pressures of the dominant fashion industry. The media constantly bombard them with images of beauty, and one of the ways to escape this enforced identification is to take a real action – to mark the body in a way that cannot be changed.

In recent years, social theory has widely discussed the issue of identity, which appeared not only as something socially constructed but also as something multiform and changeable. The discussions of performativity and sexual difference also created the impression that the subject can play with his or her sexual identity.

The paradox of the contemporary cuts in the body is that they seem at the same time to be a realization of these beliefs and a reaction against them. Making a cut in the body does not mean that the subject is merely playing with his or her identity; by irreversibly marking the body, the subject also protests against the ideology that makes everything changeable. The body thus appears as the ultimate point of the subject's identity. Since the subject does not want simply to play with the imaginary simulacra presented by the dominant fashion ideologies, he or she tries to find in the body the site of the real.

For the group of artists united in the project Body Radicals,[5] the body is today the only remaining realm over which an individual has retained power:

> Unmediated, direct access to the inner being through the artist's own blood or the feeling of pain opens up almost Artaud-like perspectives. What is happening is literal. There is no simulation. The symbolic field of the art is collapsing, bodies become black holes into which symbolic significance implodes.
>
> (Body Radicals' Home Page
> http://www.chapter.org/november97/bodyradicals/index.html)

The thesis presented in the last sentence is a very pretentious one, since the Body Radicals still call themselves artists and their artworks are usually presented in art galleries: they may not be accepted by the mainstream art community, but they none the less very much want to be recognized in the alternative spaces of the 'symbolic field of art'. This demand for social recognition already proves that, in the new forms of body art, we are not dealing with some kind of generalized psychosis or with the total collapse of the symbolic order. However, the use of the body in contemporary art does deal with the contemporary subject's problem in searching for something real in the form of his or her body.

Although the artists united in the Body Radicals use their bodies in very different ways in their artworks, one can find some similarities between them. For the purpose of my analysis here, I will focus only on the work of Orlan and Stelarc.

Orlan's[6] art consists primarily of multiple plastic surgery operations on her face, which are recorded and, with the commentary of her voice, presented in art galleries. When Orlan provides theory about her art, her primary point is that she uses her body as a site of public debate. Her art challenges the standards of beauty; it explores the variety of body-images that are outside the norms and dictates of the dominant ideology. When she plays with the images of femininity, her intention is to practice a transsexuality of woman to woman, which, however, does not follow the usual transsexual desire to have a defined and definite identity. Orlan also claims that, with the help of surgery, one can bring the internal image closer to the external one; she therefore does not need to identify with the image that nature had given her. With the help of surgery, her body is transformed into language ('flesh becomes word'). Orlan also plans to be mummified after her death and placed in an art gallery.

Orlan therefore tries to play with multiple identities, to make her body a changeable work of art and, in doing so to achieve some kind of immortality. She describes her work as a self-portrait, which is presented as an inscription in the flesh made with the help of the new technologies. Orlan's intention is to impose control, not only over her naturally given body image but also to manipulate the new technologies (like plastic surgery) and use them against the ideals of the dominant ideology.

When Orlan objects to the idea that she is performing some kind of self-mutilation, she comes very close to the defenders of clitoridectomy. Orlan claims that her body transformation augments her power and does not diminish it. Similarly, the defenders of clitoridectomy say that the ritual of circumcision actually gives women power they did not have before initiation. And when Orlan says that she transforms her body into language, she caricatures initiation rituals, which in their own ways also mark the body with language.[7]

If, in the pre-modern type of society, initiation has a very specific role in assigning the subject's sexual identity and in imposing a mark of social prohibition onto the body, then one cannot say that, in post-modern society, initiation rituals still play the same role. The insistence on clitoridectomy in the case of the African immigrants in the West or among very developed African countries, for example, can be understood as a specific answer to the deadlocks of contemporary society. The class antagonisms of post-industial society, the globalization of capital, the erosion of tradition, all brought the subject to the point of searching for some stable form of identity. The African immigrants may still respect their grand-mothers enough to allow them to perform the act of initiation, while they have an utter mistrust of other authorities in the society they live in. Here, we also have the case of disbelief in the fiction of the big Other in contemporary society; thus the insistence on old rituals of initiation must be understood as an answer to this disbelief, that is, as an attempt to find in the body a place of some stable identity.

When the body artists caricature initiation rituals or play with the same new forms of tribalism, they are trying to challenge precisely the idea of stable identity, while they none the less try to find in the body some piece of the real. In their own way, the body artists are also dealing with the deadlocks of today: with their cuts in the body, they challenge the idea that the body can give the subject the basis for an identity. So they are actually searching for what is supposed to be behind the body. If the body is just a playground for various identities, what is real here?

For Orlan, the final, unchangeable thing becomes her voice. With the help of her voice, Orlan tries to provide explanations for her art: she thus reads from theoretical texts as her face is cut and comments on the procedure of her surgery. But behind this search for meaning for her changeable face, her voice remains a constant. Orlan's voice is the drive, that is, the real, that stays the same throughout her performances. Plastic surgery of Orlan's face is painful to watch; for observers it is not only shocking to see Orlan's skin being detached from her face, but also to hear her monotonous voice reciting texts during her surgery. If Orlan were to be quiet, the observers might be able to pretend they were seeing a deeply anaes-theticized, dead-like person being cut on the stage. In this case, the shock for the observers would not be so very different from that of watching horror movies: when one does not want to see a scary scene in the film, one simply closes one's eyes. Of course, in horror movies one still hears the music and the screams, but the voice without the picture is less frightening, since the voice loses power when it is not accompanied by the picture. But in the case of Orlan, it is the voice that is the real site of horror. If one only listens to her voice and keeps one's eyes shut, one does not get relief, since Orlan's voice is the sign of deadliness and of life at the same time. As such, the voice is a death drive that always undermines the subject's identity. Orlan tries to show with her art how she can play with her identity, but her voice none the less remains the real her, as if her voice is more herself than she is.

Some other artists are trying to find a piece of the real beyond the skin with the help of computer technology, and in this endeavor they also try to replace the human voice with a computerized sound. The Australian artist Stelarc, for example, questions the role of the body in the post-industrial age. His thesis is that, with the new developments in technology, the body became obsolete, since it is biologically ill-equipped for the technological level of contemporary society. Stelarc wants to create some kind of new meta-body, which first needs to pacify and anaesthetize the existing body. With the help of genetic technology, the organs become replaceable, the skin more durable, the body starts acting without expectation; it produces movements without memory, has no desires, and so on. In this way, the self can be placed beyond the skin and connect itself with the virtual world. The body becomes a phantom body, which plays with its images and connects itself with the immortal machinery. Reproduction is substituted by redesigning and sexual intercourse is replaced with the interface between the subject and the machine. In such a virtual world it seems that we no longer have to deal with birth or death. Stelarc thus wants to make life eternal. In the end, this life would be nothing but a symbolic fiction, but a fiction that would, none the less, eliminate the trauma of the unsymbolizable real. As such, life would cease to be life, too.

Both interventions in the body – clitoridectomy and these practices of body art – pose numerous questions about the subject in the post-modern world. Some see the main problem of contemporary society as being the total erosion of the symbolic network, which results in some kind of generalized perversion or even psychosis. Others take the dissolution of the patriarchal system of social author-ities as signalling the possibility for subjects to form their own identities without submitting themselves to the imposed normative ideals. But the changed relation of the subject to the symbolic order in contemporary society should be taken neither as a total catastrophe nor as an opening up of unlimited possibilities. The disbelief in the big Other has, on the one hand, incited people's return to such cruel initiation rituals as clitoridectomy and, on the other, it has instigated the self-imposed cuts in body art. But is this the only way to respond to the fact that the Big Other does not exist? Are there no other ways of dealing with the inconsistency of the symbolic order?

Notes

1 The United Nations data shows that there are 130 million women in the world today whose genitals have been mutilated. This practice is widespread in Africa, in some Asian countries and among immigrants from these places in the West.
2 Although clitoridectomy is prevalent in communities that practice Islam, this ritual is not linked to Islam much less prescribed by the Qur'ān. In the past, clitoridectomy was sometimes also performed by Catholics, Protestants, Copts, and other religious groups. The Catholic Church never officially distanced itself from clitoridectomy: the missionaries in Africa, for example, did not condemn this practice. Only the Anglican Church, in the 1920s, denounced this ritual and advised its missionaries to prevent it (Dorkenoo 1994; Lefeuvre-Deotte 1997; Maertens 1978).
3 Note that so-called female circumcision is the mildest form of the deformations of female genitals, since circumcision removes only the prepuce that covers the clitoris. Much more severe and also much more widespread is so-called excision, which removes the whole of the clitoris. Even more common and painful is the ritual of infibulation, which means the removal of the clitoris and the labia. This practice causes numerous infections and many women die because of it.
4 The defenders of clitoridectomy who invoke the aesthetic dimension of this ritual usually say that it should be compared with the Western obsession with Western beauty ideals, which lead Western women to undergo painful plastic surgery operations, use tattoos, and so on.
5 The group Body Radicals includes such artists as Orlan, Ron Athey, Stelarc, Franko B and Annie Sprinkle. While they all use their own bodies as their artistic means of expression, their art and the explanations they give for it differ significantly.
6 For an extensive analysis of Orlan's art, see Adams (1996).
7 Artists Ron Athey and Franko B caricature various forms of initiation rituals in their performances, in which they primarily play with blood, shit and other bodily discharges.

References

Adams, P. (1996) *Emptiness of the Image*, London: Routledge.
Bloch, M. (1986) *From Blessing to Violence: History and Ideology in the Circumcision Ritual of the Merina of Madagascar*, Cambridge: Cambridge University Press.
Deleuze, G. (1991) *Masochism: Coldness and Cruelty*, New York: Zone Books.
Dorkenoo, E. (1994) *Cutting the Rose: Female Genital Mutilation – The Practice and its Prevention*, London: Minority Rights Publication.
Heald, S. (1994) 'Every man a hero: Oedipal themes in Gisu circumcision' in A. Deluz (ed.) *Anthropology and Psychoanalysis: An Encounter Through Culture*, London: Routledge.
Horkheimer, M. (1972) 'Authority and the Family' in *Critical Theory: Selected Essays*, New York: Continuum.
Lacan, J. (1993) *Ethics of Psychoanalysis*, London: Routledge.
Lefeuvre-Deotte, M. (1997) *L'excision en proces: un differend culturel?*, Paris: L'Harmatan.
Maertens, J-T. (1978) *Le corps sexionne*, Paris: Aubier.
Miller, J-A. (1997) 'Des semblants dans la relation entre les sexes', *La Cause freudienne – Revue de psychanalyse* 36.
Salecl, R. (1994) *The Spoils of Freedom*, London: Routledge.
Ussher, J. (1991) *Women's Madness: Misogyny as Mental Illness*, Hertfordshire: Harvester Wheatsheaf.

2 Mortification

Steven Connor

Why has the skin become the visible object of so many and such various forms of imaginary and actual assault: tattooing, piercing, scarification, suntanning, bondage fashions that appear to cut into or segment the skin, images of calcified, metallised or mineralised skin, along with the infliction of various kinds of disfiguring marks, actual and cosmetic? And how can this condition of jeopardy coexist with a climate of such extreme care and anxious nurture, so religiously immoderate an idealisation of the skin? What is the nature of the discomfiting (which must mean in some way comfortable) fit between a willingness to mortify the skin and the epidermic epidemic of glorified skin?

Untouchable

The skin figures. It is what we see and know of others and ourselves. We show ourselves in and on our skins, and our skins figure out the things we are and mean: our health, youth, beauty, power, enjoyment, fatigue, embarrassment or suffering. The skin is always written: it is legendary. More than the means of what we happen voluntarily or involuntarily to disclose to sight, it has become the proof of our exposure to visibility itself. It is perhaps precisely because of this that the skin has been hard to see in itself, just as it is hard to see the mirror when we are so intent on what we see in it.

And yet, it seems, the skin in itself has never been so intensely, libidinally figured as in our period. This is not just because of the ubiquity of displayed skin in our social representations; it is also because of the multiplication of skin-surfaces, of signifying screens, exteriors and supports. The first such modern skin-surface was perhaps the photograph, in which a particularly pellucid relationship was established between touching and looking, skin and image. Photographs, we dream, have been touched by the world, leaving its trace upon the surface of the photographic film. The photograph, as Roland Barthes has suggested, removes the eye from looking, and touches us:

> From a real body, which was there, proceed radiations which ultimately *touch* me, who am here. . . . A sort of umbilical cord links the body or the

photographed thing *to my gaze*: light, though impalpable, is here a carnal medium, a skin I share with anyone who has been photographed.

(Barthes 1981: 80–1; emphases in original)

Far from spectralising the world, putting it at a distance, the photograph is the modern embodiment of the contiguity between looking and grasping.

This is surely the reason for the continuing popularity of the glossy finish of the photograph. This sheen signifies the magical preciousness that we wish the photograph to retain, giving the eye notice that it is a tangible thing which can never be encompassed simply by looking. The gloss is an ideal skin, flesh transfigured, but the ideality of that skin (its intangibility) is what seems to guarantee its quality of tenderness, that word that signifies both the quality of something touched and the manner of our touching. This image has been touched and can touch us back. Perhaps it is for this reason that we feel called to handle photographs, both to caress their glossy surfaces and, occasionally, in sadness or anger, to gash and efface them. The gloss of the photograph signifies its more than human perfection, and therefore its vulnerability to the attentions of fingers, and the scratches, creases and corrupting smears of greasiness they can impart. This quality of the photograph is transmitted to the surfaces of other technological quasi-objects, such as the vinyl gramophone disc, tape (now boxed protectively in cassettes) , and the CD, in the reverent kind of touch that it seems to teach us to use in handling it, a touch in which we keep the living, vulnerable surface of the object intact, instinctively preferring to hold it by its edges. When they first appeared, we were told that CDs were incorruptible; but nobody ever wanted to believe it, and we were glad when we discovered that, like living beings, they were indeed vulnerable to erosion and to the damage wrought by our tactile attentions. The practice of 'scratching', the manipulation in live performance of vinyl records, which grew up the club culture of the 1980s, at once rescued the possibility of damage in a world of incorruptible and immaterial data and preserved this ideal delicacy in our relationship to objects, drawing attention to surfaces that would be as sensitive to our attentions as the skin of another person.

This ideal, disembodied but quasi-bodily, surface was rediscovered and extended in cinema. For perhaps the most extraordinary invention of the cinema was not its capacity to make moving images, so much as its capacity to move images anywhere, to project them in different places at different times, and to recreate the world as a series of screens or receptive surfaces. Whether this screen-creating capacity repeats the experience of the primal screen of the mother's breast, as implied by Bertram Lewin's (1946, 1953) arguments about the 'dream-screen', or whether the mother's skin is in fact hereby being retroactively cinematised, need not be in question here. But the concept of the dream-screen teaches us that the projected image always implies and, as it were, supplies itself with its own immanent screen, implicit within the image at its own focal length, on which the image will be able to come to rest. The projected images of cinema are shadowed by the techniques of reproduction and enlargement that have made the living environments of the twentieth century a phantasmagoria of signifying surfaces. If anything and everything can become a screen, then everything has the capacity to bear faces and exposed bodies. The harsh banality of brick and metal, the sides of buildings, cars and buses, are capable of being made the vehicle for visible flesh. Anything can wear a face; anything can become a *front*.

Like the life-size images of photographs that we pass from hand to hand, these cinematised public images have a tactile kind of radiance. All this visible skin, the skin of these models advertising sports shoes, ice creams, mascara and brassieres, and the secondary skins of the objects they wear, hold, caress, ingest, or recline in, all this skin *glows*, as if with its own serene, interior illumination. Touch continues to be implicated in this radiance (and it is perhaps one of the functions or effects of the ubiquity of skin to ensure the tangibility of the visible). The flesh displayed in posters and magazines, and in the electronic screens that are more and more a feature of public space, looks touchable, caressable, for what is to be impressed upon our eyes is the way that it has been touched by light; but we know that its touchability is of a higher order than the ordinary touchability of skin, the grasping touch which advertising also encourages, reaffirming constantly the association between envy and the evil eye, *invidia* and vision. Envy seems an appropriate relation to the advertisement, rather than lust or desire, since we are encouraged to want something that we should not want, and cannot ever really have. Odourless and textureless, these skins nevertheless acquaint us with a kind of higher touching, an immaculate, intactile, imperishable touch of the eye. Whenever we look at a poster or a projection on an impersonal surface, we are looking at such an idealised, generalised human skin.

But there is another kind of touch, the expression of another, harsher, kind of optics. The ideal untouchability of the image ensures that, when we can get our hands on it, we will take the opportunity to penetrate, tear and deface, as the bathing beauty in the poster advertising 'Sunny Prestatyn' is torn and defaced in Philip Larkin's poem of the same name.

Pornography brings to light the two kinds of tactile looking offered in Larkin's poem – the ideal, unbroken smoothness of the body as scene, incorruptible because untouchable, and the availability of this surface for sadistic defacement ('Huge tits and a fissured crotch/were scored well in', 1986: 35). Sadomasochistic pornography in particular combines the two modes of touching, absorbing defacement into the face. It shows the skin itself already shadowed by its disfiguration – tightly bound, caged and barred by fetishistic clothing, menaced by blade, stiletto or whip, or indeed actually bearing the marks of punishment. The last ten years have seen a steady increase in the visibility and solidification of the respectability of fetishistic and sadomasochistic imagery, in piercing and tattooing, bondage fashions involving spikes, straps and constrictions of the flesh, and cosmetic styles that stripe and slash, intensifying the contrast between the surface of the skin and the markings applied to it. Such sadomasochistic imagery takes our revenge on itself. Michel Serres suggests that the application of make-up makes the sensorium visible, highlighting the organs of sense, and thus painting on to the skin the capacity to hear, see, taste and smell (1985: 31). Sadomasochistic make-up reduces the skin to a dead, monochrome alternation of black on white, denying the display of sensitiveness, and marking the reduction of the skin to the condition of a surface to be marked. Are such assaults actual or imaginary, enacted or merely acted out? It may be suspected that this very numbing of the skin, the very playfulness or superficiality of sadomasochistic style, allows the intense libidinisation of the surface itself, and our combined craving for and rage against it.

A sizeable literature has established the connections between the violent mode of a modern epistemology and the defacing encounter between surface and marker. In *Spurs: Nietzche's Styles*, Jacques Derrida suggests that philosophical style itself is nothing but this resumed meeting of female fabric and male stylus:

> In the question of style there is always the weight or *examen* of some pointed object. At times this object might only be a quill or a stylus. But it could just as easily be a stiletto, or even a rapier. Such objects might be used in a vicious attack against what philosophy appeals to in the name of matter or matrix, an attack whose thrust could not but leave its mark, could not but inscribe there some imprint or form. But they might also be used as protection against the threat of such an attack.
>
> (Derrida 1979: 37)

Where Derrida sees an originary agony in all stylistics, Friedrich Kittler sees a more systematic, and historical escalation of violence in modernist technologies of automated writing, with the displacement of the pen by the typewriter, and then by the typewriter's analogies, phonograph, telephone and cinema. Where the pen inscribes, the typewriter impacts. In the 'discourse network' that was already in place by 1900, the intimate economy of brain, hand, eye, line and paper is replaced by the violent, blind, tactile concussion of surfaces. 'All that remains of the real is a contact surface or skin, where something writes on something else', Kittler tells us (1990: 224).

The hideous writing machine of Kafka's 'In the Penal Colony' cannot now not be read as the direct, unconscious inscription of such processes of inscription. In this self-explicating allegory, the story imprints itself as forcefully and corporeally as the very process of inscribing the law which it presents. Like the body of the condemned prisoner, the story seems to have no interiority, no curiosity or secret, no concealed or implicit backside. Law, like psychoanalysis and the other privileged expressions of the discourse network, bypasses consciousness and is made to appear directly on the body of the subject (the subject here being literally, in this story in which everything is done to the letter, the one who lies underneath, the support, the platen, the receiving bed). The text which shows all this seems itself to be inscribed by the truth it inscribes, locked between the recto and verso of its pages as immovably as the condemned man is inserted between the Designer and the Bed.

But the machine (or perhaps we should say the two machines, the device written of in Kafka's story and the machinery of that writing itself) goes wrong. Realising that the explorer, to whom he has been explicating the glories and mysteries of the machine, is not convinced of the justice of the old way of execution, the officer takes the place of the condemned man under the harrow. And then the machine appallingly, absurdly, begins to destroy itself, vomiting up its own mechanical innards in place of the human body that it ought to deliver, just in time, at the fulfilment of its sentence, and in the demonstration of the demonstration, to its ready-made grave. There is a horror and a violence in everything being brought to the surface, in everything being made a matter of surface, in the way of the old law. But the story itself seems not to be able to articulate the nature of the different horror, when the defining, violent encounter between the surface and the inscribing force fails. Does the machine of Kafka's own allegorical demonstration itself fail as a result? Or is its aim to open up a gap between itself and the mode of law's inscription? Does it know its meaning, or is its meaning written through it? The story might be available to be read, not only as the figuration of a traumatic assault on a surface, but also as the dread of a failure of the surface, the giving way of embodiment.

In his remarkable meditation on Kafka's story, Jean-François Lyotard marks out in it a conflict between two modes or moments of touching. For Lyotard, Kafka writes of the violent touch of the law, which demands to be written directly on the body, rather than merely being applied to it. Lyotard's concern is with the topography and the temporality of this typography. On what, and in what time, does the law inscribe itself? The law wants to impose its violent figuring touch upon what at first and in the end must slip through its fingers, namely an experience of an indeterminate preconceptual 'here and now' of the body that can be in no way prefigured or prescribed. This 'infant' body knows nothing of law or language, for it has not yet received their touch or taken their print. Lyotard identifies this groundless, lawless being in the here and now of corporeal experience, in which one is 'exposed in space-time and to the space-time of something that touches before any concept and even any representation', with the aesthetic:

> To be esthetically (in the sense of the first Kantian *Critique*) is to be there (*être-là*) here and now . . . This *before* is not known, obviously, because it is there before we are. It is something like birth and infancy (Latin *in-fans*) – there before we are. The *there* in question is called the body. It is not I who am born, who is given birth to. I will be born afterwards, with language, precisely in leaving infancy. My affairs will have been handled and decided before I can answer for them – and once and for all: this infancy, this body, this unconscious remaining there my entire life. When the law comes, with my self and language, it is too late. Things will already have taken a turn. And the law in its turn will not manage to efface the first turn, this first *touch*. Esthetics has to do with this first touch, which touched me when I was not there.
>
> (Lyotard 1991a: 18; emphasis in original)

What matters most about Lyotard's autistic aesthetic of self-touching is that it leaves no mark, because there is not yet a ground or surface in place to retain the trace. It is this which makes the temporality of this primal touch, the temporality upon which we must make it rest to conceive it at all, so complex. For temporality works through the making and retaining of marks and is therefore of the order of inscription. To see this first touch as *at first* – first a surface, then what comes to mark it – is mistakenly to have preinscribed it with its place in that order of temporal succession.

When it is a question of an art that would manage an encounter with this primary corporeal aesthetics, Lyotard's account has a more austere and destructive character. Discussing musical experimentation, for example, Lyotard describes a writing that would not merely apply itself to a given surface (the blank slate of the medium, or of cultural tradition), but would scour or scratch away the surface of the inscription:

> I'd like to falsify the value of the prefix 'e' to hear in *écriture* something like a 'scratching' – the old meaning of the root *scri* – *outside of*, outside any support, any apparatus of resonance and reiteration, any concept and pre-inscribed form. But first of all *outside any support*.
>
> (Lyotard 1991b: 158; emphasis in original)

The avant-garde art that would make contact with that which has no concept is characterised no longer by the lightest of caresses, but by the incendiary destruction of contact itself:

> There would not first be a surface (the whole tradition, heritage, memory) and then this stroke coming to mark it. This mark, if this is the case, will only be remark. And I know that this is how things always are, for the mind which ties times to each other and to itself, making itself the *support of every inscription*. No, it would rather be the flame, the enigma of flame itself. It indicates its support in destroying it. It belies its form. It escapes its resemblance with itself.
>
> (Lyotard 1991b: 158; emphasis in original)

The primary touch of the infant aesthetic as conceived by Lyotard has certain resemblances to what Levinas thematises as the ethical condition of proximity, which Levinas regularly represents as a pure touch or contact without mark, residue or inscription. Where, for Lyotard, the aesthetic is the touching that leaves no trace, for Levinas, the ethical relation is characterised by a contact that is too immediate to be susceptible to representation. But, like Lyotard, Levinas characterises this immediacy of contact as a rupture:

> The *ethical* . . . indicates a reversal of the subjectivity which is *open upon* beings and always in some measure represents them to itself, positing them and taking them to be such or such (whatever be the quality, axiological, practical, or logical, of the thesis that posits them), into a subjectivity that enters *into contact* with a singularity, excluding identification in the ideal, excluding thematization and representation – an absolute singularity, as such unrepresentable.

This is the original language, the foundation of the other one. The precise point at which this mutation of the intentional into the ethical occurs, and occurs continually, at which the approach *breaks through* consciousness, is the human skin and face. Contact is tenderness and responsibility.

(Levinas 1987: 116; emphasis in original)

What matters in such contact between self and other is not meaning or understanding. As with Kafka's writing machine, there is nothing but the contact itself: 'This utterance of the contact says and learns only this very fact of saying and learning – here again, like a caress' (Levinas 1987: 116).

Both Lyotard and Levinas seek from the skin figurations of the non-figural: the image of a touching without marking, a writing without residue, a weightlessness, nearness and immediacy. The skin is now reserved as that which eludes visibility, the ground on which the visible is written and which itself can thus be seen only in intimate revelatory flashes: 'The law takes a grip. . . . 'Features have to be deciphered, read and understood like ideograms. Only the hair, and the light that emanates from the skin escape its discipline' (Lyotard 1991b: 190). This is perhaps why both Levinas and Lyotard are reluctant to thematise the skin; they want the skin to remain invisible, unfigured, and yet able to touch and be touched through the blind palpations of metaphor, the nudgings and insurgences of touch into discourse.

In this, both Lyotard and Levinas work to protect something like an idealised model of the hysteric; the one who speaks through her body and cannot be made to speak otherwise, or not without a mediation that will always manifest itself as a violence. The reason for our current, continuing interest in hysteria, and perhaps also the recent revival of the concept of trauma, is surely that we so envy the symptoms which we do not have. Indeed, perhaps what we mourn and covet is symptomatology itself: the lost apparition of the symptom. This hysteria-envy surfaces clearly in Paul Virilio's recent analysis of the universal conditions of technological 'telecontact', in which everything can touch everything else, at a distance. As in the coming of the typewriter, as explicated by Friedrich Kittler, with its splitting apart of the coordination of hand, eye and paper, everything takes place at a remove from the actual individual sensorium, but this general mediation produces an overwhelming sense of the intolerable immediacy and proximity of everything, in which nothing is in fact sufficiently apart from the self or from any other thing to allow it either to exist, in the Heideggerian sense of 'standing clear' or 'standing out' against some background, or to communicate, in the sense of a making common of what is separate:

beyond the confines of proximity as we know it, prospective **telepresence** – and shared **tele-existence** with it – not only eliminate the 'line' of the visible horizon in favour of the linelessness of a deep and imaginary horizon. They also once again undermine the very notion of **relief**, with touch and **tactile telepresence at a distance** now seriously muddying not only the distinction between the 'real' and the 'virtual', as Cybersurfers currently define it, but also the very reality of the *near* and the *far*, thus casting doubt on our presence *here* and *now* and so dismantling the necessary conditions for sensory experience.

(Virilio 1997: 45; emphasis in original)

This is hysterical writing in a literal sense, which is to say, a writing that finds a certain relief in the elaborate exhibition of the typographically impassioned surface which it is telling us has vanished; bold, italic and inverted commas seem to insist on the truth of its terms, a truth that is made to seem so inescapably and self-announcingly apparent that it has gouged its way into the page we are reading, or risen up dermographically from within it.

Virilio articulates (articulates against) the nausea of edgeless exposure that follows from having broken out of our skin. There is the dread of there being no inviolate, therefore violable, surfaces any more, no possibility any more of contact or contingency, as the modernist world of traumatic impact, concussion and repercussion gives way to interfaces, interactivity and the volatile coalescence of bodies. The ideal of nonfigurable contact, whether aesthetic (Lyotard) or ethical (Levinas), may be taken both as a nostalgia for the palpable in a world in which palpability has evaporated into discourse and signification, and as an approximation of the essentially *skinless* propinquity, and immediatisation of contemporary media.

The term 'immediatisation' appears, attributed to Rémy Auxerre, a media analyst with certain resemblances to Jean Baudrillard, in Salman Rushdie's *The Ground Beneath Her Feet*, a novel in which reflections on the traumatic breaking through of worlds into each other is accompanied by forebodings of the loss of skin (1999: 485). Whether in earthquake, that governing metaphor for the 'tectonic contradictoriness' of the contemporary self, or, in the remarkable chapter entitled 'Membranes', in the natal passage from East to West, accomplished through a 'tear in the sky', which allows the musician Ormus Cama, flying from Bombay to London, to glimpse 'miracles through the gash', the novel is full of the rapture of epidermal rupture (Rushdie 1999: 339, 253). But there is also apprehension about this failure of the skin. The rock-god Ormus Cama writes: '*My greatest concern is that I feel the fragility of our space and time . . . I feel its growing attenuation.*' (Rushdie 1999: 437; emphasis in original). The narrator suggests that this attenuation encourages a primitivist return to the skin: 'It looks like it's scared us so profoundly, this fracturing, this tumbling of walls, this forgodsake freedom, that at top speed we're rushing back into our skins and war paint, postmodern into premodern, back to the future' (Rushdie 1999: 343).

In Rushdie's novel, the narrator is a photographer, and is as much concerned with photography as with the seismic powers of mass media and rock and roll. The gash in the skin is always a figured gash, even as it seems to be an assault on figurality itself, a denial of figure's ground. This may then seem to demand a further act of tearing open, or stripping away, even if this threatens the loss of skin. The alternatives of tearing and binding are not recto and verso, rather, in the Moebian topology of contemporary epidermal culture, in which everything has been turned to the front, they form a continuous surface, since what is at stake in them is the continuity of surface itself.

As its title suggests, the thematics of frontality in *The Ground Beneath Her Feet* conjoin in a specially literal way with the thematics of the underneath. In taking our print, the skin also bears our weight. As the medium of making literal, the ground upon which every figure is inscribed, the skin is often nowadays concerned with the question of weight, as it is, for example, in sadomasochistic practice and representation.

It is often as though the skin were dramatising the primary significance of the word '*bear*'. In much sadomasochistic practice and imagery, there is an obsessive interplay between the attack on shape carried out through the use of weights, or objects hung from the skin in order to stretch and distort its contours, and the display of the skin's reassuring capacity to support weight. The skin bears weight as its owner bears suffering. In one ritual practised by masochistic performance artist Bob Flanagan, a third meaning was enacted: he hung plastic babies from hooks in his skin, as a way of demonstrating the enforced bearing of children (1993: 61). Hanging objects from one's skin seems to reduce one's skin to an object, mere fleshly stuff to be played with at will and without mercy. But to hang yourself from your skin, or, as we might say, in a small but significant prepositional shift, *by* your skin, as practised, for example, by the self-modifying performance artist Stelarc, who hung himself high in the air through hooks in his skin, is to reduce *yourself* to the condition of object, or mere mass or weight. The hung person is of course reduced to an object, a mere carcass. They are wholly vulnerable and available. But they are also supported, borne up by the mortification they elect to have to bear. Suspension gives a curious compensatory sense of protection. Language gives us another literalisation here; of the person in this appalling condition, it must be said that they literally depend upon their own skin. This can be confirmed in the obsessive drive for symmetry or visible shape often evidenced in the way victims are hung or bound in sadomasochistic imagery. Like many other assaults on the skin, in weight-training, diet-restriction, body-sculpture and self-modification through mortification, the point seems to be to *keep in shape*.

So we are seeing that, alongside and within the intense longing for a scene on which to represent and make reparation for the loss of shape and surface, there is a longing for an assault upon the surface that will leave no mark, for a disfiguration that will erase – but visibly erase – the apparatus of figurality itself. Literature, performance and psychosis twist grotesquely together. The speaker in Samuel Beckett's *The Unnamable* grimly imagines himself as an organless, featureless egg in an extreme of defacement (1959: 307). A patient known as Mr. H went as far as cutting off his entire face with fragments of a mirror (Sheftel *et al.* 1986: 525–40; O'Dell 1998: 96). The face is both what is written on the face, and the faciality of the skin itself, the availability of the skin to bear inscriptions. It seemed not to be enough to remove the features of the face; the faciality of the face had to bear the brunt of the annihilating attack. But the stripping away of the features seems to reveal, even to be designed to reveal, the invariant ground of faciality, the face beneath the face, the unfigurable support of figurality.

Antonin Artaud, mistrusting his own body, colonised and infected as he felt it to be by God, language and history, just as the possessed of earlier ages may have felt their bodies to be the haunt of demons and agencies of putrefaction, sought a body remade in the immediacy of cry and gesture, a body mutilated into clamorous muteness. As Jacques Derrida has shown, this mutilation is in fact a blow against articulation, against the possibility of repetition in time and space, perhaps against the possibility of time and space as such, in so far as these are marked out on the originary ground or skin of the body. 'The body', Derrida suggests, 'must be autarchic . . . remade of a single piece' (1978: 187). Artaud thought he had discovered the condition of radical, spiritual and bodily self-making in the drug-induced Peyote ritual practised by the Tarahumara people of Mexico, with whom he spent some months in 1936. In a note added in 1947 to the narrative of his experiences that he wrote while incarcerated in the asylum at Rodez, Artaud seizes on the skin as the principle of autarchic uprightness:

> with Peyote MAN is alone, desperately scraping out the music of his own skeleton, without father, mother, family, love, god, or society.
>   And no living being to accompany him. And the skeleton is not of bone but of skin, like a skin that walks. And one walks from the equinox to the solstice, buckling on one's own humanity.
>
> (Artaud 1976: 37–8)

Here, Artaud rejects not only the spatial partition of organs across the skin, but also the top-to-bottom stratification of the body. The reimagined body of the Peyote ritual has its skin on the inside, and wears its skeleton like a second skin, or armour. This unthinkable body, at once flayed and reskinned, in which the skin bears the weight of intrinsic being rather than the traces of extrinsic meaning, allows one to be made from the inside out rather than the outside in.

The scarifier, the lacerator, the self-abuser, the piercer, all seek, like Artaud, to do violence to the primary violence that deprives me of my body, the violence of representation, naming, abstraction, the alienation of the body into significance. Theirs is an assault that goes beyond the attempt to efface and rewrite what is written on the skin: it is an assault upon the skin as the bearer or scene of meaning. It is an assault upon the apparatus of figuration, of which the skin is the privileged sign or locale. The skin is made to show, not appearance, but *apparition*, that which is immediately visible and readable, that which is, to remember the impressive, and instantly duplicable, self-mutilating performance of the lead singer of the Manic Street Preachers, shortly before his own disappearance, '4 REAL'. But all of this is, at the same time, also a rage against the loss of scene consequent upon a culture of telecontact. Hence the melodramatic excess of figurings of the skin; melodrama is nostalgic, it forces the skin into presence by forcing it back in time, as in the rituals of the Modern Primitives, seeming to testify to the fact that the skin is always out of time.

Marking time

Writing's element is time. When a mark is made, it is made, as a sound is uttered, at a certain time, and in a certain place. But the time of writing, as we have by now been so thoroughly taught, is the time, or the unpredictable many times, of its revisitations. Writing writes in anticipation of these revenances; it is pitted by the impact of all these foreseen, unforeknown futures.

Time is therefore written into writing with invisible ink. According to a traditional metaphor, the skin is written by time in just the same way as time is written into writing; its lines and furrows being said to be the work of time's pen, or chisel, or plough. Time's writing on the skin, or the concealment of that writing through cosmetics or cosmetic surgery, is our meaning: but a meaning that was never meant in the way that a written mark inscribed on a surface represents a decision. It is the way we come to mean, the meaning we come to have, through time. In this sense, the figure of time writing on the skin is itself a protective anthropomorphism, which projects a scene of here-and-now writing on a here-and-now surface – as though time could gather to a point and make its mark at a moment *in time* – to make sense of a writing of time that is really a writing through time.

If time writes the skin, then the skin can also be thought of as writing time. Assailed by marks, the skin possesses the capacity to regenerate itself, to grow out of, as well as into, disfigurement. The skin marks time partly by effacement: by the healing of lesions and the reassertion of the surface against every assault. The skin's way of writing time is indeed to write it out. The skin is a soft clock, which we wind up whenever we mark it; and when we mark the skin, and await its healing, we can make time run backwards. No other feature of our physical lives offers so magical a promise of reversibility. When we attempt to countermand time by artificially effacing its writing, smoothing out wrinkles with emollients, hitching up the face and the breasts, sucking out the fatty tissue from thighs and belly, we attempt to mimic the skin's own powers over time. So the skin *is* nothing but time, and yet, because the skin marks time, and can even reverse it, it can sometimes seem, like us, to be at odds with time, and therefore on our side against it.

It is for this reason that the mortified skin comes forward so insistently in the contemporary world, in which time, no less than place, has become multiplied and immaterialised. Mortification used to be a making visible of the here and now of the body, of the body *as* the here and now, in order to point away from it, to a longer, or different temporality. The purulence, the corruption, the visible suffering of the body, were all to be testimony to its subsequent redemption. Christ's suffering body on the cross was itself an earnest of its glorification to come, just as the breaking of the bread was the necessary part of its transfiguration into Christ's already glorified body. In Christian traditions of mortification, disfiguration is a necessary prerequisite for transfiguration.

Contemporary mortification borrows from this history, but to very different effect. Contemporary mortification does not aim to put the body in proleptic memory of its death, but to transfix the body in its presence. Medieval mortification attempted to transport the body into its redemption by accelerating its decay and death; contemporary mortification attempts to transport the body into its suffering, transfigured, ceaseless being. The body is indispensable to transcendence, for now our need is for a transcendence of the body in the body. This is not simply the replacement of a spiritual with a corporeal logic, since, to be sure, the latter is already operational in medieval mysticism, as Piero Camporesi (1988) and recent feminist explorations of female corporeal mysticism have shown (Bynum 1991, 1995). But in earlier periods, the body was capable of being thought of as plus and minus sign simultaneously, as the intersection of mortal and eternal time. For us, for whom there is only mortal time, and an immediatised present, mortification must mean a negation of the difference between the plus and the minus sign, not their aggregation, or the intensification of their difference.

For there is an intrinsic difficulty in placing or dating the time of the skin, since its function for us is to be anachronistic, or partly out of time; as the Modern Primitives movement may attest, there is a desire for the skin to figure as archaic survival, as a reminder of a different, lost way of being in one's skin. It is for this reason above all that the drive to mark the body cannot be separated from a desire to assault the very medium and apparatus of epidermal figurality, since this apparatus is temporal as well as inscriptive. By assaulting the skin, one assaults time, or the ravages inflicted on it, on us, by time.

I began with Kafka's inaugural epidermal fable. I will finish with a discussion of Joanna Briscoe's *Skin* (1997), which may be thought of as a polymorphous rewriting of that work. Where Kafka seems to reduce the body to the skin, and to reduce the skin to one single function alone, its capacity to take and retain signs, Joanna Briscoe expands the functions of the skin until it can go anywhere and be anything; it becomes an impossibly grounding figure for the polymorphousness of figuration itself. The skin is all there is, but it is everything. The narrative situation is simple: a reclusive novelist, Adèle Meier, whose beauty is beginning to fade as she approaches middle age, attempts to regain her youth through revivifying but also vampiric sexual encounters with young boys, along with a series of graphically described surgical procedures, which burn and flay away her ageing features as the narrative peels back the layers of her own personal past. It is as though the novel discovers in its narrative situation the chance, or the chance to enact the need, to show the world rewritten in terms of the skin. Here, pain, whether of actual assault, or of loss, or of realisation, is always a cutting, abrasion or infliction: 'the sight of him made a deep cut in me, infected me with pain and howling frustration' (Briscoe 1997: 56). Beauty is the mark of punishment displayed on the skin, as in 'her eyes, apricot-green pool water, bruises on the pale skin' (Briscoe 1997: 9). Love is similarly cutaneous: 'I loved her at such depth . . . rooted to the filaments of my body' (Briscoe 1997: 107), as is its failure: 'We were never knitted together' (Briscoe 1997: 107). Inertia is like a scab: 'I pick at it' (Briscoe 1997: 71). Even audibility has its epidermal register: the surgeon's voice is 'low and leatherette' (Briscoe 1997: 59). The skin bears the threat or burden of pain throughout the book, but the pain that tears into the skin is also woven into skin-like shapes and textures: after her facelift, the pain 'rung in a halo around my body'; later on,

Adèle is 'bound in a gauze web of pain' (Briscoe 1997: 115, 308). The act of writing itself is knitted into the morphology of skin: 'I scribbled notes, and larger passages, and divine plots for myself, and began to sew them together in places' (Briscoe 1997: 155): 'I've stretched the canvas in my brain so far, it's blank and only blank. When I sit down to write, it slips and fades into the grey-white shade of hospital walls, the grain a pigskin-dotted fake' (Briscoe 1997: 58).

A determined reading could easily order and articulate these figurations into male and female specialities: men being indeed associated in the novel with blades, scalpels, fists, mordant light and the sexual violence which molests the skin: 'he could have gorged new routes into her. He could have made an indelible mark on her with his penis' (Briscoe 1997: 13). Women are associated with the skin itself, or its skinlike dissimulations, webs, veils, folds, fabrics, buds, oils and the vaginated involution of hearts and flowers. But this scheme is only a recurrent attractor within a much more fundamentally turbulent swirl of associations and interconnections, which is resolvable into erotic utopia or theatre of cruelty only by subtraction. Skin migrates, for example, into other substances, notably glass and dust. Adèle is often seen with her face pressed against glass, as though her skin were taking its own photograph: 'My face, its pores and slackness, pressed against the surface. It was preserved, like an extinct species flared beneath a layer of glass' (Briscoe 1997: 68). Photography, like plastic surgery, sears and seals to do its work of preservation: but photographs are as vulnerable as living skin to the violent markings of time: 'The film is turning grey. The print is an old one, it has scratches and areas of fading' (Briscoe 1997: 236). Photography is also implicated in the drift of skin into granular indistinction that is witnessed throughout the book: 'The woman, her planes and angles and the pigmentations of her skin translated into infinitesimal grains of silver bromide, looked tarnished' (Briscoe 1997: 21–2). Dust provides the evidence that skin not only dissevers, but itself is dissolved: 'Surely grains of skin, human dust, migrate in eddies and we breathe them in, so even the essence of our neighbours tints our bloodstreams, their breath and splinters of their hair forming motes of our organic matter' (Briscoe 1997: 26). As the figure of divisibility itself, the glass-skin or the dust-skin, to specify only these, does not allow itself to be placed securely on one side or other of a male–female divide.

If anything organises the polymorphous work of figuration in which the skin is involved, it is time. Time, like everything else in the novel, is whelmed in skin. Looking back to the time of an intense and finally violently terminated affair, Adèle thinks 'of course, it's a jewel box, the memory sews events into a satin soft box' (Briscoe 1997: 75). The plastic surgery she undergoes is an attempt to get back, through an extremity of pain, the unscarred time of her beauty. Since it is in part the skin that has betrayed her, the skin must suffer to be restored to itself: 'If the face is a record of our histories, Dr. Kreitzman razed mine from me' (Briscoe 1997: 159).

Because skin takes and retains marks, it signifies irreversibility. But, as we have seen, because it not only takes and retains marks but can also erase them, it can also signify the possibility that the past might be retrievable in literal fact, in the flesh. This means, for Adèle, the surgical unwriting of the skin, and for the narration, the writing of this unwriting. We have seen that, throughout the narrative of *Skin*, the skin provides metaphorical equivalents for everything: there is nothing that cannot be expressed in terms of the look, shape, texture or aroma of skin. But, in the sections of the novel devoted to the graphic accounts of Adèle's facial surgery, this is reversed: here, the skin itself is made the object in view, that which is to be figured. In the rest of the novel, skin serves to interpret the world: here, the world is called upon to interpret the universal interpretant, to figure the ground of figuration.

> Dr. Kreitzman cut away a section of the patient's face, perfectly following the outline of the ear. As he cut, an ear-shaped template of flesh flopped onto the pillow. It hung from behind the woman's ear. He cut more away. Another strand hung from the bottom of the ear, like a long earring of flesh. He cut it off, and the nurse dropped the woman's flesh on a cloth on the table as she passed the doctor a needle holder. Later, the scissors were placed casually upon it, then it was gathered with other waste and thrown away into the incinerator bag. Groups of several flaps hanging together, like wind chimes, stuck to her neck.
>
> (Briscoe 1997: 87)

The removal of the skin from the face is accompanied by an attempt to strip away the anthropomorphism of skin. Detached from the body, like the face that hangs from the patient's skull, it is mere facticity, mere waste, beneath metaphor. It means simply itself. But figuration is necessary to this purging of figural significance. Flesh becomes its own bizarre adornment ('an earring of flesh', 'several flaps hanging together, like wind chimes'), the action of defiguration reinstates, even relies upon figural ornament. We cannot see the skin in-itself, since the skin is the hesitation between 'ourself' and 'itself'. No matter how deep one digs below the skin, there is always another skin to be found: 'Under the skin, the face's pitted surface of muscle and blood resembled another fine, bloody face; part smooth, part marbled; yellow with a crazing of blood' (Briscoe 1997: 86). This division in the book, between its erotic and its surgical sections, makes the skin neither the literal nor the metaphorical, but, as it were, the membrane which divides and joins the two.

Just in the nick of time, the novel comes to show, though never quite to tell, the primary violation that has put Adèle to sleep in her lifetime of narcotic, self-punishing beauty. We realise, literally on the last page of the novel, that the father who went missing from Adèle's family had subjected her to sexual abuse as a child. The novel wants hereby to have told a story of an original trauma, an innocence despoiled at a particular defining moment, and condemned thereafter to carry on despoiling itself in the same way, lest it lose the defining shape provided by trauma. The novel wants to lift its own veil, get under the skin of its own metaphorical preoccupations, to show what it is that the skin, in its beauty and terror, dissimulates. In doing this, the novel must reveal the ways in which, in its own narrative delays and dispersals, it has taken part in the traumatic dissimulation of trauma in which the skin is implicated. The story that this long work of dissimulation discovers is of the need for there to be a skin (which is to say, both an indelible truth and a cover-up) to bear (to carry, endure, deliver, bear out) the otherwise invisible, indivisible impact of trauma. In the end, *Skin* attempts to skin itself (odd that the English word for the removal of skin seems to contain the possibility of its regeneration – in this resembling the verb to 'bone'), identifying the primal touch that cannot be retouched, that lies unalterably beneath the 'life distilled to its extremes in rumour and quote and retouched image' (Briscoe 1997: 304).

But the need for there to have been a time and place of this touching means that the figuration of skin will continue to be necessary. Before, or underneath, the skin there must be a skin, to bear the mark of the first infliction. In the final revelation of the childhood abuse that is offered as the key to all Adèle's self-mortification, trauma becomes swallowed up in skin: 'The scream was only a dream scream, and it flopped as a rigid object gone slack' (Briscoe 1997: 317). Disfiguring the skin is a way of keeping it visible. For us, the hypervisibility of skin is an apotropaic resource which banishes the fear of its vanishing – even though the mock-hysterical hypervisibility of skin may be the very manner of its disappearance. *Skin* bears witness to the nameless suffering involved in the loss of suffering. There is a grim rhyme between the dispersal of suffering and the erotic dispersal of pleasures. To lose the place and time of experience is to lose the skin, to disclose the skin, not as a scene, but as the absence of a scene. The obscenity of the skin under assault, by contrast, gives us back the scene of suffering and pleasure, gives it somewhere to happen, and someone to happen to, a time and a place for there to be a time and a place.

References

Artaud, A. (1976) *The Peyote Dance*, trans. Helen Weaver, New York: Farrar, Straus and Giroux.

Barthes, R. (1981) *Camera Lucida*, New York: Hill and Wang.

Beckett, S. (1959) *Molloy, Malone Dies, The Unnamable*, London: Calder and Boyars.

Briscoe, J. (1997) *Skin*, London: Phoenix.

Bynum, C. W. (1991) *Fragmentation and Redemption: Essays on Gender and the Human Body in Medieval Religion*, New York: Zone Books.

—— (1995) *The Resurrection of the Body in Western Christianity 200–1336*, New York: Columbia University Press.

Camporesi, P. (1988) *The Incorruptible Flesh: Bodily Mutilation and Mortification in Religion and Folklore*, trans. Tania Croft-Murray and Helen Elsom, Cambridge: Cambridge University Press.

Derrida, J. (1978) 'La parole soufflée' in *Writing and Difference*, trans. Alan Bass, London: Routledge and Kegan Paul.

—— (1979) *Spurs: Nietzsche's Styles*, trans. Barbara Harlow, Chicago: University of Chicago Press.

Flanagan, B. (1993) *Supermasochist*, San Francisco: Re/Search Publications.

Kittler, F. (1990) *Discourse Networks, 1800/1900*, trans. Michael Metteer and Chris Cullens, Stanford: Stanford University Press.

Larkin, P. (1986) *The Whitsun Weddings*, London: Faber and Faber.

Levinas, E. (1987) 'Language and proximity' in *Collected Philosophical Papers*, trans. A. Lingis, Dordrecht: Martinus Nijhoff.

Lewin, B. D. (1946) 'Sleep, the mouth, and the dream screen', *Psychoanalytic Quarterly* 15: 419–34.

—— (1953) 'Reconsideration of the Dream Screen', *Psychoanalytic Quarterly* 22: 174–99.

Lyotard , J-F. (1991a) 'Prescription', *L'Esprit créateur* 31: 15–32.

—— (1991b) *The Inhuman: Reflections on Time*, trans. Geoffrey Bennington and Rachel Bowlby, Cambridge: Polity Press.

O'Dell, K. (1998) *Contract With the Skin: Masochism, Performance Art and the 1970s*, Minneapolis: University of Minnesota Press.

Rushdie, S. (1999) *The Ground Beneath Her Feet*, London: Jonathan Cape.

Serres, M. (1985) *Les cinq sens*, Paris: Grasset.

Sheftel, S. *et al.* (1986) 'A Case of Radical Facial Self-Mutilation: An Unprecedented Event and its Impact', *Bulletin of the Menninger Clinic* 50: 525–40.

Virilio, P. (1997) *Open Sky*, trans. Julie Rose, London: Verso.

3   Skin memories

Jay Prosser

Remembered skins

We become aware of skin as a visible surface through memory. If someone touching our skin brings us immediately into the present, the look of our skin – both to others and to ourselves – brings to its surface a remembered past. It is a phenomenological function of skin to record. Skin re-members, both literally in its material surface and metaphorically in resignifying on this surface, not only race, sex and age, but the quite detailed specificities of life histories. In its colour, texture, accumulated marks and blemishes, it remembers something of our class, labour/leisure activities, even (in the use of cosmetic surgery and/or skincare products) our most intimate psychic relation to our bodies. Skin is the body's memory of our lives. But if skin constitutes a visual biographical record, by no means is this record historically accurate. As the vicissitudes of the inheritance of race in skin colour show, skin's memory is as much a fabrication of what didn't happen as a record of what did, as much fiction as fact. Indeed, the fact that we continue to invest the legibility of identity in the skin in spite of knowing its unreliability suggests skin to be a fantasmatic surface, a canvas for what we wish were true – or for what we cannot acknowledge to be true. Skin's memory is burdened with the unconscious.

If bodies can be said to have memories, those whose bodies malfunction highlight this fact; such subjects cannot forget their bodies, but are constantly reminded of their mortality. Certain theories of illness have located the skin as one site for the body's memory. In her cultural study of cancer, Jackie Stacey draws a notion of bodily memory from trauma and suggests skin as one site for registering this trauma. As she shows, one possible side-effect of chemotherapy is to strip the body of its hair and expose the skin as a surface on which allergic reactions to the treatment are recorded: 'scratch marks become scars and stay, a permanent reminder'; 'bodily memories [that] mediate against a complete forgetting' (Stacey 1997: 84, 100). The skin is 'the body's ambassador': 'it represents the interface between inside and outside . . . it meets the world. . . . Dermographia. Skin drawing' (Stacey 1997: 84). In a similar argument, I have described transsexual sex reassignment as an attempt to re-member through skin a sexed body that should have been (Prosser 1998). Largely a process of manipulating the surface tissues of the body, sex reassignment realigns and reassigns, resexes, the skin. The difference between cancer treatment and transsexuality is illuminating, for whereas cancer-treated skin remembers the trauma that actually happened, transsexual skin remembers the fantasy that ought to have happened. Transsexuality reveals skin as a site for unconscious investment, a body memory or fantasy that failed to materialise.

Freud's bodily ego, which is a conceptualisation of body memory, gives a key role to the body's surface. Freud asserts in *The Ego and the Id* that: 'The ego is first and foremost a bodily ego; it is not merely a surface entity, but is itself the projection of a surface' (1984: 364). Didier Anzieu reads Freud's 'surface' literally as the skin to formulate his notion of the 'skin ego'. The skin ego parallels, and integrates, skin with psyche:

> The surface of the body allows us to distinguish excitations of external origins from those of internal origin; just as one of the capital functions of the ego is to distinguish between what belongs to me myself and what does not belong, between what comes from me and the desires, thoughts and affects of others, between a physical (the world) or biological (the body) reality outside the mind; the ego is the projection in the psychic of the surface of the body, namely the skin, which makes up this sheet or interface.
>
> (Anzieu 1990: 63)

The skin ego is the interface between psyche and body, self and others. The self derives from the skin, from those first touches in childhood that create a sense of ourselves as contained and social. Anzieu rereads a later metapsychological essay by Freud to show how the double-layered structure of the ego replicates the skin: as the epidermis protects, the ego is surrounded; as the dermis records stimuli, the perception-consciousness system registers memories. Through analogy to the newly invented 'Mystic Writing-pad', this chapter seeks to explain how memories can be erased from consciousness and yet retained in the unconscious; and here again, Freud gives a key role to surface. For Freud the 'more interesting part' of the writing-pad is the interface between the wax tablet and the writing, for this surface allows the writing to be recorded and erased while the wax tablet below nevertheless retains inscriptive traces. As 'the appearance and disappearance of the writing' dramatises 'the flickering-up and passing-away of consciousness in the process of perception', the unconscious retains as written traces memories that have been consciously forgotten (Freud 1984: 431, 433). It is precisely the writing-pad's/psyche's double-layered surface, what we might call the skin of the machine, that allows for this recording and erasure, this conversion of memory into the unconscious.

Anzieu's theory of the skin ego gives no stated place to memory. But as the ego is formed through our first experiences of our skin, it would seem that the skin ego takes shape through memory. Yet these memories may be unconscious, consisting of what Freud increasingly recognises as psychic reality: not memories of actual happenings, but fantasies real only in the unconscious. Anzieu's first inklings of the concept of a skin ego, which occurred while he was a psychologist on a hospital dermatology unit (Anzieu 1990), reveal skin saturated with the unconscious. He finds that those with material skin damage suffer correlative damage to their psychic envelope. More fantasmatically, thus more revealing of skin as unconscious, those with skin disorders often uncover in psychoanalysis an originating and pathogenic psychic disturbance: if damage to the material skin can be remembered psychically, damage to the psychic envelope can be remembered physically. Thus, Anzieu writes: 'skin ailments are closely related to stress, to emotional upheavals and, more importantly . . . to narcissistic flaws and inadequate structuring of the Ego . . . the irritation of the epidermis becomes confused with mental irritation' (1989: 32–33). Psychic disturbance can inscribe on the skin traumatic memories according to the hysterical symptomisations of the unconscious. Anzieu's skin analysands appear to remember in their skin conditions what they cannot consciously express. Self-mutilation, repeated self-scalding, the development of an overmuscular skin, the emission of foul smells, such non-accidental skin symptoms take Anzieu and his analysands back to a childhood memory or unconscious fantasy too traumatic to become conscious. These skin disorders appear as returns of an unspeakable repressed event.

Yet skin memories may remember, not just an individual unconscious, but a cultural one. As he believes today's typical patient suffers 'from an absence of borders or limits' – 'He is uncertain of the frontiers between the psychical and bodily Egos, between the reality Ego and the ideal Ego, between what belongs to the Self and what to others' – Anzieu identifies a confusion of borders and limits as symptomatic of Western culture at the end of twentieth century (1989: 7). In the arms race, in 'insatiable consumption' and 'the increasing disparity between the rich nations and the Third World', in our violation of nature (Anzieu 1989: 6) – and, we might add, in our own current confusion in Eastern European wars between respecting national borders and trespassing them to protect international human rights – we no longer recognise definite boundaries. Anzieu's skin ego is as powerful a global concept as an individual one and it seeks to establish limits concurrently on both fronts: 'it seems to me a matter of the utmost urgency, in both psychological and social terms, for us to re-establish limits, restore some frontiers, mark out inhabitable, liveable territories for ourselves' (1989: 8). For if somatic transgressions remember psychic ones, psychic transgressions surely remember cultural ones.

Stigmatised skins

Among Anzieu's patients with skin disorders are many who clearly cannot forget their skin. Given the function of skin as a visual surface to record, it is ironic that the cultural ideal of skin should be skin that forgets. 'Good skin' is skin unmarked by the passage of time. 'Bad skin' means skin marked both by memory and as memorable; we do not forget bad skin. But why should marked skin be a site for social memory and consciousness? What psychic investment, what cultural burdening, takes place on the skin, such that skin disorders can come to represent and embody, indeed to cause social comfort?

Erving Goffman's etymology of the term 'stigmatisation' gives flesh to the literal origination of the term. Stigmatisation begins as a practice on the skin:

> The Greeks, who were apparently strong on visual aids, originated the term *stigma* to refer to bodily signs designed to expose something unusual and bad about the moral status of the signifier. The signs were cut or burnt into the body and advertised that the bearer was a slave, a criminal, or a traitor – a blemished person, ritually polluted, to be avoided.
>
> (Goffman 1968: 11)

Stigmatisation thus begins catachrestically on the surface of the body: the material marks on the skin remember, literalising on the body and signifying in the symbolic, the subject's social difference. This catachrestic memorialising sense of stigmatisation continues in the following two stages of the term:

> Later, in Christian times, two layers of metaphor were added to the term: the first referred to bodily signs of holy grace that took the form of eruptive blossoms on the skin; the second, a medical allusion to this religious allusion, referred to bodily signs of physical disorder.
>
> (Goffman 1968: 11)

While the Christian meaning positively values the literal skin markings as remembering a symbolic holiness (Christ's sacrifice), the medical meaning sees the literal defects as producing symbolic disorder, what Goffman calls a 'spoiled identity'. But common to all stages is the catachrestic memorialisation between bodily surface and subject's social status, between cutaneous referent and social sign. Stigmatisation thus suggests that marked skin may re-member a cultural unconscious. The way in which the literal slides into sign in stigmatisation conveys condensation and displacement, two of the hallmark dynamics of the unconscious; yet the marking out in all three stages refers to the subject's cultural placement. Skin disorders may be socially stigmatising because they remember what a culture would like to repress.

Such a notion is borne out, and the notion of a cultural unconscious is thus made useful, by recognising the role that skin plays in racism; for what is racism if not the categorical form of stigmatisation? At once the most epidermal study of racism and the most psychoanalytic – thus forging a link between skin and the unconscious – Frantz Fanon's *Black Skin, White Masks* argues that racism is better described as the 'epidermalization' of inferiority than its 'internalisation' (1967: 11). A black subject in a racist encounter is reduced to and through his surface. '"Dirty Nigger!" Or simply, "Look, a Negro!"'; in Fanon's dramatisation the interpellation fixes the black subject 'in the sense in which a chemical solution is fixed by a dye' (Fanon 1967: 11). S/he becomes precisely *coloured* in that moment, a body re-membered by the racist white subject as only skin: 'the corporeal schema crumbled, its place taken by a racial epidermal schema' (Fanon 1967: 112). Fanon's account, which extirpates the unconscious roots of racism and its soma-topsychic sustenance, suggests that racism is perpetuated in its unconscious form – surely its most pernicious – in no small part through the skin, skin re-membering constituting social membership. If stigmatisation begins as a memorialising cata-chresis, as Goffman's account indicates, is it not possible, in accordance with the confusion between literal and signifier in catachresis, that differently marked skin (and this includes differently coloured skin) comes, not just to signify, but to call for and justify – and in the unconscious to cause – different symbolic treatment? This is not, of course, to justify racism; rather it is rather to grapple with the soma-topsychic dimension of racism that perpetuates it ruthlessly in the unconscious.

Two narratives may be invoked here to support this proposition about the role of skin colour in the perpetuation of unconscious racism. One is Toni Morrison's thesis that the entirety of American literature – and of American history – has constructed white American subjectivity by re-membering blackness as otherness, a blackness that it yet seeks to repress and subject to a national amnesia (Morrison 1993; Morrison 1994: 256–7). The other narrative consists of the response to the Stephen Lawrence report in Britain which, following the racist murder of the black teenager, was the first public document to condemn institutional racism in Britain (Macpherson 1999). The night of the report's publication, Lawrence's (black) memorial stone in Eltham, South London was daubed with white paint; this act that sought to white out, literally and symbolically, the realities of racism in contemporary Britain, was symptomatic of the desire to forget at the very moment the country was enjoined to remember what a nation couldn't bear to have rendered conscious – its racism. Both narratives, which are equally literal and literary, reveal skin colour as a crucial canvas for the construction of racism and then for its repression, for the unconscious dimensions of racism in two nations's cultural memories.

If the black subject is stigmatised in a racist unconscious, are the subjects who bring to the surface this stigmatisation of skin, skin 'disorder' threatening social disorder, light-skinned black subjects? Like skin-disordered subjects, such subjects, perhaps for not very different reasons, are burdened with their own and others' skin consciousness. Though by definition their skin is not marked out – some can blend in, some can pass – it is precisely their blending and passing that literalises transgressed boundaries. In her account of what it means to be a 'white black American,' an African American with white skin, Judy Scales-Trent describes how her skin colour remembers – recalls and materialises – transgressed racial bound-aries. 'Living on the margins of race . . . black and white at the same time', she is a 'skinwalker'. Her movement through the world exposes and violates a dual con-struction of race: 'this system of rigid dualism . . . fosters so much anxiety when people don't fit into the categories neatly, when people "transgress boundaries"', yet 'in order for me to exist I must transgress boundaries' (Scales-Trent 1995: 7, 32, 12). Scales-Trent's 'skinwalking' powerfully suggests the historical reasons behind the anxiety over interstitially coloured skin. Originally, light-coloured black skin enabled passage from the master's plantations into his house and then perhaps from there to freedom, this literal skinwalking involving transgression of broken boundaries. But *Notes of a White Black Woman* is moving for the way it peels back the layers of pain and guilt impacted in racial stigmatisation. Helpless to prevent an involuntary passing, Scales-Trent suffers, toward black African Americans, 'the guilt of a survivor' (1995: 17). She wonders how many light-skinned blacks 'like I, went into the civil rights field, in some measure as a means of expiating our sin – of how we look' (Scales-Trent 1995: 69). Her coming out as white black woman (it is important that it is white that is the subordinate modifier here) and her work as a black civil rights lawyer is perhaps, she bravely acknow-ledges, an unconscious attempt 'to atone as a way of escaping the rage of our darker brothers and sisters' (Scales-Trent 1995: 69). She is still unconsciously atoning for the stigmatisation of her light-coloured, transgressive skin.

Vitiligo incarnates the transgression of the colour boundary. Consisting of the death of melanin cells in the epidermis, though it can strike any race, vitiligo threatens greater loss for those with dark skin because the loss of colour is greater and thus more noticeable. Rather than attempting to posit an uncutaneous intra-psychic self, vitiligo self-help publications encourage an acknowledgement of the investment of psychic self in skin by urging a process of mourning in vitiligo sufferers (Lesage 1997). Such a concern suggests a coloured skin ego – a racial skin ego. As they lose their colour, what memory of self, of skin, of race is shed? Some folklore beliefs about vitiligo, however, suggest that cultural stigmatisation is enmeshed with these psychosomatic recognitions of the investment of self in skin – Goffman's thesis with Anzieu's. Medical sociologist Anne Hill Beuf documents one belief among African Americans that vitiligo is God's punishment for those blacks who wished they were white; the skin disease is, in this rendition, a deserved realisation of unconscious, unspeakable desire to transgress (Beuf 1990). And the fact that in East India, vitiligo is seen as prefiguring leprosy, and that both vitiligo and leprosy are collapsed into 'leukoderma' (Beuf 1990: 45) – literally meaning 'white skin' and a term that can equally refer to Caucasian whiteness – again shows how light-coloured skin comes to carry the weight of the stigmatisation of racial transgression in a cultural unconscious.

If even for white subjects skin disorders are stigmatising, is it because in a cultural unconscious so concerned with literal and symbolic boundaries, skin disorders unconsciously (again condensing and symbolising – catachrestically) re-member a skin that refuses the borders of that foundational cultural divide – of race? Surely what is transgressive (and thus deserving of stigmatisation) about such differently marked skin is that it shows – forces into consciousness – the fact that racial difference, the alignment of race with black and white, is but a fantas-matic construction, not a real border at all, but precisely one repeatedly produced and memorialised in a racist unconscious.

Autobiographical skins

If the concept of stigmatisation inscribes or writes out a psycho-sociosymbolic signifier on the skin, this catachresis is reversed when skin-disordered subjects write out their skin in autobiographies; here the 'dermographia' or Freud's inscriptions on his mystic writing-pad are literalised and literarised. I use the term 'skin autobiographies' to group autobiographies, patent or legible as such, in which the author's skin disorder figures in some important way, in which the writing is a representation of skin disorder. Although it may seem eccentric to form a group from such a bizarre and apparently exceptional subject, such texts, which are not in fact so exceptional, do work as a group with shared conventions and concerns and in a form peculiarly appropriate to autobiography. The subject's marking out with skin disorder is reflected, symptomised, in the writing of autobiography which, as Georges Gusdorf (1980) suggests, is always symptomatic of the self's sense of being marked out, the subject's self-consciousness. And the fact that autobiography emerges generically from the religious tradition of confession, and that confession remains a legible thread even in modern autobiography, renders autobiography the ideal vehicle for working out the layers of guilt and sin in stigmatised skin disorders. Writing autobiography uncannily 'fits' the psychic dimension of skin disorders like a second skin.

With remarkably few exceptions, skin autobiographies associate skin disorder with sin. Writing of his psoriasis in his aptly titled memoir *Self-Consciousness*, John Updike casts himself as a 'pariah', 'a sin-soaked anchorite of old'; his skin marks him out as stigmatised, socially untouchable (1990: 52, 45). Dennis Potter's psychiatrist in *The Singing Detective* make a similar connection:

> The skin, after all is extremely *personal*, is it not? The temptation is to believe that the ills and the poisons of the mind or the personality have somehow or other erupted straight out on to the skin. 'Unclean! Unclean!' The leper in the Bible, yes?
>
> (Potter, 1986: 56; emphasis in original)

Although Dr Gibbon dismisses this theory of stigmatisation as 'nonsense', Potter's screenplay shows that it is the psoriatic author-figure's 'confession' of his memories in analysis with Dr Gibbon that works out his protagonist's skin disorder, and thus realises this 'temptation' (1986: 56). Indeed, as studies of these affects show, where are shame and guilt remembered in the body but on the skin? In blushing, in the sudden flushing of the face with colour, skin is indeed the 'ambassador' of the psyche, sending the signifier guilt via the skin ego into the world. Psychologist Silvan Tomkins (1963) regards skin as particularly important for conveying shame; and Andrew Strathern in his anthropological study of shame concludes that shame is on the skin because skin 'is the immediate point of contact with the physical world ... and can also conveniently symbolise the point of contact between [people] and the social forces that surround them' (1977: 101). As with Anzieu's skin ego, these formulations of shame reveal skin as a catachrestic interface that forces the transgressions of psyche and the social into the soma.

Autobiographical skins are flushed with shame; the writing is a body narrative coloured with authorial self-consciousness. 'Scab-picking' is how Updike describes the act of autobiography, adding: 'It pains me to write these pages. They are humiliating' (1990: 44). But if revealing the skin in autobiography is as stigmatising as revealing the skin disorder in the flesh, why write the autobiography? What comprises these stigmatisations, what sins lie behind these autobiographical skins? What shame or guilt is so internalised that it can be flushed out only on the skin, and then in the autobiography, in writing?

Family s(k)ins

In *The Shell and the Kernel*, another topography of the psyche which originates in dialogue with Freud's attention to the surface of the ego, Nicolas Abraham writes that the 'shell', what Freud describes as 'a protective layer, an ectoderm, a cerebral cortex', is only really interesting for what it encloses (Abraham and Torok 1994: 80). '[T]he shell itself is marked by what it shelters; what it encloses is disclosed within it' (Abraham and Torok 1994: 80). The kernel enclosed and disclosed within the shell of the psyche is the unconscious, which explains the equivocation: what is enclosed is at once disclosed, according to the dynamics of the unconscious, displaced and simultaneously signified. The unconscious, which is of course the kernel of psychoanalysis, comprises repressed transgressive sexuality: 'the Sexual . . . concerns the totality of the Kernel' (Abraham and Torok 1994: 89). The unconscious is in fact constituted by the repression of this transgressive sexuality, namely by the repression of the Oedipus complex. It is the successful repression of this desire, this incorporation of a desire awakened in familial relations and made shameful by a prohibition, that ensures the subsequent correct trajectory of our desire and our 'civilisation'.

In collaboration with Maria Torok, Abraham has described this incorporated secret of repressed desire as a crypt. The crypt contains, entombs, a phantom, 'an undisclosed family secret handed down to an unwitting descendant' (Abraham and Torok 1994: 16). In a process that Abraham terms with the richly suggestive 'transgenerational haunting', the crypt contains a family secret passed down from earlier generations because it is unspeakable, too humiliating to be told. But the 'shameful silence of several generations' can be disclosed in 'the symptoms of a descendant' (Abraham and Torok 1994: 22). In a form of psychosomatic illness Abraham and Torok call 'self-to-self affliction', certain psychosomatic illnesses can re-member in the body the incorporated family secret. While their self-to-self afflictions do not include the skin, Abraham and Torok's topography of the shell and the kernel is no better illustrated than by skin disorders that symptomise the unconscious, as in Anzieu. In a form of 'designification', the crypt of the kernel can be unconsciously signified in the shell. This is less a return than an 'eruption' of the repressed, this term again wonderfully literalized in skin disorders. This symptom on the surface/shell is the 'memory trace' of the unconscious – as Abraham and Torok write in a figure recalling Stacey's skin 'ambassador', 'the appropriate emissaries enact a passage each time from a Kernel to its Periphery' (Abraham and Torok 1994: 91). What erupts in the trace is the encrypted transgression: family shame.

If '[t]he symptom is a memorial that bespeaks a willfully disregarded event'

(Abraham and Torok 1994: 92), then what wilfully disregarded events do we find memorialised in skin disorders in skin autobiographies, which as autobiographies are anyway memorials that inevitably have a space – a crypt – for family history? What memory is too traumatic, too stigmatising to be expressed other than through the skin – and then through the revelation of the skin ego in the auto- biography? In keeping with the psychoanalytic notion that the repressed memory is always sexual and familial, skin autobiographies transgress the bounds of the sexual and familial; they transgress them first of all by locating the sexual *in* the familial. More variously these transgressed boundaries concern those between child and parent, belonging and departure, self and other, memory and the present, fantasy and reality. In speaking of such transgressed boundaries and leaking family secrets into the public domain, skin autobiographies transgress them even further.

Hereditary skin disorders explicitly tie skin stigmatisation to family memory. Updike's first memory of his psoriasis in *Self-Consciousness* is of his inheritance of it from his mother. *Self-Consciousness* is thoroughly concerned with skin difference and heredity; a later chapter parallels Updike's stigmatisation of his psoriasis with what he imagines to be the future of his half-black, half-white grandsons. But while he believes his grandsons' skin embodies the transgression of an interracial taboo, his first memory of his own skin associates his psoriasis with the transgres- sion of a much more primal taboo, namely the sexual boundary between mother and son. The memory is suffused with sexual desire. It consists of Updike as a small boy:

> lying on the upstairs side porch of the Shillington house, amid the sickly oleaginous smell of Siroil, on fuzzy-warmed towels, with my mother, sun- bathing. We are both, in my mental picture, not quite naked. She would have been still a youngish woman at the time, and I remember being embarrassed by something, but whether by our being together in this way or simply by my skin is not clear in this mottled recollection. She, too, had psoriasis; I had inherited it from her.
>
> (Updike 1990: 39)

What was Updike embarrassed by in this memory that meant he could no longer remember even here in the memoir, this work of memory? What has he unconsciously repressed – if not precisely the intimacy of this picture, the intim- acy of a son with his youngish mother, both not quite naked? What is the effect of the memory if not to enmesh the aetiology of psoriasis, its very origins and cause, with a desire that cannot be fully remembered and expressed *because* it is transgres- sive? Certainly in the final chapter, which Updike is writing while waiting for his mother to die and when he once more feels imminent conjunction with his mother, this union comes to him again in association with psoriasis. But the intimacy is now frightening, offensive even, boding not the awakening of sexual desire, but his own death. Looking at his mother in hospital, now no longer a youngish woman but close to death, he recalls how some family friends had told him how much he resembled her:

I felt slightly offended, as though a dirty secret were being advertised. Standing there in the bright medical center I was aware of the little flecks of psoriasis at the edge of my mother's white hair, and in the wings of her nostrils, and of all the spots of actinic damage mottling her skin, which had once been as smooth and fair as [my own as a boy]. My mother was my future, as well as my past.

(Updike 1990: 231)

The psoriasis again sends to the surface transgressed boundaries between mother and son – 'a dirty secret' – their relation, their closeness, the inevitable line of inheritance. I am not suggesting of course that any 'desire' Updike feels for his mother in the earlier scene is conscious. On the contrary, the recollection's description as 'mottled,' a word that in the birth-of-psoriasis/desire is converted in the waiting-for-death scene to refer to the mother's psoriatic skin, suggests precisely that these are unconscious memories, as marred and flawed as the skin they remember. Memory in autobiography is as much unconscious as conscious, and the awakening of desire for the mother in the son – what Updike claims he can't consciously remember – surely comes through unconsciously in Updike's intimate, sensual writing of his boyhood scene.

In Dennis Potter's *The Singing Detective* the autofictional persona Philip Marlow first develops his skin disease, the same psoriatic arthropathy from which Potter suffered, simultaneously with the guilt he feels at his parents' separation. Sitting with his mother in an Underground station after their move to London from the Forest of Dean, a trajectory that mirrors Potter's own early life, the boy Philip pesters her about his father's absence: 'When's him a coming? . . . Mum? When's our Dad going to come?' (Potter 1986: 231). When Mrs. Marlow snatches his arm to get him to stop, he reveals his first sore: 'He rolls up his sleeve. On his forearm is a big red and silvery white patch. She is astonished, not knowing what it is. (In fact, a first psoriatic lesion.)' (Potter 1986: 185). Coinciding with Philip's childhood trauma, the psoriatic lesion is a 'message' from Philip's unconscious. In Marlow's case, the kernel in the unconscious is a transgressive primal scene: at the centre of his unconscious is the boy Philip's witnessing of his mother's adultery. This is a terrifyingly carnal experience. Philip sees his mother 'flat on her back. The skirt of her thin and flowered dress is pulled up to her waist. Her legs are apart. Her heels are digging into the soft ground.' The man's 'bare backside' as he 'grunts and labours on top of her' is 'more visible than his face' (Potter, 1986: 113). From Philip's perspective, as from that of Freud's Wolf Man's, the 'lovemaking seems akin to violence, or physical attack' (Potter, 1986: 113). As the adult Marlow recalls the memory from his hospital bed, the scene merging seamlessly with his present-day surroundings and his psoriasis (as with Freud's hysterics who suffer mainly from reminiscences, Marlow is 'enmeshed in a complicated melancholy', 'memory crashes into him again' Potter 1986: 116, 158), his repressed memories of this taboo sexuality inscribe themselves as symptoms on his body. The moment of the psoriasis's inception renders it literally a 'self-to-self afflicted' attack on Philip for his own part in witnessing the sexual attack. He bears (or bares) the shame for her adultery, guilt for his parents' split, and for his mother's subsequent suicide that quickly follows their move to London. 'Who? Who? Which one? Who is it?' (Potter 1986: 144): the imputation of blame runs throughout *The Singing Detective* with Philip the child unable to process adult events and helplessly pointing the accusatory finger at himself. Incorporating the secrets of his parents' unspeakable trauma, Marlow's skin dramatises or 'speaks' its kernel according to the unconscious dynamics of hystericisation of the skin ego.

But, as suggested by the trajectory from Anzieu to Goffman, skin disorders in skin autobiographies can remember a stigmatisation that is as much cultural as familial – indeed a closer reading of race boundaries in Updike and class boundaries in Potter would reveal as much. In Anne Karpf's (1996) account of the effects of her parents' experience of the Holocaust on her life, her eczema, like Updike and Potter's psoriasis, is a way of speaking an unspeakable family secret that is a explicitly a cultural memory; her eczema is a memorialisation – or in Marianne Hirsch's (1987) evocative term for the effects of survivors' memories on the next generation a 'postmemory' – of her parents' unspoken memories of the Holocaust. Living in the repression of their Holocaust experience but with her childhood everywhere marked by its ineluctable presence, Karpf grows up with her parents' memories leaving their mark literally on her skin. 'The Holocaust had become enmeshed in our parents' personal subjectivity and was part of the family tissue', she writes, and the historical 'tissue' inscribes itself on her tissues (Karpf 1996: 96). At 27 she begins a relationship with a non-Jewish man. Simultaneously she develops eczema, her body enacting on its literal boundary her symbolic transgression of boundaries – between Jew and gentile, between her own memory and her parents' – that her parents' experience has rendered uncrossable. Her eczema speaks the guilt in her unconscious, 'the desecratory feel of the relationship' –'My mother . . . told me I was doing what Hitler hadn't managed to – finishing off the Jewish race' – is shown on her desecrated, desiccated skin (Karpf 1996: 97). As she 'chafed at' her parents (Karpf 1996: 97), her body enacts this chafing:

> I tried repeatedly to reconcile these warring views until, eventually, it all extruded through my hands, unerring somatic proof (the body being an incorrigible punster) that I couldn't in fact handle it. Beads of moisture appeared, trapped beneath the skin, on the palm of one hand, and with them came a compelling urge to scratch. Then I started to claw at my left hand with the nails of my right until the blood ran. This mania of scratching continued until the whole surface of the hand turned raging, stinging scarlet and there came, despite the wound (or perhaps because of it), a sense of release, followed immediately by guilt.
>
> (Karpf 1996: 98)

The cycle of repressing and articulating the guilt, the notion of the body as ruthless punster colliding psychic and social signifier with corporeal referent, reveals the catachresis of stigmatisation at work on the skin. Indeed, of her eczema wounds, which become 'florid with yellow and green crests of pus', Karpf writes, 'they seemed like self-inflicted stigmata, visible and so particularly shaming' (1996: 98). And as the masturbatory sequence of scratching followed by release followed by immediate guilt suggests, this Holocaust-postmemory skin disorder is still sexual. Karpf's eczema symptomises her transgression, which according to her parents' memories – and it is their memories that her skin speaks – is compounded by the fact that her sexual partner is not Jewish. A message from the phantom of her 'transgenerational haunting', her skin speaks her parents repressed memory as her own. When a friend points out to Karpf that the place on her arm which she has been scratching is the very place on her mother's that is tattooed with her concentration camp number, Karpf remains 'unconvinced' of the symbolism (1996: 106). But her refusal of this symbolism, and the very fact that she notes it, is a sure sign of its unconscious truth. For if her eczema is her 'unconscious self . . . trying to articulate its distress' (Karpf 1996: 103), the distress it articulates is not hers but the unspeakable family memory that has haunted her childhood.

Of all skin autobiographies, Tim Lott's *The Scent of Dried Roses* is the most encrypted. Like Karpf's *The War After: Living with the Holocaust*, Lott's is an auto/biography, a story of the self that sees that self as inseparably formed, 'storied' by family memory. Lott's account describes his own depression as inextricably entwined with that of his mother and her suicide. But the skin disorder here is the parent's not the child's; and it is the skin disorder itself that is encrypted. Lott writes of both his mother's skin disorder and her depression but never connects them; he does not recognise the role skin disorder plays in his mother's depression or her suicide. This is a failure to see that repeats the encrypting of Jean Lott's skin disorder in her life. Jean suffered from alopecia areata, although Lott didn't know this until late in his adult life. Jean kept the fact that she was totally bald secret, even from her husband, wearing a scarf or wig all the time, even in bed – '[Jack] had never seen her without hair' (Lott 1996: 2). Yet though Tim Lott makes little consciously of this secrecy, or of what it surely indicates, namely the terrible psychic trauma suffered by a woman of 23 who permanently loses all her hair, *The Scent of Dried Roses* leaves the reader with an unavoidable sense that Jean Lott's baldness played a central role in her depression and death. Including as throwaway remarks such surely crucial details, as the fact that Jean had planned to be a hairdresser, and that she had mentioned to a friend that 'if the hair went, she would be a monster, a circus lady' (Lott 1996: 117), Lott's auto/biography *unconsciously* releases baldness from Jean's crypt. The book begins and ends with Jean's baldness, hair forming the unwitting shell of the depression narrative. In the beginning we are told that the onset of Jean's alopecia coincided exactly with the difficult pregnancy with Tim. Jean begins taking tablets for her alopecia while pregnant. The tablets don't work, and when Tim is born with major physical problems Jean's hair speeds up its loss: 'slowly, as in punishment, [Jean] moulted. By the early 1960s she had lost all her hair. No one could ever find out; and not even Jack could see' (Lott 1996: 3). Lott ends *The Scent of Dried Roses* with his mother's medical notes, which make further crucial revelations about her alopecia, but again he fails consciously to take them on board or factor them into his story. The medical records show his mother seeking treatment, not just for the physical, but the psychic symptoms of her alopecia. She is prescribed tranquillisers for what the records note are 'the emotional factors playing a part in continuing this reaction' (Lott 1996: 273). The verb 'play' is fittingly complex: Lott remarks (but again makes nothing of) on the fact that the steroids used to treat the hair loss could result in depression. But the hair loss itself surely produced psychic distress, as evidenced (and surely exacerbated) by the fact Jean kept her baldness totally secret, even from those most intimate with her. 'Play' even leaves open the possibility that psychic disturbance – depression – might have been a contributing cause of the hair loss. In short, the hair loss and depression, of which Lott claims to be telling the story, are fundamentally enmeshed. As the records conclude, the hair loss is diagnosed as unpreventable, the patient is fitted with a wig and is to be prescribed anti-depressants 'indefinitely' (Lott 1996: 273).

What Tim Lott does consciously trace the root of his mother's depression to – her sense of gradual displacement, the transgression of the solid lines of white English lower-middle-class life in demographically changing Southall, West London – is itself connected to Jean's baldness and suggests possible reasons for her secrecy. The transgression of a cultural boundary sees the transformation of the utopian suburbs, to which Jean's interwar generation aspired to belong, into an urban Asian community from which Jean longs to escape. Jean's dream – and Lott's nightmare – is of 'subtopian' England with its net curtains, carriage clocks on the mantel piece, stodgy puddings and overcooked vegetables, pastel-colour clothing, Saturday car-washing routines and tennis clubs on Sundays. The dream is displaced by an immigrant England of, 'Curried Halal Meats, the Queens Style Carpet Centre, the Shahi Nan Kebab, Fine Fabrics: Specialists in Sarees and Dhuptas . . . the plaster melted wedding cake of the Southall Mosque' (Lott 1996: 26). Jean's desires to blend in – 'the England Jean perhaps imagined she wanted to belong to – warm, slightly eccentric, innocent, quiet, decent, quaint, a bit pompous . . . It is the sense of an impossible, genteel, romantic, imagined England' (Lott 1996: 34) – are thwarted by the influx of immigrants to Southall. But Jean's idealisation of and desire for the white middle-class norm cannot be divorced from her own bodily difference and perhaps helps explain her reason for keeping her baldness such a secret. Her own fears of being marked out, of exposure, are reflected in and compounded by the changing skin of Southall ('I hate Southall', she writes in her suicide note: 'I can see only decay, I feel alone' (Lott 1996: 24)); she now feels culturally displaced. What might be read as Jean's ethnocentrism or even racism is surely a message of what she keeps buried in her own crypt: her monstrous, circus-lady baldness.

Skin autobiographies send messages from the unconscious to the surface of the body and the text. Writing of the relation between the psychic and the material body, the unconscious and its symptoms, Abraham designates their interface, in an exceptional use of this term, 'the somatic'. He locates this somatic most referentially on the skin: 'The *somatic* must be something quite different from the body proper. . . . The *somatic* is what I cannot touch directly, either as my integument and its internal prolongations or as my psyche, the latter given to the consciousness of self' (Abraham and Torok 1994: 87). Neither body nor psyche proper, the 'somatic' is that interface that cannot be touched directly. This psychic dimension of the body, or corporeal dimension of the psyche, the psychic integument or skin ego, can be touched and known only by the unconscious sending out of messages onto the skin: 'the somatic is that of which I would know nothing if its representative, my fantasy, were not there to send me back to it, its source as it were and ultimate justification' (Abraham and Torok 1994: 87). If behind the somatic is the crypt of the unconscious – 'It is the Somatic which dispatches its messengers to the Envelope, exciting it from the very place the latter conceals' (Abraham and Torok 1994: 87) – then skin autobiographies decrypt what would otherwise remain unopened and untouched.

Skinscapes

Autobiography works like a skin; it is the skin the author sends out that at once conceals and reveals the self. Skin autobiographies form an alternative skin. Writing skin is obviously an attempt to work out, to express (that is both to articulate and thus to expel) a stigmatised skin/sin. The importance of writing for expressing skin disfigurements is addressed by Anzieu in dialogue with fellow analyst Micheline Enriquez in relation to Enriquez's patient Fanchon (Anzieu 1989; Enriquez 1984). Adopted as a baby, Fanchon is subjected by her adoptive parents to a fictional lineage that stigmatises her biological parents: the implication is that she is the illegitimate child of a mother who was herself an outlaw, in some tellings because she was Jewish, in others because she was a sexual collaborator with the Nazis (the overlaying of these plots is of course doubly stigmatising: a collaborating Jew). Growing up with these (post)memories of maternal impropriety, Fanchon attempts to purge herself of her parents' uncleanliness, literally washing out the stigmatisation from her skin with excessive cleaning rituals that leave her body damaged. She washes her hair until it falls out, mutilates her breast, scars her own hands and in a recurrence during analysis in one night develops pustules on her face and pulls out half her hair (her actions seem to repeat the physical stigmatizations of both sexual collaborators and camp survivors, though neither Enriquez nor Anzieu pursue the intriguing cultural dimensions of stigmatisation in this case). Stigmatising herself catachrestically, Fanchon becomes her mother.

She takes control of what Enriquez calls this 'défiguration' (1984: 201) with what we might call a process of refiguration. The stigma inscribed on her face – 'le mal . . . est inscrit sur sa figure' (Enriquez 1984: 188) – is written out as representative writing. Representative writing consists of Fanchon writing what she sees around her; it enables her to recover her self and her memory, to reconstitute the traces of herself: 'reconstituer des traces d'elle-même' (Enriquez 1984: 201). Moving from inscribing text in the body to inscribing the body in text – 'C'est le corps du texte' (Enriquez 1984: 204) – Fanchon forms a skin of words that recovers her skin. As she says, 'C'est comme si cette écriture m'avait permis la récupération d'une peau' (Enriquez 1984: 213). Anzieu concludes *The Skin Ego*: 'The spoken word, and even more, the written word, has the power to function as a skin' (1989: 231).

Skin autobiographies show writing skin as cathartic. Writing recovers a skin ego damaged in the original skin/sin memory. As Potter's Marlow lies in bed and remembers his novel *The Singing Detective*, effectively narrating his way back to health (Marlow's psoriasis is so appalling he can't even hold a pen, but his reminiscences are, he insists, writing), he recovers his original unafflicted skin. Updike in *Self-Consciousness* represents his writing as an attempt to compensate for his own damaged surface. The prolificity and smoothness that are hallmarks of Updike's prose distract from and reconstruct as flawless a flawed bodily surface: 'I have never cared, in print, about niceness or modesty, but agonize over typos and factual errors – "spots" on the ideally unflecked text' (1990: 70). In Updike's short story 'From the Journal of a Leper' a potter with terrible psoriasis produces 'blemishless' pots (1980: 182). Once his spots are cured his pots are spoiled. If perfect art compensates for imperfect skin, the reversal of one side of the catachresis threatens the other.

As unconscious memory, messages from the kernel, writing skin disorders in skin autobiographies does not reflect memory but draws on the fictional, the fantasmatic of the unconscious. Autobiographical skins are 'skinscapes', to use the name of Marlow's fictional bar, an imagined space for working out and staging memories or fantasies buried in the unconscious. Skin memories in autobiographical skins are fantasmatic returns of the repressed. They are 'rememories' rather than memories – to borrow Toni Morrison's term for the ghost in *Beloved* (Morrison 1991). Beloved is the 'rememory' who returns fantasmatically to allow her mother to work through the trauma of infanticide: it is the scar on Beloved's skin where Sethe slit her throat that demands Sethe finally recognise the true identity of the ghost she has encrypted, the shell that forces the crypt to spill its contents. As unconscious memories, skin autobiographies are not mimetic but are explicitly between fiction and autobiography, or between autobiography and biography – either way the story of the self, as a story of the other (or Other). More obviously than other autobiographies, they are not representational stories of the self; in their exposure of skin, they are manifestly, on the surface, invested with the unconscious. Revealing another layer beneath the autobiographical skin – like the layers to Freud's mystic writing-pad which, as a description of how the unconscious retains as 'memories' (but really fantasies) what is consciously forgotten, can work as a model of autobiography – skin autobiographies reveal an/ Other story. One version of this Other story transgresses the boundary between fiction and autobiography. Updike and Potter incorporate into their texts fictional elements, to differing degrees, that leave their autobiographical skins moving in and out of revelation and concealment. Thus in *Self-Consciousness*, exceptionally for an autobiography, Updike includes numerous footnotes that cite his own fiction. While this might appear to reveal the autobiographical in the fiction, in fact since the fiction was written first and preceded the real, *Self-Consciousness* reveals the fictional in the autobiographical. If autobiography feels like 'scab-picking' because it reveals too much skin, fiction covers it over. Updike writes, '[t]he fabricated truth of poetry and fiction makes a shelter in which I feel safe, sheltered within interlaced plausibilities. . . . Out of a soiled and restless life, I have refined my books' (1990: 220). Fiction interposes precisely a fabric of fabrication over the authorial skin that allows for greater revelations, a more profound because unconscious truth. And while Potter refused to write his autobiography because he believed 'autobiographies are a complicated series of lies' (Cook 1995: 126), *The Singing Detective* is precisely this lying autobiography, this unconscious auto-biography. Its ostensible fiction parallels so much in Potter's own life that, like Updike's psoriatic memoir, it layers onto the author's scabrous autobiographical body the cloaks of fiction. These layers of fabrication for self are present in Lott's and Karpf's memoirs though in different form. The second strand of skin autobiographies intercalates fiction, not with autobiography, but with biography. Lott and Karpf tell the story of their parents interwoven with their selves, but their memoirs have the same effect of concealing that *autos* with the Other.

Skin autobiographies are as layered as the skin itself. Into skin, they intercalate, not simply memory, but memory as it is fictionalised and fabricated in the unconscious. Indeed, that the skin is a surface for the investment of unconscious memory is a truth of which we are not conscious – until they remind us of it.

References

Abraham, N. and Torok, M. (1994) *The Shell and the Kernel: Renewals of Psychoanalysis*, vol.1, trans. N. T. Rand, Chicago: Chicago University Press.

Anzieu, D. (1989) *The Skin Ego: A Psychoanalytic Approach to the Self*, trans. C. Turner, New Haven: Yale University Press.

—— (1990) *A Skin for Thought: Interviews with Gilbert Tarrab on Psychology and Psychoanalysis*, London: Karnac.

Beuf, A. H. (1990) *Beauty is the Beast: Appearance-Impaired Children in America*, Philadelphia: Pennsylvania University Press.

Cook, J. R. (1995) *Dennis Potter: A Life on Screen*, Manchester: Manchester University Press.

Enriquez, M. (1984) *Aux Carrefours de la Haine: Paranoïa, Masochisme, Apathie*, Paris: Épi.

Fanon, F. (1967) *Black Skin, White Masks*, trans. C. L. Markmann, New York: Grove Press.

Freud, S. (1984) *On Metapsychology: The Theory of Psychoanalysis*, trans. J. Strachey, London: Penguin.

Goffman, E. (1968) *Stigma: Notes on the Management of Spoiled Identity*, London: Penguin.

Gusdorf, G. (1980) 'The Conditions and Limits of Autobiography' in J. Olney (ed.) *Autobiography: Essays Theoretical and Critical*, Princeton: Princeton University Press.

Hirsch, M. (1997) *Family Frames: Photography, Narrative, and Postmemory*, Cambridge, MA: Harvard University Press.

Karpf, A. (1996) *The War After: Living with the Holocaust*, London: Heinemann.

Lesage, M. (1997) *Vitiligo: Understanding the Loss of Skin Colour*, London: Vitiligo Society.

Lott, T. (1996) *The Scent of Dried Roses*, London: Viking.

Macpherson, W. (1999) *The Stephen Lawrence Inquiry: Report of an Inquiry by Sir William Macpherson*, London: The Stationery Office.

Morrison, T. (1991) *Beloved*, New York: Penguin.

—— (1993) *Playing in the Dark: Whiteness and the Literary Imagination*, New York: Vintage.

—— (1994) 'The Pain of Being Black', interview with B. Angelo, in D. Taylor-Guthrie (ed.) *Conversations with Toni Morrison,* Jackson: University Press of Mississippi.

Potter, D. (1986) *The Singing Detective,* London: Faber and Faber.

Prosser, J. (1998) *Second Skins: The Body Narratives of Transsexuality,* New York: Columbia University Press.

Scales-Trent, J. (1995) *Notes of a White Black Woman: Race, Colour, Community,* University Park: Pennsylvania State University Press.

Stacey, J. (1997) *Teratologies: A Cultural Study of Cancer,* London: Routledge.

Strathern, A. (1977) 'Why is Shame on the Skin?' in J. Blacking (ed.) *The Anthropology of the Body,* London: Academic Press.

Tomkins, S. (1963) *Affect, Imagery, Consciousness: The Negative Affects,* New York: Springer.

Updike, J. (1980) 'From the Journal of a Leper', in *Problems and Other Stories,* London: Deutsch.

—— (1990) *Self-Consciousness: Memoirs,* London: Penguin.

4 Skin-tight

Celebrity, pregnancy and subjectivity

Imogen Tyler

Pregnant bodies – even clothed – are sources of discomfort and disgust in popular culture.

(Stabile 1994: 84)

. . . posing for photoshoots while pregnant has become an almost compulsory celebrity rite of passage.

(Jones 1999: 35)

Despite a history of intense medical scrutiny and regulation, until recently the pregnant woman has been conspicuously absent from popular visual representation.[1] This changed dramatically in August 1991, when Annie Leibovitz's photograph of the naked and heavily pregnant Hollywood actress, Demi Moore, graced the front cover of the American style magazine, *Vanity Fair*, accompanied by the caption 'More Demi Moore' (Plate 4.1). Since the publication of this photograph, there has been a proliferation of similar images of pregnant celebrities in fashion and lifestyle magazines.[2] These photographs have, in turn, been the catalyst for a new visibility of pregnant women across a range of different cultural media, a visibility which demands a reassessment of the supposed taboo surrounding the representation of the pregnant body in contemporary Western cultures. It is impossible to understand the extent of the widespread public response to the appearance of this photograph of Moore, without first recognising the power of the cultural taboo which previously regulated mainstream representations of pregnant women. Similarly, it is difficult to grasp the significance of the subsequent photographs of pregnant celebrities without an awareness of their reference to the *Vanity Fair* photograph.[3] Yet, despite the fact that this could be argued to be one of the most significant photographs of its era, there has been no sustained close reading of it and its broader impact on definitions of the female body in contemporary visual cultures. This chapter offers such a reading in relation to the project of 'thinking through the skin'. It asks: How has pregnant embodiment been figured within cultural theories of the subject? How might we read the Moore photograph in the context of the previous invisibility of the pregnant body? How does this photograph of pregnant embodiment relate to the history of foetal imagery?

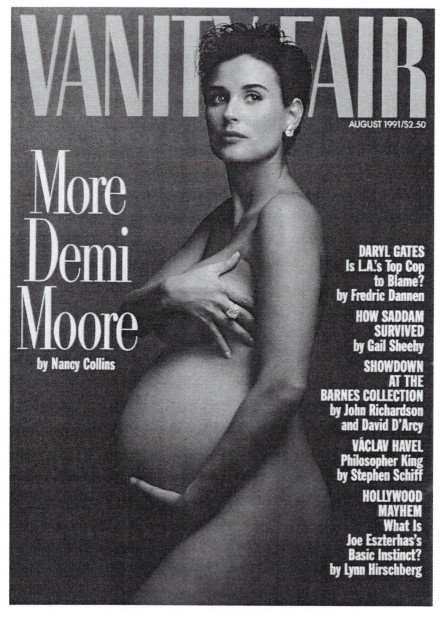

Plate 4.1 Demi Moore on the cover of *Vanity Fair*, August 1991

Annie Leibovitz/Vanity Fair

A key theoretical context for my reading of this photograph is the notion of flexible subjectivity, which has been increasingly foregrounded in theoretical debates about the body and identity. In these debates, subjectivity has been redefined through concepts such as 'the performative' (Butler 1993), 'the nomadic' (Deleuze and Guattari 1988; Braidotti 1994) and 'the cybernetic' (Plant 1998). In this chapter, I shall consider what distinguishes the elasticity of pregnant subjectivity from other understandings of the flexible subject. I shall explore the ways in which thinking through the skin of the pregnant subject questions individualistic notions of 'a body' and 'a skin'. My exploration of the visual and the theoretical representations of pregnant embodiment will suggest that the elastic subjectivity of pregnancy needs to be distinguished from other forms of flexible becoming.

What the Demi Moore and the post-Moore photographs of pregnant celebrities have in common is a shared visual emphasis on the naked stretched skin of the pregnant body. This emphasis contrasts with popular cultural representations of the maternal body as the site of internal and threatening fluidity. I suggest that this construction of the maternal body, as that which must be abjected and/or disciplined, has been part of the operation of the cultural taboo surrounding the pregnant subject. I argue that this taboo in part created the conditions of possibility for the (imaginary) foetal subjects of the twentieth century. In contrast, the Moore photograph constructs the tight external surface of the pregnant body as an idealised desirable sign of female subjectivity. I shall suggest that the emphasis on the exposure of skin characterises a difference from the previous 'veiling' of pregnant bodies and pregnant subjects within popular culture. My reading of the front cover photograph of Moore serves as a point of connection to thinking through the implications of this visibility in relation to the theoretical invisibility of the pregnant subject. In order to analyse the significance of the skin of the pregnant subject in this photograph, I shall employ Didier Anzieu's theory of the Skin Ego (1989). The fetishistic emphasis this photograph places on the skin's surface is constituted through a set of complex and contradictory discourses. On the one hand, what is represented through the exhibition of a discrete bodily surface is the presence of an integral subject: 'the very image of unassailable impenetrability' (Connor 1999: 48). This contrasts with the cultural and theoretical construction of the maternal body as a site of undifferentiated loss and lack (see Creed 1993). On the other hand, this emphasis on the surface of the body simultaneously invokes the familiar construction of femininity as nothing but surface: the visual construction of women as desirable objects for the male gaze. In this chapter, I shall ask how this particular photograph, and by implication those that have been published since, can be read as a symptom of the intensification of medical and legal intrusions into and control over the pregnant subject. I shall analyse this photograph as an image of a 'body which wears its depth on its surface [thereby] folding out [. . .] the imaginary "assaults" upon it' (Connor 1999: 48). It is this complex relationship between the skin as surface and the subject as depth, and between visual culture and cultural theory, that guides my thinking.

The skin ego

In *The Skin Ego: A Psychoanalytic Approach to the Self* (1989), Anzieu outlines a thesis that goes, 'against the grain of most post-structuralist theories of the body informed by psychoanalysis' (Prosser 1998: 65). Anzieu critiques Lacanian revisions of Freud, which have placed increasing emphasis on the relationship between the unconscious and language. He offers a return to the Freudian model of the ego and the unconscious as inherently bodily. Central to this reconsideration of the body is Anzieu's redefinition of the ego as the skin ego.[4] Jay Prosser usefully summarises Anzieu's concept thus:

> His concept of the 'skin ego' takes the body's physical skin as the primary organ underlying the formation of the ego, its handling, its touching, its holding – our experience of its feel – individualizing our psychic functioning, quite crucially making us who we are. [. . .] It holds each of us together, quite literally contains us, protects us, keeps us discrete.
>
> (Prosser 1998: 65)

Anzieu's theory of the skin ego provides a potentially valuable resource for theorising the stretched and expanded subjectivity of pregnancy. But is this theory of the skin ego flexible enough to account for the more than oneness of the pregnant subject, and does the skin of the pregnant subject, its handling, holding and touching, have an 'individualising psychic function'? For in pregnancy, the body's skin surface no longer straightforwardly performs the function of separating self from not-self. The skin is the site (and sight) of change in pregnancy. It softens, becomes more elastic, stretches and is stretch-marked; it mutates and expands, growing new skin inside of itself.

Anzieu's account represents the pregnant woman (and indeed the mother) as 'the maternal environment' who is, 'so called because *it* surrounds the baby with an external envelope made up of messages' (1989; 62 my emphasis). He thus constructs the pregnant woman, not as a subject, but as the container of new life. The story of ego-acquisition Anzieu outlines is one in which the maternal serves as 'the common skin' which must be disavowed in order for the ego to come into existence. Like other psychoanalytic theories of ego-acquisition, Anzieu documents the birth of the ego from the perspective of the emergent 'I'. This story is never relayed from the perspective of the ego, the body or the self, which facilitates the production of the other self from within herself. Anzieu's skin-ego thus relies on a familiar 'phantasy of self-engendering', which in turn operates as a denial of the subject position of the pregnant woman and the mother. What remains untheorised within this account is the skin ego of the pregnant subject. The skin ego of the pregnant subject does not simply hold together an individual and it does not simply protect a self, as she is already more than one and is indivisible into ones. Therefore the skin ego of the pregnant subject does not fit individualist models of ego identity. As Sarah Franklin notes:

The very term 'individual', meaning one who cannot be divided, can only represent the male, as it is precisely the process of one individual becoming two which occurs through a woman's pregnancy. Pregnancy is [. . .] the exact antithesis of individuality.

(Franklin 1991: 203)

Philosophical and psychoanalytic theories of subjectivity have historically been modelled on a notion of an *indivisible individual* (Tyler 2000). In her work on motherhood, Julia Kristeva argues:

if we suppose that the mother is *the subject* of gestation, in other words the master of a process that science, despite its effective devices, acknowledges it cannot now and perhaps never will be able to take away from her [. . .] then we acknowledge the risk of losing identity.

(1993: 238; my emphasis)

Following this analysis we can extrapolate that the taboo surrounding the representation of pregnant women, specifically as 'the subjects of their gestation' is linked to the divisibility of the pregnant body. Thus the taboo surrounding pregnancy is related here to the unsettling effect which pregnant embodiment has upon dominant cultural understandings of the individuated or individual self. According to psychoanalytic theory, to be a subject is to be subjected as an individual to the culture, language and symbolic order of a particular discursive regime. Within this framework, subjects who are not successfully individuated from the mother at the time of entry into symbolic culture are at risk of psychosis. For Freud, madness or psychosis is a result of failing to distinguish between the ego and the id. Hence, following Freudian orthodoxy, to acknowledge or represent the mother as 'the subject of gestation' is to risk 'losing identity' itself. Pregnant subjectivity thus 'threatens to collapse a signifying system based on the paternal law of differentiation [as it] automatically throws into question ideas concerning the self, boundaries between self and other, and hence identity' (Doane 1990: 170).

Despite reiterating many of the assumptions of Freudian theory of which numerous feminists have been so critical, Anzieu's concept of the skin ego is nevertheless useful for theorising pregnant subjectivity. For what the theory of the skin ego insists upon is that the presence of skin is crucial in ascertaining and distinguishing the discrete self. A feminist theory of the skin ego would allow the conceptualisation of the skin ego in relation to the specificity of sexually differentiated subject positions. It would open up a space for a critique of Anzieu's conception of the maternal as environment and for the theorisation of the gendered subjectivity of pregnancy. As French philosopher Luce Irigaray suggests in her work on female subjectivity, alternatives to the disavowal of the woman-mother as a subject might emerge through a questioning of the orthodox psychoanalytic assumption that this absence is structurally integral (and somehow necessary) to Western culture (Irigaray 1985). Indeed, Irigaray suggests that in order for the woman – mother to be reconfigured and represented as a subject, she must re-envelope herself with herself. This means creating a skin ego that would allow the pregnant subject to differentiate herself from the subjectless position to which she has been theoretically and culturally subjected.

Thinking through the skin of the pregnant subject thus requires rethinking the skin ego as non-individualistic and subject to transformation and change. The pregnant subject has a skin ego capable, not only of expansion and retraction, but of giving birth to other selves. As Hélène Cixous notes it is, 'not only a question of a transformation, of rhythms, exchanges, of relationship to space, [and] of the whole perceptual system', but the 'specific power to produce something living of which her flesh is the locus' (Cixous and Clément 1996: 90). Neither one nor two, it is the fleshy in-betweenness and irreducible simultaneity of pregnant subjectivity that marks the critical difference. The problem is, however, as Christine Battersby writes, that 'we are lacking models to explain how identity might be retained whilst impregnated with otherness and whilst other selves are generated from within the embodied self' (1997: 227).

The difficulty of conceptualising pregnant embodiment within theories of subjectivity, which privileges only those bodily selves that conform to individualist notions of the self, highlighted in the work of Battersby and others, parallels the striking taboos around the representation of the pregnant body in visual culture. Thus the 1991 August issue of *Vanity Fair* presents the opportunity to develop theoretical and conceptual responses to what can only be described as a groundbreaking photograph.

'More Demi Moore'

Photographed in profile on *Vanity Fair*'s front cover, Moore's right arm and hand is shielding her breasts, her left arm and hand frames and cradles her heavily pregnant belly. Moore's flawless, taut, tanned skin is lit in such a way as to glow and has an intensely luminous quality. For Richard Dyer, this use of lighting is intimately connected to whiteness. As he writes: 'Idealised white women are bathed in and permeated by light. It streams through them and falls onto them from above' (1997: 122). In this way, the lighting emphasises that Moore's whiteness is a crucial part of her ideality. She is a 'glowing pure white woman' (Dyer 1997: 122). In the photograph, the light lingers on her made-up face and the taut skin of her pregnant belly. Her head is tilted upwards and turned to face the spectator. The photograph employs the conventions of 'photographic art': it is a highly stylised image employing elaborate lighting and high-resolution, high-quality printing. The only items Moore is wearing in the image are diamond earrings and a large diamond ring, both of which are emphasised through the position and extension of her hand. The diamonds signify wealth, success, class and stardom. This use of 'props' makes reference to the iconography of classical portraiture, in the fine art traditions of painting and photography. Moore's gaze in the photograph is indeterminate; she is neither looking at the camera nor away from it. As a result, the image lacks any clear point of identification for the spectator. Read in the context of classical portraiture, Moore's indeterminable gaze is reminiscent of Julia Kristeva's descriptions of the gaze of the Virgin in Giovanni Bellini's paintings: 'The faces of his Madonnas are turned away, intent on something else that draws their gaze to the side, up above, or nowhere in particular' (1993: 247). Despite the obvious differences between this image – a photograph taken in 1991 of a heavily pregnant actress – and those of Bellini's fifteenth-century paintings, such a comparison is nevertheless enlightening, since Bellini's Madonnas are the Virgin mothers of sons: submissive, passive and devoid of sexual desire.[5] In contrast, this statuesque representation of pregnant embodiment is incongruously sacred, maternal *and* erotic. Her glowing white purity has an ambivalent relationship to the sexuality her pregnant body simultaneously exudes.

Moore's indeterminate gaze can be read as an attempt to give this photograph an acceptable and familiar lineage in fine art. If Moore had been shot directly returning the gaze of the spectator, if her gaze had broken through the shiny surface of the photograph, this image would have been more difficult to accept, as it would have been more readily interpreted as inappropriately sexually inviting.[6] However, although Moore does not return the gaze of the voyeur directly, her gaze *towards* the spectator, when taken together with the enclosing poise of her body, particularly the shielding of the nipples from view, identifies her as a subject who is aware she is being looked at. In this photograph, Moore invites the look of the voyeur, but demurely, *with a little class*. Her ambivalent gaze thus perplexes, 'an act of looking that would simply make her body an object' (Connor 1999: 45).

When the August 1991 issue of Vanity Fair was published, many newsagents in the US placed it on the top shelf alongside pornographic publications, precisely because there was no received way of interpreting and classifying such an image. Given the general invisibility of pregnant bodies in popular media this photograph was highly unusual when it was first published.[7] This was the first time a celebrity figure had posed heavily pregnant for a high-profile publicity photoshoot and it was and still is an image that is difficult to 'read'. This difficulty in interpretation was apparent in the unprecedented and highly contradictory public responses to it and media interest in it. The cover 'provoked the most intense controversy in *Vanity Fair's* history: ninety-five television spots, sixty-four radio shows, 1,500 newspaper articles and a dozen cartoons' (Stabile 1994: 84). It became the best-selling single issue in the magazine's history, even though in the US alone about two dozen newsagent chains made the decision that the issue was unsuitable for 'family stores', and refused to carry it.[8] On publication the front cover photograph was immediately circulated and reprinted around the globe and was considered significant enough to make the headlines on news bulletins across the US, Europe and Japan. Clearly sensing the controversy this cover would provoke, and undoubtedly trying to capitalise on it, the magazines publishers, Condé Naste Publications, sent out many US copies of the issue sealed in a plastic bag, with a sheet of paper demurely veiling the pregnant torso, leaving only Moore's face and the *Vanity Fair* title visible. This veiling reiterates the taboo status of the naked pregnant body, which the photograph in turn challenges.

Moreover, this process of veiling and unveiling also relates to the attention to surface that is a key feature of this photograph. What the magazine's brown wrapper cover veils is an image of Moore's skin. However, once unveiled, the photograph itself can be seen to represent the body's surface in such a way that Moore's pregnant body is both hyper-visible and yet concealed through surface. Steven Connor (1999) writes about this ambivalence of surface in terms of shiny skin:

> Like the modernist building faced in glass, the shining skin is able to hide in plain sight [. . .] The shine of the skin deflects and diffuses the perforative, punctual line of sight across the horizontality of the planar body. The skin thus becomes a sort of mirror, borrowing the mirror's depthlessness and invisibility (the mirror offers everything to the eye but itself, for you can only ever look in a mirror, never at it). [. . .] The skin mirror effaces itself in its visibility, but also retains a certain opacity.
>
> (1999: 45)

Moore's skin is presented through the use of lighting, the pose of her body and the colour of the print, in such a way that it takes on the unreal and depthless quality that Connor outlines above. Moore's skin is immaculate, perfect. She appears to be clothed by her skin. She is wearing her skin. This concealing wearing of the skin frustrates the spectator's desire to see all. There is a play between nakedness and nudity, between visibility and invisibility in this image, which entices the spectator to peer at the display of the pregnant body, while simultaneously offering a body surface that offers none of the satisfaction of depth. This perplexing play of surface, 'operates as an impossible "flat depth" of viscous liquidity, a diffulgence that never divulges itself to the eye' (1999: 46). The realist claims of the history of photographic practice, promised to reveal all, and yet here in the reflective shiny surface of both the magazine cover and Moore's skin itself, what we anticipate seeing is precisely shielded from view. This photograph and its presentation to the spectator thus play with the relationship between surface and depth, which might be said to characterise photography as a visual form. Through its deployment of reflective surfaces, this skin-tight image of pregnancy displaces the cultural imaging of the maternal as open, porous and undifferentiated. Skin operates in this image as 'a kind of visual immune system' (Connor 1999: 47) against the penetrative gaze. Interestingly, for Connor, this operation of the shiny skin surface as a shield against the objectifying gaze, evokes 'a masculinised conception of the body surface. [. . .] a kind of hardness that would enclose, canalise or otherwise discipline the threatening fluidity attributed to the female body or the feminised interior' (1999: 46). The opposition between masculine exteriority and feminine interiority is apparent in the familiar theoretical and popular representations of the maternal as the abject inside, which threatens the skin-boundary of the individualised (masculine) subject. Given this, it is important to consider how the maternal body has been constructed as that which must be abjected by the (masculine) subject.

The abject maternal

Significantly, the 'skin' figures at the beginning of Kristeva's theory of abjection. In *Powers of Horror: An Essay on Abjection* (1982), Kristeva uses the analogy of skin on the surface of milk to explain the experience of abjection. It is when, she writes, 'the eyes see or the lips touch that skin' that a gagging sensation ensues (Kristeva 1982: 2). The process of gagging is a physical enactment of the psychic process of abjection in which the 'I' abjects (and thus distinguishes itself from) that which it is not. To use her metaphor, when the skin of the milk touches the skin of my lips, it threatens the border between the object milk and the subject, 'me'. What Kristeva suggests here is that when the subject/object boundary is breached, the object is transformed into the abject object. Human skin is always involved in abjection; it is the border zone upon which self and not-self is perpetually played out. It is the bodily site at which abjection occurs. Connor notes that our 'skin is the vulnerable, unreliable boundary between inner and outer conditions and the proof of their frightening, fascinating intimate contiguity' (1999: 52). One function of the skin is that it signifies, as abjection enacts, the capacity of the subject to maintain the distinction between outer and inner, ego and other. For Kristeva, the corpse or a wound with blood and pus are common abject objects, things in or through which the skin border has disintegrated or been punctured in some way so as to expose the subject to the limits of self. As Connor writes, '[t]he wounded lacerated flesh must be kept apart from the rigidified armature of the male phantasmal body' (1999: 47). However, at the same time, the fantasy of the dangerously fluid and fleshy must persist, in order to protect the fantasy of bodily integrity. It is thus not surprising that abjection is often intimately linked to the absence and presence of skin.

This link, between abjection and the presence and absence of the skin, is perhaps most visually apparent in the horror film. In this genre, the maternal is frequently invoked as the site of abjection. For example, in the film *The Brood* (1979), the site of horror is a massive womb, which is on the outside of the woman's body. In the science fiction film *Aliens* (1986), we are confronted with the horrifying site of the Alien's womb, externalised in the form of a deathly birth chamber. Barbara Creed argues that horror films bring to representation the patriarchal phantasy that the 'womb is horrifying per se'. Significantly, though, it is not the fact of pregnancy and its embodiment *per se*, but the absence of the skin, which allows the spectator to be 'confronted directly with the scene of horror' in these films (Creed 1993: 49). The absence of skin, which distinguishes many representations of the maternal in horror films, can be understood both as a visual instance of the disavowal of the pregnant subject's skin-ego and as a visual reminder of the fantasy of masculine impenetrability. As I argued previously, these representations of the maternal find equivalencies within psychoanalytic theories of subjectivity. For example, in the Lacanian theory of the mirror stage the mother is figured as 'the undifferentiated plenitude into which the sharp alienation and singularity of the mirror stage cuts' (Connor 1999: 37).

However, a distinction needs to be made between the categories of mother, maternal and pregnancy here, since my concern in this chapter is to differentiate pregnancy from motherhood, precisely to enable a theorisation of pregnancy as a transitional form of subjectivity. Motherhood already implies a self/other, mother/child distinction, which does not exist in any simple binary form for the pregnant subject. If we return to the cover of *Vanity Fair* with this problematic in mind, we might now read the photograph of Moore as facilitating a theorisation of the specificity of the pregnant subject, which seems so elusive within the theoretical models of subjectivity discussed above. The caption 'More Demi Moore' constructs the meaning of the photograph, not as a photograph of a mother or a photograph of the impending birth of a child, but as an image of a pregnant subject: More Moore. The use of light, to reflect on Moore's skin, directs the spectator's gaze to the surface of the body in such a way as to emphasise the external form of the pregnant body rather than its (imagined) contents. In representing a clearly differentiated body, but not an individual one, Moore is positioned as a subject who is the embodied site of her own transformation and gestation. It is thus the visual emphasis on the surface of Moore's body in this photograph that enables us to think through the skin as the site of pregnant subjectivity.

The skin shield: re-enveloping the foetus

Whilst such a reading of the Moore photograph is suggestive of new directions for theorising the subject of pregnancy, nevertheless the problem remains that this reading turns upon the skin as the privileged site of subjectivity. Such an investment in skin in this instance cannot be separated from the more general preoccupation with the skin which, for Connor, has become a symptom of the shock of modernity. As Connor argues, 'assailed by shock and sensory discomfiture of every kind, a modern subjectivity comes to be organised around the imperative need to filter, screen and block out excitations' (1999: 51). Given this, he suggests that 'the intense libidinisation of the skin in contemporary cultural practises and representations is inseparable from a desire for psychic integration through the skin' (Connor 1999: 50).

Following Connor, the visual emphasis on skin in the Moore image may enable a theorisation of skin as the site of subjective presence, but we cannot ignore the broader cultural context which has produced a libidinal investment in the skin of the pregnant celebrity. For such an investment must be read as a symptom of the shock effects of the increasing technological intervention into the pregnant body, which has produced the foetus as a subject at the expense of the pregnant woman's own visibility. The function of skin in the Moore image is therefore inseparable from the impact of the visual technologies that have penetrated beneath the pregnant woman's skin in contemporary culture: indeed, it may be read as a response to them. In the final section of this chapter, I shall thus analyse this photograph as a symptom of the intensification of the intrusions into a woman's pregnancy. In particular, I shall consider this photograph's clothing of the pregnant body in skin in relation to the effacement of the pregnant woman in foetal photography. Correlatively, I shall examine how this photograph of a pregnant subject contrasts with the imaging of the foetus as the official subject of reproduction.

There is now a substantial body of feminist work which offers a critical interrogation of the cultural impact of new visual technologies. Theorists such as Barbara Duden (1993), Sarah Franklin (1991), Valerie Hartouni (1997) and Rosalind Petchesky (1987) have argued that the visibility of the foetus, who has been bestowed the status of a subject by fact of this visual 'independence', is achieved at the cost of the increasing invisibility of the pregnant woman as the actual subject of gestation. For example, Carol Stabile suggests that 'with the advent of visual technologies, the contents of the uterus have been demystified and have become entirely representable, *but pregnant bodies themselves remain concealed*' (1994: 84; my emphasis).

Like much scientific and medical imaging technology, foetal photography does not lay bare its devices. As Franklin writes:

> The position of the spectator constructed by [foetal] images is most significantly defined by the structuring absence of the mother, who is replaced by empty space. Equally invisible are the means by which these images were produced, which must have involved highly invasive technological manoeuvres.
>
> (Franklin 1991: 195–6)

There is often little suggestion that it is a photographic practice which involves dead foetuses which are then presented as 'alive'[9] or as a practice which takes place *under the skin* of a pregnant woman.[10] The disappearance of the pregnant body within foetal imagery 'renders female and male contributions to reproduction equivalent' (Stabile 1994: 89).

This process of displacement relates to skin in two ways. First, it is accomplished through the disappearance of the pregnant woman's external skin, and second, through the construction of a foetal skin. Both are crucial to the imaging of foetal personhood. Foetal skin is 'visually constructed' through the practices of foetal photography, so that the foetus can be differentiated from the other fleshy material within the pregnant woman's womb. For although, according to Anzieu, the foetus does develop a skin-like type membrane within the first two months of development, and 'before the other sensory systems' (1989: 14), this early skin remains transparent and diffuse. Crucially, this skin is not a part of the perception-consciousness system until after birth. New born babies learn where the surface of their body ends and the world begins as they become slowly conscious. Despite the fact that the actual foetus does not develop what we would fully recognise as a skin of its own until it reaches a fairly late developmental stage, it must nevertheless be imaged photographically as having a skin in order to be imagined as a discrete being. Anzieu notes that a common synonym for the word membrane is *pia mater*, meaning literally skin mother or mother skin, 'clearly conveying the pre-conscious notion that the mother is the first skin' (1989: 13).

The pregnant woman's external skin is the boundary between herself, as a discrete being, and the world. Within this external skin, there is a membrane or skin sac within which the foetus floats. The membrane that coats the foetal body is both part of her skin and the skin of an other who is not yet a separate self. It is very difficult to distinguish between her skin and the foetal skin while the foetus is alive; the pregnant woman experiences the foetal skin as part of her-self. As Anzieu notes, 'subjectivity is not just about having a physical skin; it's about feeling one owns it: it's a matter of psychic investment of self in skin' (cited in Prosser 1998: 73). A foetus has no such investment in its skin-self, whether dead or alive.

It is precisely the function of the construction of foetal skin to make us, the spectators, invest in the foetus as a subject. In order to replicate life through dead foetuses and in order to construct the discrete skin surface necessary for the project of imaging foetal personhood, foetal photographs, such as Lennart Nilsson's famous photographs for *Life Magazine* (1965 and 1990), use complex lighting effects. Through back lighting and the deployment and removal of parts of the woman's body, such as the womb, the placenta and the embryonic sac, the effect is created of a live discrete being. As Hartouni notes, the foetus is presented as a 'discrete and separate entity, outside of, unconnected to, and, by virtue of its ostensible or visual independence, in an adversarial relationship with the body and life upon which it is nevertheless inextricably dependent' (1997: 67). There are two significant ways in which this construction of the skin (and the correlative signification of there being a subject present), takes place within foetal photography. Early gestational pictures often show the foetus floating within the embryonic sac: a spherical container that stands in for the skin and marks the foetus as separate and self-contained. In these images, the mother's body is not only absent, but is replaced as 'the container' of the foetus by this skin-like sac. Later gestational photographs of the foetus more clearly depict it as a being with a skin: close-up shots are lit in such a way as to highlight its translucent covering, revealing the veins below the surface that signify aliveness. These close-ups, often of the face, hands and feet, effect an intense (emotional) identification provoked in part by the transparency and delicacy of the skin pictured. This fragility of the outer covering of the foetus has been extended in the construction of the foetal subject as a vulnerable child in need of protection. What is disavowed within these images is not only the *pia mater*, the mother's skin, but also, and as a consequence, the pregnant woman who is the structuring absence of these photographs. As Hartouni notes, we are in danger of losing sight of the fact that 'pregnancies, when they occur, occur in women's bodies (1997: 67).

Indeed, as some have argued, the disappearance of the woman's body from sight has been paralleled by the emergence of the foetus, not just as a visible entity with a personhood, but as a celebrity. Given the highly complex special effects that foetal photography employs it is perhaps not surprising that the 'spot-lit' foetus, the epitome of innocent childhood, has obtained the status of a celebrity.[11] As Berlant writes, for the foetus, 'like all celebrities, the identity its body co-ordinates exists fully in the public sphere of superpersonhood, where it radiates authenticity and elicits strong identification' (1997: 124).

The structural absence of the pregnant woman's subjectivity, which I have identified within psychoanalytic theory and within popular visual cultures (until the publication of the Moore photograph) is thus repeated anew within the practices of foetal photography. All of these sites operate around a taboo that has disavowed pregnant subjectivity. Indeed, the displacement of pregnant embodiment in the foetal narratives of the late twentieth century demonstrates a clear political need to theorise and reframe pregnant women as the subjects of gestation. The taboo-breaking publication of the Moore photograph thus presents the opportunity to address the absence of the pregnant subject within existing theoretical frameworks and to begin to imagine her presence. This photograph can thus be read as a shield against the imaging of foetal personhood and a refusal of the mother/child dichotomy that monopolises discourses around reproduction. Through my reading of the cultural significance of skin I have suggested that the Moore photograph re-envelops the foetus within the pregnant body, an envelopment which can be theorised and in turn can present ways for women to re-envelop themselves as the subjects of their own gestation.

Notes

1 Images of pregnant women have historically been confined to medical and associated health literature and a sub-category of pornography. It is significant that there has been a broad increase in the number of 'lifestyle' magazines since 1991 and that the portrayal of pregnancy in these magazines has shifted away from traditional material and medical images. For instance, they now regularly feature glamorous images of pregnant celebrities

2 Since the publication of Leibovitz's photographs of Moore there has been an explosion of post-Demi images of pregnancy in the United States and the United Kingdom, most of which appeared in the late 1990s. These photoshoots were the primary site in which new representations of pregnant embodiment were elaborated and they impacted commercially in terms of the creation of new markets for pregnant women. The presence of pregnant women across a range of different cultural sites suggests that the visibility of pregnancy is increasingly acceptable. For example, in the UK the pregnancies of even minor celebrities are seized upon as the opportunity for a photoshoot and an appearance in such celebrity lifestyle magazines as *Hello* in much the same way as a celebrity marriage is felt to be of public interest and is seen as an opportunity for publicity.

3 Notable amongst these pregnant photographs are those of Pamela Anderson, US actress and model, pictured on the cover of the British celebrity magazine *OK!* (issue 10, May 1996), Lisa Rinna, US soap star, *Playboy* (September 1998) as well as pop star Melanie Blatt who appeared in close copy of Demi pose on the front cover of the British tabloid Newspaper *The Sun* (1 August 1998). Supermodel Elle Macpherson appeared in a skin-tight black leotard with a Milk Moustache, for the US Milk Marketing advertising campaign, which was featured on billboards, buses and in newspapers and magazines across the US. Supermodel Cindy Crawford posed naked, seven months pregnant, on the front cover of American fashion magazine *W* (May 1999), a photograph which was considered notable enough to reprinted on the front cover of the British tabloid newspaper, *The Mirror* (Wednesday 12 May 1999) with the caption 'Cindy does a Demi'.

4 For Anzieu, the infant's acquisition of an ego, a skin ego, falls into three main stages, each of which involves the acquisition of key imaginary structures or phantasies. In the first of these the infant denies or represses his/her birth through the acquisition of a phantasy of an extended interuterine existence. In the second stage, the infant and mother are bound together within a phantasy of a common skin. As the child develops, in the third stage, the suppression of the common skin must take place in order for the child to envelope him/herself in his/her own skin (ego). This is the 'recognition that each has his or her own skin, his or her own ego, a recognition which does not come about without resistance and pain. It is at this point that phantasies of the flayed skin, the stolen skin, the bruised or murderous skin exert their influence' (Anzieu 1989: 63) If the mother and/or child fail to relinquish and repress the common skin 'the structure [of the skin ego] is not acquired or, more usually, is distorted' (Anzieu 1989: 4–5).

5 These adjectives could serve equally well in descriptions of medical and popular health manual depictions of the pregnant body prior to the publication of this photograph in 1991. The pregnant body was and is often decapitated (and thus de-subjectified) within the frame, with the focus of the image being the torso alone.

6 Annette Kuhn notes that pornography often depicts women 'gazing away' in order to facilitate and heighten the pleasure of the voyeur, allowing the spectator to imagine that they are 'sneaking a look' (1995: 273).

7 Prior to the publication of these photographs of Demi Moore, the British pop-star Neneh Cherry had caused a stir in the United Kingdom through her first appearance on the British music programme, *Top of the Pops* in 1989: she was eight months pregnant and wearing skin-tight lycra. She was also photographed pregnant in the British music press. It is unclear what impact the visibility of Neneh Cherry's pregnancy had on later representations of pregnancy in the United States and United Kingdom. However this incident is always referred to in subsequent interviews with Cherry (see for example, *Rolling Stone Magazine* 4 February 1993).

8 Local as well as national papers reported on the 'impact' of the front cover image. The *Seattle Post Intelligencer* ran an article entitled ' "Family" Stores Want Less of Moore: QFC and Target chains pull magazine featuring the semi-clad Demi' (July 20th 1991), in which business owners and other local people were reported to be outraged by the issue, and deemed it inappropriate for 'family stores' (article at: http://www.geocities.com/Hollywood/Agency/5560/mags/van91_2.html.) Other stores across the US and Europe held the magazine 'behind the counter' or put in 'on the top shelf' alongside pornographic publications.

9 I am referring specifically to Lennart Nilson's presentations of dead foetuses as alive, for example in his in 'The First Pictures Ever of How Life Begins' (photo essay), *Life*, August 1990. See Stabile (1994) for a close reading of Nilson's two *Life* photo essays.

10 For a detailed analysis of the mechanisms of this disavowal see Hartouni 1997.

11 In using the category of 'foetal celebrity', I am referring to the use of these photographs in anti-abortion campaigns. See Peggy Phelan's analysis of this use of foetal imagery in *Unmarked* (1993).

I would like to thank Jackie Stacey for all her help and advice with this chapter, and Fiona Summers for checking references for me.

References

Anzieu, D. (1989) *The Skin Ego: A Psychoanalytic Approach to the Self*, New Haven: Yale University Press.

Battersby, C. (1997) *The Phenomenal Woman: Feminist Metaphysics and Patterns of Identity*, Cambridge: Polity.

Berlant, L. (1997) *The Queen of America Goes to Washington City*, Durham: Duke University Press.

Braidotti, R. (1994) *Nomadic Subjects: Embodiment and Sexual Difference in Contemporary Feminist Theory*, New York: Columbia University Press.

Butler, J. (1993) *Bodies that Matter: On the Discursive Limits of 'Sex'*, London: Routledge.

Cixous, H. and Clément, C. (1996) *The Newly Born Woman*, trans. B. Wing, Minneapolis: University of Minnesota Press.

Connor, S. (1999) 'Integuments: The Scar, the Sheen, the Screen' *New Formations* 39: 32–54.

Creed, B. (1993) *The Monstrous–Feminine: Film, Feminism and Psychoanalysis*, London: Routledge.

Deleuze, G. and Guattari, F. (1988) *A Thousand Plateaus: Capitalism and Schizophrenia*, London: Athlone Press.

Doane, M. A. (1990) 'Technophilia, Technology, Representation, and the Feminine' in M. Jacobus, E. F. Keller and S. Shuttleworth (eds) *Body/Politics: Women and the Discourse of Science*, New York: Routledge.

Duden, B. (1993) *Disembodying Women: Perspectives on Pregnancy and the Unborn*, trans. L. Hoinacki, Cambridge, MA: Harvard University Press.

Dyer, R. (1997) *White*, London: Routledge.

Franklin, S. (1991) 'Fetal Fascinations: New Dimensions to the Medical-Scientific Construction of Fetal Personhood' in S. Franklin, C. Lury and J. Stacey (eds) *Off-Centre: Feminism and Cultural Studies*, London: HarperCollins.

Hartouni, V. (1997) *Cultural Conceptions: On Reproductive Technologies and the Remaking of Life*, Minneapolis: University of Minnesota Press.

Irigaray, L. (1985) *This Sex Which Is Not One*, trans. C. Porter with C. Burke, New York: Cornell University Press.

—— (1993) *An Ethics of Sexual Difference*, trans. C. Burke and G. C. Gill, London: The Athlone Press.

Jones, D. (1999) 'Pop Belly', *Sunday Times* 28 February, pp. 32–40.

Kristeva, J. (1982) *The Powers of Horror: An Essay on Abjection*, trans. L. S. Roudiez, New York: Columbia University Press.

—— (1993) *Desire in Language: A Semiotic Approach to Literature and Art*, L. S. Roudiez (ed.), trans. T. Gora, A. Jardine and L. S. Roudiez, London: Blackwell.

Kuhn, A. (1995) 'Lawless Seeing' in G. Dines and J. Humez (eds) *Gender, Race and Class in the Media: A Text Reader*, London: Sage.

Petchesky, R. (1987) 'Fetal Images: The Power of Visual Culture in the Politics of Reproduction' in M. Stanworth (ed.), *Reproductive Technologies: Gender, Motherhood and Medicine*, Minneapolis: University of Minnesota Press.

Phelan, P. (1993) *Unmarked: The Politics of Performance*, New York: Routledge.

Plant, S. (1998) *Zeros and Ones: Digital Women and the New Technoculture*, London: Fourth Estate.

Prosser, J. (1998) *Second Skin: The Body Narratives of Transsexuality*, New York: Columbia University Press.

Stabile, C. A. (1994) *Feminism and the Technological Fix*, Manchester: Manchester University Press.

Tyler, I. (2000) 'Reframing Pregnant Embodiment' in S. Ahmed, J. Kilby, C. Lury, M. McNeil and B. Skeggs (eds) *Transformations: Thinking Through Feminism*, London: Routledge.

Walker, M. B. (1998) *Philosophy and the Maternal Body: Reading Silence*, London: Routledge.

Part II

Skin encounters

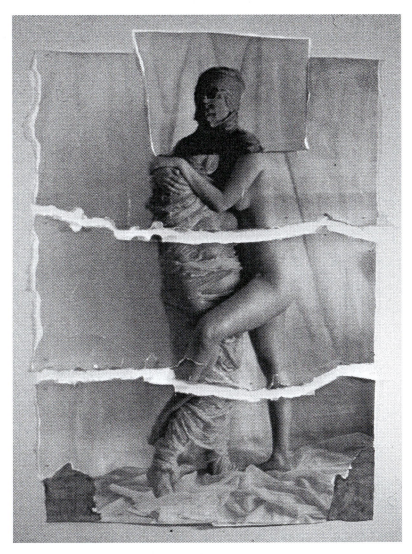

Frontispiece 2 'The Re-integration of Self'
Toned photographic mural print with oil, from installation *Writ(e) of Habeus Corpus*, 5 ft × 5 ft
Susan McKenna and Elizabeth Hynes

5   Eating skin[1]

Elspeth Probyn

When I first arrived, having migrated from Canada to Australia, the overwhelming jumble of impressions, the gaps of knowledge, the constant pressure of ignorance, the incommensurability of ways of knowing; all these I felt in my guts: '*les tripes* as research protocol' (Probyn 1996: 155[2]). As is often the case, I have ingested my experience, turned my stomach into a research project, and in the course of studying food and belonging, I have eaten my way into slices of Australian identity. Rare kangaroo and smoked emu, Barossa chooks and beautiful steak, lamb, fish, lemongrass and paper bark. I now have an alimentary acquaintance with Mod Oz.

It is only recently that I have noticed changes in my skin. It has become both toughened and overly sensitive. In the changing rooms, I look with no great pleasure at my unclothed body. An English girl, a passing acquaintance from the gym, joins me and we stand naked, white skins reflected in the pocked mirror. I ask her how she likes being here, and she says that she finds 'the Aborigines depressing'. Stunned, I wait for more, I blush, I mumble, I search for the right reply. No elaboration comes from her, no coherent reply from me. Was her comment clumsy sympathy, casual racism or an aversion to seeing anything that might make her uncomfortable, *pas bien dans sa peau*? I leave feeling depressed, inept and thin-skinned. I'm beginning to think that as a white in Australia it helps to have thick skin. Thick, hard skin as protection against implication in the living memory of the country, the brutalities of colonisation still so vividly worn by some, hidden on others.

Any investigation of skin must start here. It must start in the present in order to seek ways of connecting to the past. It must start in the acknowledgment of the fact that skin matters, matters viscerally, and in different ways. It must begin in an acknowledgment of the different shades, textures and feel of skin, of skin as testimony both to the subjective state of individuals and to the histories that have moulded them: of fair Aboriginal skin as a document of the planned erasure of black skin; of the muddied skin of the white working class; of the reddened, cancered skin of farmers; of the albino whiteness of the classic 'bluey'; of the clear white skin of the affluent suburbs; of the skins of those allowed in only relatively recently – breaching the previously impenetrable skin of the White Australia policy.[3] Skin becomes a living proof of the ways in which individuals seek to inhabit this land.

Skin is that fine membrane that must be made porous to itself, to its own histories. Skin offers a myriad of connections, but it also reminds us of the disconnections, and of the limits of good intentions. To rework Donna Haraway's (1990) question about why skin has to end at our bodies, this is to remember that in general terms our skins end at our histories of racism, violence and indifference, forming hard barriers between skin marked white, black, coloured. For whites, skin offers no blueprint, no blanket insurance against guilt. But if we are to make them, the connections must be as subtly different as the skins of the land. Those from here will find their own ways to connect to the colour of skins that carry the histories of the nation, as well as moments of interracial friendship, of love not rape: skins that may be made to breathe with the possibility of coexistence, respect and maybe even care.

But my task is different: How as a white migrant from a white settler nation to live within the present order of another white settler nation? How to connect two distant parts of the world, and their different white and black histories, without merely transposing the one upon the other (thus blurring the differences), without proposing parallels (so that the lines never meet)? How to live ethically, which is to say fully situated, when I have no roots? Or rather, how to make roots other than those tap roots of familial and national history; to make roots like those that spread from the skin of potatoes, branching in all directions, breaking up solidified soil?[4] For I am here. I sit in my home in Redfern, aware that I inhabit precariously a site drenched in the meanings of the past and present. A place where, for the Gadigal and other Aboriginal people, the kangaroo fed, a place of plenty now levelled as the most visible reminder of what two hundred years of white occupation has produced.

Redfern has the largest urban concentration of Aboriginals. It is also known for its high unemployment and crime rates, drug use and other signs of poor living conditions. As the last inner city suburb in Sydney to be gentrified, there is a disparate mix of inhabitants: different waves of migration, especially Lebanese and Korean, and now the affluent seeking cheap houses that they can 'do up'. But it is first and foremost marked by the presence of the original occupants of Australia.

The mural on the Redfern railway bridge sighs '40,000 years is a long time', asserts, '40,000 years and still here', as the Block[5] is rendered a police state. There are, of course, a number of straightforward actions that white-skinned newcomers like me can take: I must do my homework better, read and learn more about both sides, all sides, of this country. I must remember to walk in the country, and not through it, in my haste to know the land. I must try not to stare into the eyes of Aboriginal friends and new acquaintances as if I could pry from them knowledge that would save me. All of this and more. Yet it is useless if merely learned by rote, gobbled up to be spat back in the thrill of passing tests. Done in this way, the skin will toughen, allowing me to navigate the hazards of reconciliation untouched. Skin registers, but what to do with its wants, and refusals, its silences, its exigencies?

In thinking about the uses of skin, I want to work skin on a number of levels.

On one level, skin seduces as metaphor: colonialism as the process of laying a foreign skin upon the land, making its indigenous inhabitants wear their own skins uneasily, become ashamed of them, making them wear them in imitation of the white man. But under the skin of colonialism lie other stories of how whites try to make the land their own, sometimes loving it as their own. There are small instances where coloniser and colonised touch skin to skin.[6] On another level, skin as metonym, or more aptly synecdoche: as the most literal part of the whole process of colonisation, skin records the structural imposition of policies and practices. And on yet another level, can thinking through skin be used to figure other forms of relationships, of being within the historical present of countries like Australia and Canada struggling to make sense of themselves? Eating skin as a way of living well with the present: feeling its bite, feeding its future? To add another level of enquiry, my preoccupation here is to find a way of using skin as a way of engaging in the present history of my adopted country. For me, this means reflecting on the history of my own skin, and how I live here with the ghostly skin of my forebears. To put it another way, how can my skin form rhizomatic roots, joining where I am, where I come from, all conducted in an abyss of the past rendered present, all engaged in the exigency of participating viscerally in the processes of reconciliation, in the hopes of coexistence?

At times, it all seems so hard that it hurts my brain, cutting deep lines into my brow. Couldn't it be easier? What if skin were merely the fact of bodies, of hers and mine: five feet, nine and half inches against another five, six and a half? Skin as the longest organ, then stretched again by another's? What if skin signified only desire, pleasure and the ease of body upon body, oiled skin and skin? And eating skin, the taste of pools of passion? Could the very smoothness of our skins cause difference to slide away, erasing the markings of black and white, past and present, here and there? My desire for her skin, for its shades of history and difference, her desire for mine: as my skin eats hers, and her skin eats mine, could we find a way of desiring that doesn't erase my whiteness, her blackness, but that through osmosis lets us learn to be together differently?

She calls me 'blue', and I in surprise say that at least she got a real white girl, not some Aussified mixture of white. She laughs at something I say: 'you're talking Koori now'. I redden and admit to taking on accents as easily as clothing, that I am after all a mid-Atlantic bastard whose tongue loves long 'a's. 'True, eh': such a comforting phrase that I want to lick it into my own vocabulary. She tells me stories, she asks me to tell mine. I do, but they seem inconsequential, the lovers' talk tracing trajectories. The story I itch to tell also shames. The broad family history of white colonisers might have kept us fatally apart, placing me forever on the side of empire and class privilege. From my father's side, I carry the name that still signifies to some links to parts of the world I have never visited. But the story I want to tell her concerns my more enlightened maternal side, my mother's solidly socialist father and her socially concerned mother. I know that in the telling it will become more complicated than these blanket categories. I finally blurt out to her, as she looks with calm waiting eyes, 'My grandmother liked to inhabit the skins of others'. My grandmother's poem in which she masquerades as a Native

Canadian woman – a squaw in her words – rattles. And I am silent before the chasm this opens between this new love and me. All she says is, 'That's interesting, go on'.

*   *   *

A poet, my grandmother took on the bodies of those arranged around her: Native Canadians, Japanese, Chinese and Dukabor – the remnants of workers that Canada no longer needed for clearing land and building roads who then did housework for her, or the decimated fragments of First Nations cleared from the land into reservations near where she lived. For her, 'going native' seemed to mean taking on the exotic in a visceral manner. In my family jokes were told of her desire to take on the other, to speak the other (who sometimes responded bluntly; we suspected that a Chinese scroll given to her said 'bugger off white woman'). When I first came upon her poems, I blushed at their intent and their dated turns. On the other side of the Pacific, I wonder now at her desire, that seems to shadow mine as surely as our first names and red hair. Named for her, I stare in shock at the way in which my signature imitates hers. Writing on skin, it would be easy to disown our intimate history, so that my own desire would bubble up purely in a denunciation of hers. Do I also envy her the freedom with which she donned other bodies? Years of feminisms and critiques of feminisms tie my tongue and bind me in a cramped corner. I am free to speak of the Other but only as a political/ethical/epistemological problem. In certain circles, in other corners, I could claim a unity in difference. In yet further corners, I could assert that being a woman joins me with others. I can pontificate on the skin but I cannot inhabit it. But hope tugs: Could skin be the site where difference becomes intense, where it sucks both ways and rearranges the present?

But of course it won't be that simple. In any case, I don't want a simplicity that would exfoliate difference, strip desire. I would, however, like an elegant solution to skin, a model or a figure that translates a myriad of complexity into one line: eating skin. Why eating, and not caressing, stroking or even grafting skin? In part, I use this figure because I really love to eat skin – the sheer pleasure of crackling, creme brulée, crispy duck and roasted potatoes, the enigmatic delight of the skin on milky coffee. Eating skin is unavoidably sensual. The figure of eating skin also suggests for me a way of being overwhelmingly close to difference, without subsuming difference into the same, or the same-other. I think of Georg Simmel's comment about the paradox of eating: an act that marks out radical incommensurability ('what the individual eats, no one else can eat under any circumstances') and commensality (eating together as the fundamental basis of sociality) (Simmel 1994: 346). Eating skin is a way of recognising absolute difference, yet at the same time it is an act that demands you roll up your sleeves and get stuck in.

Eating skin: the phrase immediately forefronts the consumption of difference. More often than not, this is taken to be the eradication of difference, difference turned into commodity.[7] Yet such interpretations ignore the ways in which one is changed by eating, made bigger, smaller, healthier, sicker, happier, fearful. Skin is the most obvious of social markers, yet it evades attempts to speak of it in terms both sociological and desirous. Despite being a touchy subject best avoided in certain contexts, we must none the less learn to grapple with it, get our hands sticky with questions not easily answered. Eating skin is that fine line that divides and brings together so many categories and incongruities: the bruising of violence and intensity, the clichés of inner and outer. But what of skin as a way of thinking through difference, to some place beyond the triteness of self-same, self-other, to a space where eating skin unravels statements about assimilation and authenticity? Could we make eating skin an act of such intensity that it burns out the fear that makes us hide behind abstraction? More precisely, and within a clashing arrangement of contexts, I want to know how to eat skin, the skin of the other: to eat skin well, and to hope for my skin to be well eaten.

To eat skin well is both a question of theoretical amplitude and one that gnaws daily. At the first level, the question of eating well has already been broached by Derrida, who tells us that

> the question is no longer one of knowing whether it is 'good' to eat the other or if the other is 'good' to eat, nor of knowing which other. One eats him regardless and lets oneself be eaten by him.
>
> (Derrida 1991: 114)

In some ways, his formulation is daunting in its simplicity:

> The moral question is thus not, nor has it ever been: should one eat or not eat, eat this and not that, the living or the nonliving, man or animal, but since *one must* eat in any case and since it is and tastes good to eat, and since there's no other definition of the good (*du bien*), *how* for goodness sake should one *eat well* (*bien manger*)?
>
> (Derrida 1991: 115; emphasis in original)

As Derrida himself immediately asks, 'What does this imply?' In simple terms, eating well for Derrida demands respect, but a respect that can be glimpsed only at that moment when the teeth and tongue are already touching the skin. In a rush of compulsion, 'one must', 'one must eat well', he says that 'respect for the other [is evoked] at the very moment when, in experience . . . one must begin to identify with the other who is to be assimilated, interiorized, understood ideally' (Derrida 1991: 115).

Derrida's use of eating is metonymical, so we hear his injunction to eat well at the same time that it darts from tongue to ear, from eating to speaking: to address 'oneself to the other', to 'speak to him in words that also pass through the mouth, the ear, and sight' (Derrida 1991: 115). This movement soon deserts the taste of the other, but it is not metaphor, and his argument causes the mind to stretch, to reach after the sense of this respect. 'The sublime refinement involved in this respect for the other is also a way of "Eating well", in the sense of good eating but also doing well to eat.' (Derrida 1991: 115.) From these images Derrida fabricates a more involved plan of engagement. Reconnoitring gratitude and recognition:

reconnaissance before and in the world. But this moment of eating well must be conducted in the shadow of merely eating: the possibilities of the respect produced out of eating well are ghosted by the memory of the imperative that 'I must, I must eat'. With this, Derrida brings us down to earth to face the question of what we can actually do, under these circumstances, now.

Derrida's movement orchestrates eating, and eating well. To replay this in more corporeal terms, think of being hungry, of starving. Images of starving reverberate in this country of plenty: the first whites who would not countenance eating the food of Aboriginals, who in fact placed Aboriginals on the same level as the kangaroo and emu they would not eat. The first whites who got over their disgust and then quickly killed off the game, emptied the sea of fish, thus ensuring the starvation of black Australia, who poisoned the food and water. To roll the phrase around the mouth, eating well in this country insists on that moment of contact when I eat the other and she eats me, and also almost immediately recedes into a heavy horizon. History is that horizon from which rise up memories of that moment of contact over two hundred years ago. Middens of oyster shells are the reminder of Aboriginal feasts, and are recounted today as evidence of a line of connection based on 'foods loved by original Australians, convict Australians, New Australians and modern Australians' (Newton 1998).

Eating oysters, connective tissue that joins the indigenous, the convict, the new and the modern. This makes sense only if eating is understood in its intensity. Think carefully of how one eats oysters: peering closely to see if they look all right, smelling them in order to ascertain their provenance, then with an index pulling the flesh from the shell and sliding it into the mouth, where of course it tries to confound, to make us question what is being eaten, and even who or what is eating whom. Eating then foregrounds the conjoining of very different entities, marking the moment of excessive recognition. Another way of putting this is to ask what happens if we specify *what* one eats when one eats well. To insert skin into the equation, what would eating skin well imply? To eat *skin* well. . . . the idea sinks flatly into the soil of a sunburnt country that might evaporate the white and black shades of shame in a present filled with bad blood when our prime minister cannot utter the words, 'we are sorry'.

This is the base line that reverberates. A point of departure, a touchstone and a suffocating horizon under which I turn to another story, to a line that ties my skin to those I find here, that allows me to inhabit a space proffered by eyes that see freckles and Anglo-white skin suturing me into Australian history, that cannot be silenced by cries of innocence: 'But I'm not from here'. Caught squirming within layers of history that I do not yet, will never quite, comprehend, I want foreign accents to return to my tongue: 'I am a migrant, my hands are clean, my intentions pure'. However, this is not a story, only an excuse. It is not until I have looked at difference with an intent to eat well that I can truly taste the abyss between good intentions and something else. That 'something else' nags us: 'We think we know a lot of things but do not really know them at all'. As Michael Ignatieff writes of the processes of reconciliation, 'We can know something in our heads without knowing it in our guts. . . . What we know in our heads must become something we know in our guts; what we know in our guts must become something we know in our heads' (Ignatieff 1998: 168). Ignatieff's point coincides with the pauses we can hear: 'eating . . . well', 'eating . . . skin . . . well'. To return to Derrida's argument, eating well requires that one begins by identifying with the other. This is an identification that precedes but also underpins the fact that one identifies with the other 'who is to be assimilated' (Derrida 1991: 115). This is, of course, a Frenchman, who from afar can speak with ease of assimilation. Here in Australia his ideas must be greeted with the knowledge of the ways in which assimilation and 'identifying appropriation' have worked. The horror of recognition before facts: the facts that fill over six hundred pages of the report, *Bringing Them Home*.[8] This model of 'biological absorption' was a resolution to the problem of feeding and settlement:

> the key issue to [Chief Protector] Neville was skin colour. Once 'half-castes' were sufficiently white in colour they would become like white people. After two or three generations the process of acceptance into the non-Indigenous community would be complete, the older generations would have died and the settlements could be closed.
>
> (*Bringing Them Home* 1997: 108)

It is human to repel such facts. What can I say to the woman, roughly my age, who remembers that in the 1970s 'we was bought like a market', a woman 'from a family of 13 siblings all removed who was raped by her foster father and forced to have an abortion' (*Bringing Them Home* 1997: 90). 'Sorry' is paltry, there is no part of my experience that can be made to match up to this. At the same time, I cannot merely ingest these facts, as if they could be taken in, defecated out, leaving no trace. As they burn like acid down the alimentary tract, they must be digested. They must, and this sounds strange in such contexts, be eaten well. For it is in the face of horror that Derrida places the possibility of respect, and the concomitant responsibility that one must take in eating well. There is a fervour in his cry for an excessive responsibility. Speaking of what he calls ' "the" question . . . "the" figure of responsibility, namely, Auschwitz', Derrida chides those who would speak 'in such an instrumental fashion and in order to say nothing . . . to give oneself a good conscience, so as not to be the last to accuse, to teach lessons, to take positions, to grandstand' (Derrida 1991: 118). Against this 'eloquence of denunciation', he proposes a 'surplus of responsibility' which will, he promises, 'never authorize any silence' (Derrida 1991: 118). He stresses the import of this: 'I repeat: responsibility is excessive or it is not responsibility' (Derrida 1991: 118).

Such responsibility is possible only in an excess of recognition. I'll meet Derrida's cry with my own: what surplus of recognition and responsibility might greet the eating of skin? Having ducked responsibility by leaving my country of birth, my desire to be enmeshed in this new country may be the zeal of the immigrant. In any case, and in both Derrdia's and mine, the question is begged of where all this responsibility is to be directed, in what form is it to be found. To recognise is to be brought into contact, to lose the possibility of ignorance. Perhaps, rather than reconciliation, we whites need to hold on to recognisance, until we observe the conditions of our existence. To recognise is to acknowledge this existence, and to show appreciation for it. I'll hazard that an excess of responsibility must be met by an excess of both recognition and representation, and an excess in representation. These three 'r's send us in several directions all at once. They must be observed, not in piety – they do not proffer absolution, only more responsibility, recognition, representations. In this model, skin knows no single dimension, and eating skin opens vistas difficult to chart. As the French expression has it, being *à fleur de peau*[9] means never knowing quite what will rage upon the skin, of where the proper boundaries of my skin end and another begins.

A fleur de peau, I return to the opening of this essay where I am placed – goosebumps rising from the confrontation of my grandmother's wish to inhabit the skins of others, and my desire to eat the skin of a lover, of an adopted country, to let the both in through the pores, and to sweat with hope for a meeting place: of skin and teeth and tongue and knowledge held in guts and head and skin and teeth and tongue.

*   *   *

In an old manilla folder marked in my grandfather's tight hand, 'Mother's poetry', are the remnants of my grandmother's career as a poet. The pieces of paper vary: typed poems marked with metal biting the paper, poems cut from the newspaper, poems in her handwriting. Many by-lined: 'Elspeth Honeyman Clarke, in the *New York Times*', but none are dated. Hardly an archive, and historians, professional or amateur, would have a fit. From a childhood of constantly moving from one rented house to another, they can be fabricated tenuously to the past. Somewhere in boxes stored away after my grandfather's death there might be other bits of evidence of the Clarke family, now all dead. I saw those boxes once, huge containers of debris – old pots and pans, an ironing board shoved in with my father's military medals and a large collection of Penguin paperbacks. There were boxes and boxes of photographs but hard to say of whom, and with my mother and uncle gone there is no way of knowing. I read her poems, not as a literary critic nor even as a sleuth; I read them with a granddaughter's eye turned inwards to a remembered itinerary of their movements, a cautious eye focused on a faraway wish to make sense of this excess. An outrageous desire to connect up the dots is immediately stalled by the title of one of the poems, 'Half-breed'. 'Half-breed', the word threatens to block any contact between granddaughter and grandmother, but the rhythm of her writing draws me in, into a story of deep rupture between mother and daughter. The dots that I wished to connect up dissolve into white representations of pain as my grandmother imagines herself into the grief of broken Native families. The first time I read it in shame: surely she knows that what she does at will mocks what others were forced to do? But shame in this case doesn't leap both ways, and as I hear the words again my skin reverberates with their sound.

HALF-BREED

I have lost her, my daughter, and never
As long as this body may love
Shall I see her again. In this body
She grew, and I bore her with gladness
And fed her with pride. [. . .]

Late at night, tho' I slept as I read
I taught her, and sweetly she grew.
I brushed her soft hair with a rapture
Too keen for delight; it was fair
Like her father's and shone in the sunlight,
And she wore but the finest of muslins,
With lace that the Sisters had made me
At the neck and the hem. So time passed
And I saw her one day as a maiden,
Slender, dark-eyed and proud as a queen.

Then she left me to go to the city
And train as a nurse; it seemed best. [. . .]

Graduation,– I sent her a trinket
And all I could spare for her flowers.
They told me her room could not hold them,
Later on, when I went there to ask –
To ask, for June came, and she came not,
Nor the next, nor any month after.
And all my blood was burnt up with my longing,
And fear, like a knife, stabbed my soul.

Still she came not. At last I could stay here
No longer. I dressed myself slowly,
Thinking, so might she wish me to look,
Though I knew no mere garment could alter
The face of a squaw, such as I.
[. . .]

In a suburb, I found her. My knock
Mocked the pounding that throbbed in my side,
And she came. Her face froze when she saw me,
Then she asked what I wanted. 'Elaine!'
But she answered, too loudly, 'No baskets,
No thank you, no baskets today.'
And I saw through the door a white table,
And flowers, and a young man's fair head,
Before the door closed on 'No baskets,
No thank you, no baskets today.'

She is gone. Aie – aie! I am lonely.
There is nothing in life or in death
For me now. God be good to her only,
And spare her this pain, my Elaine.

*   *   *

She was, evidently, a striking woman. In the only photograph I have of her, she is
flanked by stern proud parents; friends remark on her beauty that I cannot see.
For years the family stories told about her block my vision: the exciting ones of
how she fell in love with a remittance man, incredibly called Mr Bliss. And of how,
when the scoundrel went back to England with her heart, she and my great
grandmother followed him, chased him down to a corner of Devon or Cornwall.
The upper-class remittance man and the Canadian colonial beauty: an echo of
love in colonial times, permitted in the periphery and then shunned once back in
the heart of Empire. The path of that story ends there, although there was
something about them coming back on the boat before the *Titanic*, their lives in
exchange for her lost English love. Another story begins sort of mid-sentence, with
a tale of my grandparents eloping at an advanced age. When I was little, in my
grandfather's orchard, hiding in the crook of my mother's favourite apple tree, I'd
try hard to imagine them climbing down a ladder late at night. By then she had
become a palpable absence: there were faded photographs of an upright woman
with hair plaited and bound around and around, there was a locket with snippets
of that once flaming gold hair dulled to reddish brown, there were traces of her
carved into a plank in the kitchen which catalogued all our heights, and that my
mother said lied: my grandparents were marked off at the same line – 'Tom and
Elspeth', fudging the fact that she was considerably taller than her wiry husband.
Chalk and cheese: she was a committed Anglophile, he a socialist with hatred for
the English ruling class honed in the trenches, perhaps further fed by his wife's
past romance. Past images of her lying on the horsehair chaise-longue, either an
invalid, or in my father's opinion, a nasty hypochondriac. But they never liked
each other. Did my grandmother prickle at my mother's marriage to yet another
upper-class Englishman? In any case, there was bad blood between them. To the
point that my christened name was replaced for decades by a pretty diminutive.
To the point that when my mother was to follow my father on a posting to
Germany, she is reported to have said, 'Calista if you leave me you will never see
me again'. And true to her word, she died before we returned. 'Spare her this
pain, my Elaine.'

   But this is a nimbus of a familial making, hazing the part that I want to follow.
Past the maternal machinations that rendered my uncle a broken man: 'No, you
cannot marry a Filipina, Bill', and he obeyed. Past the love that seems to have
been stinted on her own beautiful dark-eyed daughter. Past her husband who
worshipped her: a painful gulf between my namesake and I when in very old age
he confused us. Past the poem on fading blue airmail paper written 'from Elspeth
C. to Elspeth P.': 'Nourish her, and cherish her; Name her stately – Goddess,
queen, most beautiful – None so dear as she!' Past the feuds and the broken family

ties, past the extinguished name of her family, I try to follow her into the space she creates, slipped under the skin of a squaw mourning her daughter, vanished by the white man's ways: 'she went to the city . . . it seemed best'.

She wrote the words for a song that seems to have had some success. It looks very grand printed by Arthur H. Stockwell, Ltd. of Ludgate Hill, EC4. A friend comments on the intricacy of the melody, on the fact that it is in B minor (an off key for the triumph of the frontier). I read it in order to follow her part way into the stretches of British Columbia. Called 'The Cariboo Trail', the cover drawing comes straight from the pen of an Englishman domesticating from afar the wild land that my grandfather was in a more efficient way taming by paving. Laying down roads like skin on the country, the land heats and freezes buckling them; the skinned land that won't quite be tamed. Her lyrics are already looking back at when the Cariboo trail was battered down in the chase for gold:

> Who were they that came riding, riding, Over the Cariboo Trail? Horses and mules, Wise men and fools, merchant, thief; Kloochman, chief; soldier, sailor, parson, jade; (This is the way that a trail is made.) . . . All of them coming to Yale in the end. Barkerville, Lillooet, Yale in the end, Over the Cariboo Trail, Over the Cariboo Trail. What did they come to look for? Gold? But the river runs swift and dark and cold, And who can tell what the river might hold, for those who come a-seeking?

Contrasted with the romance of gold, I find the reason that she was there: 'They have blasted and hewn a New Road, By the side of the old, old Trail, They have built their bridges of stone and steel, They have laid their grades for a swifter wheel' ('The Cariboo Trail' 1932).

So there they all are, my grandparents, my mother and uncle, living on the side of the new road that plunges into the interior and up north. Living in tents for the whole of the children's childhood and adolescence, what did they possibly do to pass the time, as one new road after another led them further and further north? A write-up of my grandmother yellows, cut from a newspaper of who knows what year. The journalist is making a point, using her as example 'to show that an ordinary, hard-working wife and mother, leading and enjoying a full life and having the instinct to make poetry will probably make a better job of it in the long run than some of the yearning sisters who get all eager and het up'. In tones of backlash that are repeated at the end of the century, he holds up my grandmother against those of my ilk – feminists. The prescience is uncanny. 'This thoroughly normal woman does not go about swapping soulful strophes with other poets and addressing societies.' 'Quite the contrary' writes the journalist:

> For many years her husband's profession of a civil engineer led her into the far and wilder parts of the province, living in tents and wikiups where, with real pioneer spirit, she undertook the education of her two children from matter supplied by the department of education at Victoria, and made a good job of it.

Yet, as she presumably performed her wifely duties and educated her children, no sign of family enters her poems to disturb. I look in vain for her dark daughter, for her brother married to an Indian wife (I don't bother asking my father which Nation; it would be as useful as his description of my mother as 'touched by the tar brush'). In her poems, I find lines that streak across: 'Cry of loons across the lake –/Should a heart that's mended, ache?' ('Resolution'). Vestiges of displacement that cannot be placed: 'They are building a house/(Shut them in!)'. But who is shut in, who has lost the land, to whom does she address this advice?

> Make the doors and windows fast,
> Try who may!
> Lest the little folk at night
> Steal away their heart's delight.
> Call it a blessing, cross your heart
> And come away.
>
> ('The New House')

The cry of the loons as haunting as the curlews that might take away the souls of children. The rain that beats upon the house that shuts in, keeps safe, keeps out, reproaches, reminds of impossible wishes: 'Sharp needle-pointed rain/Striking the window-pane,/Breaking the silence,/Stabs heart and brain' ('Rain'). I read too much in, get lost between the lines, and am faced with an immense gulf of my own making. The constant ache that the country won't quite let her in, that existence will always be fitful, that it will always coexist with layers of the dead, the disappeared:

> Lady, if beneath your pillow
> Men are lying dead,
> They would wish you peaceful slumbers
> In your narrow bed.
>
> ('Song of the rails')

        *   *   *

A white woman sleeping on the dead, sleeping with her family on the side of a new road that will conquer the interior of British Columbia. These are not quite the brave images of pioneering popular with generations of white Canadians. They are wedged in-between my sketchy knowledge of the more insalubrious aspects of my grandfather's career: in charge of camps where the Chinese and Japanese dispossessed of their homes and businesses were herded during the Second World War. Previous to that he had managed the work camps for the unemployed of the Depression era. As he sent them off to labour on the roads, did she write her poems in the boss-man's tent? Or did she wander the countryside trying to find a spot not ravaged by the picks and shovels, trodden down by the feet of those stripped of citizenship forced to work for food? It is obvious that she saw the beauty, but how did she make herself at home? How does a white woman write herself into the land? How does she make room for herself? Why does she want to? She inhabits the land warily, and yet still she sits, writes herself into the skin of an indigenous woman whose daughter does not want her.

The question looms: What do I want of my grandmother, and of her stories of the other? As I sit on the other side of the Pacific with her poems laid around me, bits of papers inscribed with her hand but undated, unreferenced, I wonder about her longing, and mine. What sort of politics can such desires feed?

In the terms of contemporary debates within cultural studies, it's hard to deal with questions of this genre with much subtlety. But then, how subtle is the desire to make of one's grandmother an exemplar of the fraught relation of white settler women within colonised land, how gentle the act of inhabiting the body of a Native woman? Perhaps one can be too subtle, too clever in elaborating 'solutions' to the everyday problems of living in stolen land. The bluntness of certain critics is salutary. For instance, in her essay, 'Eating the Other', bell hooks is unequivocal about contemporary trends in interracial sexual desire, the ways in which black women constitute the 'unexplored terrain, a symbolic frontier . . . fertile ground for their reconstruction of the masculine norm, for asserting themselves as trans-gressive desiring subjects' (1992: 25). This is but one ploy; another, perhaps more feminine, certainly insidious, is the 'process of yearning for that one has des-troyed'. 'The desire to make contact with those bodies deemed Other, with no apparent will to dominate, assuages the guilt of the past, [and] even takes the form of a defiant gesture where one denies accountability and historical connection' (hooks 1992: 25).

Within this frame, my desire for another pants loud, a bull in a china shop of complicated relations. Black versus white; these starkly opposed categories are removed from the skin and from the land that breeds them. Closer to skin, it may also be that more delicate and difficult questions need to be posed about the racialised skin relations of past to present. Evidently skin is different here in Australia than in America. Produced from a different history, black and white claims are also different. There, a slave economy of skin but also a system of treaties, here the thin hope of Native Title that might allow for coexistence of black and white on the same land. Contested in the courts, in the battles over mining and grazing, the affect of skin and land is written at street level: 'SHAME! SHAME!' reads the graffiti on a clapped-out building on Redfern Street. In 'uncanny Australia' (Gelder and Jacobs 1998), skin twists and turns. But to tell the story as only tragic is to ignore the ways in which in the face of it all Aboriginal Australia has survived, and in certain cases thrived. After all, 2 per cent of the population produces the symbols that the world recognises as Australian. In the face of this, in some circles it is now admitted that 'whiteness is a state of incompleteness', that 'the "non-ethnic" experience is, by implication, a negative, a lack, not much of an experience at all'.[10] Does this explain why so many white writers and artists masquerade as black? Or is it that as whites we've run out of stories, and look longingly at the ways in which, as Jackie Huggins says, 'Aboriginal writers have a sense of purpose, an urgent task on behalf of their communities and a wealth of material and themes' (1990: 170). Compared to such courage, generosity and ingenuity, I feel that I'm hiding behind my grandmother's skirts, obsessed with her pen scratching the skin of another? Scratches through time; I find her ahead of me searching for subjects, acknowledging the ambiguity of her situation: 'We poets cannot write/our songs anymore/We make scratching noises/on our slates/When we try./And some leave squeaky pencils'.

Abandoned pencils: to stand looking on with envy, or to pass on the burden of representation that the other has always had to subsume, that, I'm afraid, would be a deferral, not of respect but of abdication. And while in today's configurations some of the strategies that my grandmother deployed would, quite rightly, be seen as mimicry, a literary black-facing, others are excessive in different ways. An excess of identification with the Native woman is complicated by the zealous dredging of dead bodies that disturb the sleep of unconscious ladies; a lady writes while others sleep. To condemn from afar is fatuous. But it's hard to know what to do with these stray fragments that hail from the past and present of another country, but a country connected in a myriad of ways to the one in which I now live. I can hear clearly how she tries to enter the skin of the other, how hard she attempts to depict as fragile and porous the land that is being paved over, the loons' cries that echo like her heartbreak.

These are, of course, madly romantic depictions on both our parts. Representations of recognition, they are like skin, vulnerable to critique: they would bruise, and heal, and bruise and heal again. In a similar way, I want to think about eating skin well as a process of recognition that produces representations that are porous, that breathe, that let the inside out and leave glistening marks of interior hopes upon their surface. Skin is, after all, expansive; it stretches and then retracts, always showing the traces of its own processes. It is also expensive; and a skin economy of reading and writing has its cost. Reading as eating skin, writing as eating skin is a luxury that indulges the shifts and the desires that are at play; it is also a necessity if we are to get closer to reasons that render skin clear, or sallow, penetrable or hide-like. This is one way of making difference matter, one response to the calls to move 'the Western feminist away from an ethics of *universal judgment* . . . towards an ethics where judgments are made possible only through *specific engagement*' (Ahmed 1998: 57; emphases in original).

I can only agree with Ahmed's impulse even as I question the abstract figure of the Western feminist who will now engage specifically. As a prescription, it points in the right direction but needs to be met by figures of engagement, figures that do engage – ones like eating skin well that compel connection, that collapse the usual distance required by representation, abstraction and ethics.[11] It is in this vein that Derrida offers his critique of Kant, his metonym of eating well. That point of contact when one eats the other, when one addresses oneself to her. In turn, I want to insist on the fact that when I eat skin, skin eats me. When I read my grandmother's poems of desire, of colonial fear and desire, I read them as I eat skin: close up, the tongue tasting pores, pores eating the surface of tongue – they eat into me. These poems stitch me into a history of violence, at the same time that they bring me into the feminine domain of an everyday making do (Giard 1998). This very closeness imposes a connection and compels difference. She is not the Native woman she longs to inhabit; I am not my grandmother, yet her blood is in my veins, on my name, colours my skin. But to eat skin well is to ingest the line that binds a family history into an acknowledgement of playing a part in the history of white settlement and invasion. If I can eat that skin well perhaps I can now act on her words of recognition. To eat skin well is to turn that line of skin into an excess of recognition, propelling action even as the teeth of the past bite.

I could of course have used other figures and modes to trace the connections and disconnections between here and there, then and now.[12] The blush of shame, or the rush of guilt and resentment against those who cause these affects to flush my skin. The silence of good intentions, the clamour of denunciation – all these would have done. But faced with the fact of structural blockages, the impossibility of getting under the skin of colonial histories and presents, the act of eating skin well makes recognition, respect and responsibility an everyday matter, and an ongoing process. I must, I must eat skin . . . better.

At the end of this telling of the story, I turn towards my patient listener, and read in her smile what she is too generous to say: 'Yes, Blue, you've got a few things to learn.'

Notes

1 I would like to acknowledge the thoughtful comments of several people. To Wendy Brady whose listening and talking deeply mark this essay, and to Line Grenier, Val Morrison and Natalya Lusty and others, my gratitude. I also remember my family and give thanks.

2 In *Outside Belongings* I argue for a type of sociology of the skin.

3 The White Australia policy stemmed from the *Immigration Restriction Act* of 1901, and included a set of policies that ran from 1901 to the early 1970s. It denied or restricted immigration, and forced the deportation of some residents, including Pacific Islanders and Chinese. See *Australian Race Relations* (Markus 1994), especially Chapter 5, 'White Australia: 1890–1945'.

4 The idea of the potato plant as an example of a rhizome was raised in my Ph.D. seminar on Deleuze and Foucault by students who also usefully pointed out that potatoes are sometimes planted in order to break up hard soil. In Deleuze's description, rhizomes are contrasted with arboreal models of depth: 'unlike trees or roots, the rhizome connects any point to any other point, and its traits are not necessarily linked to the same nature; it brings into play very different regimes of signs, and even non-signs' (Deleuze 1993: 35). The principle of the rhizome therefore allows for many types of connection, but also insists on dis-connection and rupture: 'A rhizome may be broken, shattered at a given spot, but it will start up again on one of its old lines, or on new lines' (Deleuze 1993: 32). In part, this essay is an attempt to forge rhizomatic lines amongst different states, and to pick up on old and new lines.

5 'The Block' is the piece of land in central Sydney bordering on the railway line in Redfern that is managed by the Aboriginal Housing Commission. It is now a site of destitution, and one of the major drug sites in central Sydney. It has also become a shameful and shaming political football. Inhabitants were moved out, sometimes forcibly, when it was 'cleaned up' for the 2000 Olympics. See Jones 1996. Redfern holds a particular significance for many Aboriginal people. It has also been home to many poor white migrants. It is now being gentrified, is increasingly inhabited by people like me.

6 In terms of the reconciliation process, we urban whites need to remember the ways in which some farmers have embraced the idea of coexistence and, based on their own love of the land, recognise the long history of Aboriginal care of the land.

7 Elsewhere I examine the links between eating and consumption of difference, which have also been extensively documented by others. Here I wish to go beyond the metaphoric slide which aligns eating with difference and the assimilation of otherness. See Probyn 2000, Probyn 1999.

8 The report details evidence given by 535 Indigenous Australians concerning their experiences of the removal process, and there are countless others who also form part of what in Australia is commonly known as the Stolen Generations. Succinctly put, the Report recounts the practices that were current from the beginning of the century and into the 1970s aimed at removing Indigenous children, especially those who were deemed to be fair. The goal of these policies was clearly stated in a newspaper editorial of 1937: 'Perhaps it would take one hundred years, perhaps longer but the race was dying. The pure blooded Aborigine was not a quick breeder. On the other hand, the half-caste was' (*Brisbane Herald*, 1937). In the words of an historian, by removing Indigenous children, 'this mixed descent population would, over time, "merge" with the non-Indigenous population' (Henry Reynolds, cited in *Bringing Them Home*, p. 29). The President of the Human Rights and Equal Opportunity Commission, Sir Ronald Wilson has qualified the policy of removal as genocidal.

9 *A fleur de peau* is to be sensitive, or more precisely *sensible*: a state of being acutely, tangibly and physiologically aware. *Le Robert/Collins Dictionnary* defines 'être sensible' as 'sentient being' and follows it with 'univers sensible' producing the semantic possibilities of 'existing as a sentient being within a sensible universe'.

10 This is Gelder and Jacobs's (1998) response to Peter Cochrane's claim that even the ethnicising term Anglo-Celt is not ethnic enough.

11 Following Pasi Falk's argument, such a collapsing of distance can also bring on disgust. See Falk 1994. Lest it be thought that eating skin is simply pleasurable or that closeness is an easy panacea, it should be remembered that touch and closeness have historically been interwoven with the coloniser's disgust at the other. In my *Carnal Appetites* (2000) I attempt to think through the connections between eating, disgust and touch.

12 Elsewhere I have explored other practices, such as cannibalism. I have also tried to think about the ways in which we have been categorised in terms of what whites expect others to eat. See Probyn 2000.

References

Ahmed, S. (1998) *Differences that Matter: Feminist Theory and Postmodernism*, Cambridge: Cambridge University Press.

Bringing Them Home. Report of the National Inquiry into the Separation of Aboriginal and Torres Strait Islander Children from Their Families, Commonwealth of Australia, 1997.

Deleuze, G. (1993) 'Rhizome Versus Trees' in C. Boundas (ed.) *The Deleuze Reader*, New York: University of Columbia Press.

Derrida, J. (1991) '"Eating Well,", or the Calculation of the Subject: An Interview with Jacques Derrida', trans. P. Connor and A. Ronnell, in E. Cadava, P. Connor and J-L. Nancy (eds) *Who Comes After the Subject?* London: Routledge.

Falk, P. (1994) *The Consuming Body*, London: Sage.

Gelder, K. and Jacobs, J. M. (1998) *Uncanny Australia: Sacredness and Identity in a Postcolonial Nation*, Melbourne: Melbourne University Press.

Giard, L. (1998) 'Doing Cooking' in M. de Certeau, L. Giard and P. Mayol (eds) *The Practice of Everyday Life*, vol. 2, trans. T. J. Tomasik, Minneapolis: University of Minnesota Press.

Haraway, D. (1990) 'A Manifesto for Cyborgs' in L. Nicholson (ed.) *Feminism/Postmodernism*, New York: Routledge.

hooks, b. (1992) 'Eating the Other: Desire and Resistance' in *Black Looks: Race and Representation*, Boston: South End Press.

Huggins, J. (1990) 'Response' in S. Janson and S. Macintyre (eds) *Through White Eyes*, Sydney: Allen and Unwin.

Ignatieff, M. (1998) 'The Nightmare from which We Are Trying to Awake' in *The Warrior's Honor: Ethnic War and the Modern Conscience*, London: Vintage.

Jones, P. (Project Co-ordinator) (1996) *Guwanyi: Stories of the Redfern Aboriginal Community*, Historic Houses Trust of New South Wales.

Markus, A. (1994) *Australian Race Relations*, Sydney: Allen and Unwin.

Newton, J. (1998) 'Eating in Sydney from Middens to Mysterious Mushrooms', *Australia's Table Tomorrow*, Food Forum hosted by the Food Media Club Australia Inc, Sydney.

Probyn, E. (1996) *Outside Belongings*, New York: Routledge.

—— (1999) 'Indigestion of Identities' in *M/C: A Jounal of Media and Culture* 2, 7: http://english.uq.edu.au/mc/

—— (2000) *Carnal Appetites: Food Sex Identities*, London and New York: Routledge.

Simmel, G. (1994) 'The Sociology of the Meal', trans. M. Symons, *Food and Foodways*, 5, 4: 345–50.

6 Open wounds

Tina Takemoto

The wound is the boundary between life and death, but also refuses to be the boundary and allows life and death to communicate in an alarming space.

(Parveen Adams 1998: 63)

If something is to stay in the memory, it must be burned in: only that which never ceases to *hurt* stays in the memory.

(Friedrich Nietzsche 1967: 61; emphasis in original)

Is there a melancholy of illness? People say that the severe illness of a loved one puts one's life and one's work in perspective. But in attempting to cope with, make sense of and endure this circumstance within my own life, I seemed to lose all sense of perspective. It was as if the proximity of loss rendered all too visible the fragility and irreplaceability of relationships so easily taken for granted. How can one maintain the suspension of disbelief necessary to withhold despair, to believe that what one can do or say matters, against the knowledge that it may not make a difference? Perhaps these are thoughts that should be preserved for a private register, one that is more profound, and ought not to figure in a formal essay. Yet it is precisely these circumstances that have forced me to rethink the relationship between mourning and grief as well as what is at stake in working on the subjects of illness, race and the politics of collaborative performance. While collaboration often implies a unique form of working together, a melding of minds with seamless intentions, those of us who work collaboratively also know that it can be one of the most frustrating, ambivalent, overinvested, under-appreciated, unbalanced, unequal, conflicted, co-dependent and downright debilitating ways to make art. In writing about collaboration, then, it is also toward those things that get left out, that go unsaid or unexpressed – toward what Toni Morrison (1989) has called those 'unspeakable things unspoken' – that I would like to direct this chapter.

This chapter tells the story of two skins and considers *Her/She Senses Imag(in)ed Malady*, a collaborative project that Angela Ellsworth and I began in 1993 when Angela was diagnosed with lymphoma. Through this project we documented the experience of illness within the dynamic of a long-distance friendship and artistic relationship. Although Angela has long since completed radiation and chemotherapy treatments, this project continues to raise questions regarding the shifting physical and psychological effects of cancer on two women's bodies. Perhaps it is only now that Angela's cancer has been in remission for some years, and within the space of theoretical reflection, that I can begin to consider some of the more difficult personal, ethical and conceptual questions raised by our collaboration. Initially, for instance, the fact of our racial difference appeared to be irrelevant to a project about illness; it is only recently that I have begun to rethink the extent to which the 'coincidence' of our racial difference continues to complicate what it means to identify and perform across bodies marked by illness, gender, and race.

Imag(in)ed malady

In 1992 Angela and I began performing together under the collective name Her/She Senses. We presented a number of live performance pieces that addressed the representation of women, particularly in relation to the body and race. In *Her/She Senses Misfit Attire*, Angela spent three hours pulling the marshmallow tops off a pile of pink Hostess Snowballs and stuffing them into her fishnet stocking. Her leg ended up large, heavy, pink and lumpy – looking a bit like a misshapen stuffed animal or a multi-breasted goddess figure (see Plate 6.1). Meanwhile, I sharpened hundreds of wooden chopsticks in an electric pencil sharpener bound up in my hair and stuck them, hara-kiri-style, into my dress. After three hours I had the look of a porcupine or human pincushion (Plate 6.2). In another performance, Angela clipped dozens of clothespins to the flesh of her face while I ate Top Ramen noodles out of a clay pot on my head. In these absurd displays of consumption and accumulation of materials on our bodies, we were primarily concerned with how to negotiate stereotypes through the presence of our bodies, how to confront scopic regimes that render 'overweight' and racialized, gendered bodies as other. This interest in the status of the visual was most forcefully affected in December 1993 when Angela was diagnosed with Hodgkin's disease, a form of cancer that affects the lymph system and had formed a large tumor in her chest. What has occupied our minds since is, not only the question of overdetermined visibility, but also that of invisibility: the visible bind of the body caught within institutionalized schemes of racial and gendered subjectivity complicated by the invisibility of those territorializations that occur within bodies: the invisible and unknowable form of illness realized by the fact of illness and made vivid the moment it becomes personal.

Eve Kosofsky Sedgwick (1993) observes how the diagnosis of her advanced breast cancer completely altered her perception of herself, her work, and her relationship to her friend Michael Lynch, who was at the time very sick with AIDS. She notes how, at the often arbitrary and unexpected moment of diagnosis, it is the newly realized fact of illness, and not the illness itself, that produces seemingly irreversible perceptual and identificatory shifts. Circumstances and relationships that once appeared most clear (her health, his illness) become totally opaque. Sedgwick speaks at length about Lynch's white glasses and her 'fetishistic

Plate 6.1 Misfit attire (A.E. hostess snowball leg)
Performance still, NJ, December 1992, from *Her/She Senses Imag(in)ed Malady*
Angela Ellsworth and Tina Takemoto

crystallization of him through those white glasses' (1993: 253). She becomes obsessed by the idea of getting a pair for herself and describes her desire to appear in and see through his glasses. When she finally finds a pair, she notes that although she 'felt like Michael' while wearing them, she also realized that to others she still did not look like Michael. The desire for and impossibility of bridging this 'gap between the self we see and the self as whom we are seen' mark the difficulty and equivocality of identifications made across gender, sexualities, and what Sedgwick calls the 'ontological crack between the living and the dead' (1993: 257).

For Angela and me, our long hair became the object of our identification. Hers was brown, curly, subject to changes in the weather. Mine was black, straight, always the same. During the early stages of her diagnosis, the doctors were pretty sure that the tumor in her chest was malignant and would require aggressive treatment. Based on the little that we knew about cancer at the time, the only thing that we could foresee was that she would probably lose her hair and spend a lot of time feeling nauseous. When we decided to cut our hair together, I was living in Rochester, New York and Angela had just moved from New York City to Phoenix, Arizona. Her biopsy, which would help determine the status of her

Plate 6.2 Misfit attire (T.T. chopstick dress)
Performance still, NJ, December 1992, from *Her/She Senses Imag(in)ed Malady*
Angela Ellsworth and Tina Takemoto

tumor, was scheduled for the first week in January. A couple of days before the New Year I joined her in Arizona. We spent an evening chewing piece after piece of Bazooka bubble gum, sticking wads in each other's hair, and cutting them out. With the help of a barber we ended up with short, just-below-the-ear hairstyles. The 'success' of this project seemed proof of our agency, our ability to outsmart and out-art the effects of illness. I left Arizona optimistic, exhausted and relieved, as if the incapacitating shock of illness had been replaced by a potential for action.

It was under quite different circumstances that we cut our hair the second time. Angela's cancer had metastasized to a large portion of her lymph system and the tests indicated that she was in the 'third stage' of Hodgkin's disease. By February she began a chemotherapy program that resulted in various unpredictable side effects. But her hair did not fall out immediately as we had all expected that it would; she had been losing hair gradually for weeks until one day, as Angela described it, her hair follicles just 'gave up'. On that day, Angela called me on the phone from Phoenix and told me that she had rolled up her remaining hair in soft pink curlers, cut them out, and saved them on a plate. The next day I repeated the procedure in my bathroom in Rochester, this time with plastic pink curlers. Yet, in the back of my mind I wondered if all this was indeed a show of force against malady or just an absurd masquerade. As Angela's health began to worsen, the agency we initially felt through our collaborative efforts gave way to figuring out how to cope, how to respond at all.

In his essay 'Mourning and Militancy', Douglas Crimp (1990) speaks of the ambivalent relationship between mourning and activism, particularly in light of the HIV/AIDS pandemic. Crimp observes that within the context of gross political negligence the activist decree, 'turn your grief to anger', can function as an urgent and necessary call for action that 'assumes not so much that mourning can be forgone as that the psychic process can simply be converted' (1990: 234). Yet after nearly a decade of attempting to cope with the AIDS crisis, Crimp (1993) notes how the devastating effects of personal loss have tempered the promise activism once held when ACT UP was first formed in 1987: 'unlike that moment, when the very fact of our growing activism afforded the hope that we could save ourselves, very few of us still believe that the lives of those infected can be saved by what we do'. 'Mourning becomes militancy', then, appears as a necessary political response and also as a displacement or suspension of despair. What troubles Crimp is the extent to which this displacement of grief might also deter activists from acknowledging their own potential at-risk status as well as recognizing the psychic significance of their own mourning. Within the private register of *Imag(in)ed Malady*, I began to wonder if our desire to make art had as much to do with an attempt to make sense of the situation as a need to hold off despair.

The coincidence of race

In the summer of 1992 Angela switched from chemotherapy to radiation treatment and I returned to Phoenix for a visit. In celebration of our reunion and her newly growing hair, we decided to bleach our hair blonde and to produce a number of poolside images entitled 'Lemon Heads'. A few weeks earlier a friend quite tactfully asked me how I thought the collaborative work might relate to some of my earlier interests in race and identity, particularly in relation to notions of mimicry. Quite defensively I asserted that this was a project about illness and friendship and, as such, had little to do with my 'other' work on racial difference. It was only after two quite disparate incidents that I was able to reconsider the force of this inquiry. Both incidents occurred outside of the context of the project and both were comments on my 'blondeness' – an appearance change that, after so many hairstyle alterations, had become for me just another 'phase' in the project. The first comment came in the form of a compliment from a close friend who remarked, 'I don't know quite how to say this, Tina, but since you've become blonde it is as if you've lost your ethnicity.' The second remark had the tenor of an accusation; I was walking with a friend when a person across the street yelled to my friend, 'Hey, don't let her fool you. I can *see* what she is. She's Chinese.'

Outside the context of a project about illness, a blonde Asian appears as another figure of mimicry, remarkable for succeeding or failing to become white.

Homi Bhabha reminds us that the, 'excess or slippage produced by the *ambivalence* of mimicry (almost the same, *but not quite*) does not merely "rupture" the discourse, but becomes transformed into an uncertainty which fixes the . . . subject as the "partial presence"' (1994: 86; emphases in original). At once 'resemblance and menace', she is 'almost the same but not quite, almost the same but not white'. Among the many subtle and less-than-subtle encounters with racism we experience in our daily lives, there are those that we learn to shrug off and forget. That these two incidents come to mind is, perhaps, a reminder of the extent to which race matters and continues to matter, particularly within interracial identifications based on mimicry.

Visual rhymes

One aspect of our project was conceptualized around the theme of thinking through the skin. We produced a series of 'visual rhymes' in which photographs of Angela's body were coupled with reconstructed images of my body. During the course of her medical treatments, Angela photographed the various changes occurring on her body and sent them to me. I staged a number of photographs in which I attempted to repeat these images on my skin, using the most inadequate means possible. Following a biopsy procedure entering through her neck, the Polaroids of her healing scar sent me searching for visual equivalents. A worry doll with scotch tape, a live leech, and an office clip were photographed on my neck as surrogates for the scar on her neck (see Plates 6.3 and 6.4). *Blown Veins/ Jelly Hands* was produced while Angela was in the midst of receiving chemotherapy treatments. After so many injections, she complained that her veins were

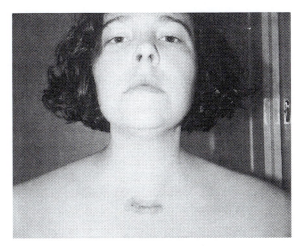

Plate 6.3 Neck marks (A.E. with biopsy scar)
Photo document, AZ, January 1994, from *Her/She Senses Imag(in)ed Malady*
Angela Ellsworth and Tina Takemoto

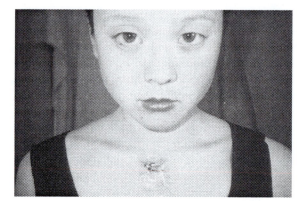

Plate 6.4 Neck marks ii (T.T. worrydoll w/scotch tape)
        Photo document, NY, March 1994, from *Her/She Senses Imag(in)ed Malady*
Angela Ellsworth and Tina Takemoto

beginning to fail her; their frequent use caused them to harden, burst or recede from the skin's surface. After days of staring down at the healthy state of my own hands, I stole raspberry jelly packets from a diner, clear-taped them to my hands, and photographed them as I burst them open (Plate 6.5).

Skin was the primary site of our visual rhymes. Didier Anzieu (1989) suggests that the function of skin is threefold: it operates as an envelope of the self, a protective barrier against the outside, and a means of communicating with others (1989: 40). Through his concept of the 'skin ego', he demonstrates how skin can take on psychic dimensions that are directly related to the experience of the surface of the body. For Anzieu skin not only designates the psychic and corporeal boundaries of the self, but also provides the interface for 'establishing signifying relations' with the outside world by offering an 'inscribing surface' for marks left by others (1989: 40). In cancer treatment, the traces of warfare against illness (and not the illness itself) leave their marks on the body's surface. Jackie Stacey notes that in cancer the 'skin is overburdened. . . . Without its protective covering of hair it is exposed. It must work harder' (1997: 84). As a result of chemotherapy and radiation treatments, the skin develops rashes. Scratching leaves scars on the body, permanent reminders of illness in the form of what Stacey calls 'dermographia' or 'skin drawing'. Angela and I could not see the tumor shrink or the cells stop multiplying, but we noticed the skin pale, the hair thin, the rashes and lesions come and go. We became most interested in the traces left on Angela's body by medical intervention, the scars and wounds that marked the entrances to the body and made her body both receptive and vulnerable to medical treatment. Re-imaging these wounds on my body using toys, food and other quotidian objects was intended to underscore our absolute inability to produce an adequate visual rhyme.

Is it the lack of sufficient visual signs that arrests the mind in metaphoric

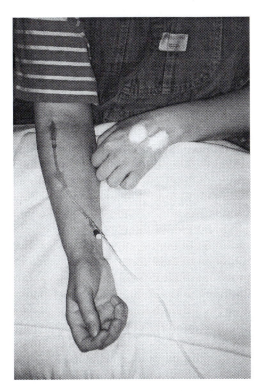

Plate 6.5 Blown veins (A.E. chemotherapy)
Photo document, AZ, June 1993, from *Her/She Senses Imag(in)ed Malady*
Angela Ellsworth and Tina Takemoto

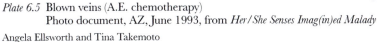

thinking? Provokes the imagination? How can I explain my persistent fascination with size, shape, density and weight? Our respective interests in the body seemed to wax and wane in inverse proportion to Angela's illness and my health. While she became less obsessed, though ceaselessly annoyed, with the bruises, rashes, scars and lesions occurring on her colonized body, I became transfixed by descriptions, listened carefully for symptoms, searched endlessly for equivalents. What governs the logic of this project? I am reminded of that 'special form of neurosis' that Luce Irigaray describes as the 'one condition to which the female condition is assigned: that of mimicry' (1985: 125, 151). Irigaray suggests that mimicry can function as a means 'to convert a form of subordination into an affirmation . . . so as to make "visible", by an effect of playful repetition, what is supposed to remain invisible' (1985: 76).

Through playful repetition mimicry makes visible the inadequacy of its own repetition and demonstrates the impossibility of direct equivalence between sign and referent, self and other. Within the conceptual framework of our project, the visual rhyme always missed its mark. It was a woundless wound that intentionally failed to re-present the scars left by medical treatments. Our visual rhymes produced some unexpected readings. Despite the physical differences between Angela and me (white/Asian, ill/well) and our mismatched pairing of physical traces and objects (scar as toy, blown veins as jelly packets), some viewers believed that both images were of Angela whereas others feared that I was also sick or in danger of contagion. Stacey (1997) observes that cultural anxieties over representations of cancer bear a striking resemblance to those surrounding same-sex identification and desire. The reproduction of cells in cancer, like the doubling of femininity in lesbianism, 'signify sameness, an excess of sameness that goes against the natural order. Deviant cells and deviant desires both generate a horror of (as well as a fascination with) the presence of the undifferentiated' (Stacey 1997: 78). Did the reactions to our visual rhymes reflect similar fears of abjection – fears of what Julia Kristeva (cited in Stacey 1997: 79) calls 'death infecting life'? It was as if the dual presence of our images blurred and doubled the 'normal' figure of the individual body. Charles Green likens this collaborative presence to a '*döppelganger*' which he describes as 'an apparition associated with death, sometimes experienced historically as a shadow or as the double of a living person' or a 'phantom extension of the artists' joint will, rather like a phantom limb' (2000: 37). In constructing our visual rhymes what kind of *doppelgängers* had we produced? To what extent did this practice of body doubling go beyond the realm of empathy, cross the threshold of identification and create specters of illness outside of our control?

Story of wounds

As the boundaries between illness and health, self and other, became increasingly blurred, I became overwhelmed by nightmarish visions of illness and the compulsion to repeat them on my body. On 23 March 1995, I taped five matches to my right arm and lit them in an attempt to 'rhyme' the cumulative effects of Angela's chemotherapy injections. I had become so involved in the internal logic of the project that I began to lose sense of the limits of health and safety. Telling the folks in the emergency room not to worry because it was just an art project gone awry almost landed me in the psychiatric ward. Within the collaboration, the body's surface had become a literal and corporeal register of our difference and a site of identification. Yet, the extremity of this act caused a crisis in our collaboration and raised significant questions regarding the trauma of illness, the ambivalence of identification and difference, and the ethics of response and responsibility.

Parveen Adams reminds us that although a scar may be healed 'it nevertheless opens you up continuously to the previous time of the open wound, a continuous reopening of the wound' (1998: 63). Yet in recalling the circumstances of my own wounds, I still find it difficult to explain how my preoccupation with Angela's illness resulted in this act of self-harm. For Adams, the signification of the wound is unlike the cut that functions as an inscription or writing on the skin. Rather, the wound marks the boundary between life and death and acts as an unwriting of the skin that is not fixed (Adams 1998). This suggests that the wound can function

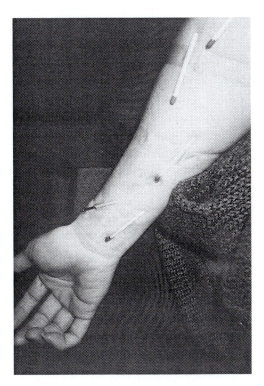

Plate 6.6 Arm burn (T.T. w/matches)
        Photo document, NY, 1995, from *Her/She Senses Imag(in)ed Malady*
Angela Ellsworth and Tina Takemoto

as a site where medicine enters the body to restore life or as a site where death nearly realizes itself in an accident or an act of self-harm. While the scars left on Angela's skin recall the months of medical intervention when her body was made porous to numerous treatments, my scars attest to a more ambivalent tale. Can wounds testify to more than we are willing to say? What can they tell us about the bonds of friendship, the trauma of illness, and the boundaries between self and other? It is precisely the unspeakable nature of this act that has forced me to rethink the relationship between mourning and illness as well as what wounds can tell us about the difficult process of confronting the illness of a loved one.

The act of wounding serves as a point of departure for considering the relationship between grief and illness, particularly in light of Jacques Derrida's work on mourning (1986) and Sigmund Freud's work on mourning and melancholia (1963). Although mourning often refers to the process of bereavement after loss by death, I suggest that an analysis of mourning also enables us to consider the force of grief present in confronting the illness of another – a force of suspended mourning that both resists and anticipates the possibility of loss. Of specific interest is how wounds figure in Freud's concept of melancholia and Cathy

Caruth's theories of trauma and traumatic awakening (1996). Taken together, these works demonstrate how the act of wounding provides one instance where grief and trauma intersect and offer some insight into the difficult process of confronting the illness of a loved one. Finally, I consider some of the implications of mourning and mimicry in light of interracial collaboration: how the presence of racial difference complicates what it means to identify and perform across two bodies.

Ethics of mourning

What constitutes the work of mourning? For what and to whom is it destined? Are we capable of mourning, and have we the right to mourn? In 1984 shortly after the death of his friend Paul de Man, Derrida reflects on friendship and the ethics of mourning. He describes two forms of mourning that are each marked by a particular ethical inadequacy:

> Is the most distressing, or even the most deadly infidelity that of a *possible mourning* which would interiorize within us the image, idol, or ideal of the other who is dead and lives only in us? Or is it that of the impossible mourning, which, leaving the other his alterity, respecting thus his infinite remove, either refuses to take or is incapable of taking the other within oneself, as in the tomb or the vault of some narcissism?
>
> (Derrida 1986: 6; emphasis in original)

While 'possible mourning' requires an interiorization and thus an appropriation of all that one wishes to preserve in memory, including the body and image of the departed friend, 'impossible mourning' – a certain refusal of mourning – entails making no gesture at all out of respect for the other's 'infinite remove'. Derrida suggests that the aporia of mourning binds one to an impossible obligation to interiorize the other and to resist his or her appropriation. Mourning is doomed to fail because there is always something of the other that resists incorporation, and it is out of respect for this excess that one must recognize the inadequacy of one's own memory in order to preserve the other's difference. For Derrida, it is this impossible choice between taking the other within oneself and leaving the other his or her alterity that constitutes the ethics of friendship and the dilemma of mourning.

Although Derrida focuses on the process of grief after the loss of a friend, he suggests that the recognition of mortality is never outside of friendship. The possibility of the death of the other exists before the moment of its occurrence, and it is constituted upon the initiation of friendship itself. It is what goes without saying (and what cannot be said), but is nevertheless inscribed in our relations to others. Reflecting on his relationship with de Man he writes, 'It suffices that I know him to be mortal, that he knows me to be mortal – there is no friendship without this knowledge of finitude' (Derrida 1986: 29). Friendship entrusts the memory of each one to the other before and beyond their separation. But it is only when confronted with the fact of death or its imminent possibility that one turns toward memory – toward the possibility that memory will be entrusted solely within me or within us – only to realize, yet again, the utter inadequacy of its reserve:

> Upon the death of the other we are given to memory, and thus to interioriza-
> tion, since the other, outside us, is now nothing. And with the dark light of this
> nothing, we learn that the other resists the closure of our interiorizing mem-
> ory. With the nothing of this irrevocable absence, the other appears as other,
> and as other for us, upon his death or at least in the anticipated possibility of
> a death, since death constitutes and makes manifest the limits of a *me* or an *us*
> who are obliged to harbor something that is greater and other than them;
> something outside them within them.
>
> (Derrida 1986: 34; emphasis in original)

Confronted with the absence of the departed friend, we learn that the friend's presence cannot be reanimated through any act of memory because any attempt to re-present or re-member the past only makes clearer the futility of this gesture. Thus, the possibility of death makes visible the boundaries of subjectivity pre-cisely at the moment when the other appears as other – when the departed friend can no longer join the us that constitutes the law of friendship. Despite this, or perhaps for this reason, we appear obliged to 'harbor something that is greater and other than them; something outside them within them' (1986: 34). For Derrida, it is the force of this obligation that governs the law of friendship and the ethics of mourning. And yet how are we to understand the ambivalence that also accompanies friendship and grief? How can we reconcile the force of our obliga-tions to others with the desire to sever our attachments in order to go on living? In light of these questions I now turn to Freud's analysis of mourning and melancholia.

Open wounds

Reflecting upon the work of mourning, Freud (1963) makes the distinction between mourning as the normal process of grief that enables a person to over-come the loss of a loved person, and melancholia as a pathological form of mourning that responds to a loss that cannot be overcome and that often results in self-punishment. Mourning, he observes, usually takes place following the finite occurrence of loss by death. Freud describes it as the painful process through which the subject eventually comes to terms with the reality of loss and the ego is 'persuaded by the sum of its narcissistic satisfactions in being alive to sever its attachment' to the dead in order to go on living (1963: 176). Melancholia, by contrast, responds to a 'loss of a more ideal kind' in which the subject suffers from an intense loss but 'cannot clearly see what has been lost' (Freud 1963: 166). He asserts that as long as the nature of loss remains unknown, the subject appears to have no means of overcoming it: 'The complex of melancholia *behaves like an open wound*, drawing to itself cathectic energy from all sides . . . and draining the ego until it is ultimately depleted' (Freud 1963: 174; my emphasis added). In melancholia, then, a crisis of the ego occurs because the subject can neither consciously apprehend the source of loss nor sever attachments to the object of loss.

I would like to suggest that this description of melancholia helps us to consider the force of grief present in confronting the illness of a loved person. In both cases the process of grief is complicated by the anticipation of loss, and both revolve around a crisis that simultaneously defies and demands a witness. In confronting the illness of another, a person can neither imagine life without the other nor sever attachments to the living. Suspended between thoughts of the not-yet and the this-will-be, the subject must continually negotiate between the proximity of loss and the incomprehensibility of death. Is there a melancholy of illness?

Before turning to this question, let us first consider what Freud's work on grief can tell us about the ambivalence of loss and the relationship between processes of grief and acts of self-injury. For Freud, melancholia is characterized by a conflict of ambivalence that is either constitutional to the relationship between subject and object or related to the threat of losing the object. He suggests that the threat of losing a love-object, such as a person whom the subject loves, has loved or ought to love, can produce such a crisis of the ego that arises from the inability to express the ambivalence caused by the overwhelming possibility of loss. In order to preserve attachments to the other person, all conflicts of ambivalence must remain excluded from consciousness, are then incorporated into the ego, and finally reappear in acts of self-punishment.

What interests Freud is how self-reproaches of the subject can also be understood as 'reproaches against a loved object which have been shifted on to the patient's own ego' (1963: 169). He argues that only after the regression of the libido into the ego occurs, that is, only after the subject has incorporated the ambivalence over loss into the ego, does the process of melancholia become apparent. While melancholia 'appears in consciousness as a conflict between part of the ego and its self-criticizing faculty', he suggests that this internal conflict is symptomatic of an external conflict with a loved person that cannot be consciously acknowledged (Freud 1963: 178). In one of the most disturbing passages of the text, Freud observes that:

> sufferers usually succeed in the end in taking revenge, by the circuitous path of self-punishment, on the original objects and in tormenting them by means of the illness, having developed the latter so as to avoid the necessity of openly expressing their hostility against the loved ones.
>
> (Freud 1963: 172)

According to this scenario, the subject uses self-punishment as a means to get back at and torment those who represent the original source of anguish. Freud insists that the violence directed within can be understood as violence directed without when it is recognized that the ambivalence of melancholia revolves around the need to express opposite feelings of love and hate. Denied on the level of consciousness, the subject's ambivalence over loss reappears on the site of the body in the form of self-harm. For Freud, melancholia provides one of the few instances where he begins to understand the 'riddle of the tendency toward suicide'. He writes, 'an analysis of melancholia shows that the ego can only kill itself when . . . it can treat itself as an object, when it is able to launch against itself the animosity relating to the object' (Freud 1963: 173). The act of suicide thus becomes possible when the ego is so overwhelmed by ambivalence over the object that it will destroy the object (and the ego) in order to overcome it. Melancholia both behaves like an open wound (by drawing energy from all sides) and becomes apparent to consciousness through the act of wounding (by denigrating and ultimately depleting the ego). Paradoxically, it is through the active debasement of the ego (enabled by the ability to objectify loss and then to act against it) that the subject eventually breaks free from loss. Attacking the object of loss from within appears to be the only means of arresting the cathectic power of melancholia as an open wound.

By comparing the process of grief with acts of self-punishment Freud is able to link the work of mourning with that of melancholia. He writes:

> Just as the work of grief, by declaring the object to be dead and offering the ego the benefit of continuing to live, impels the ego to give up the object, so [in melancholia] each single conflict of ambivalence, by disparaging the object, denigrating it, even as it were slaying it, loosens the fixation of the libido to it.
>
> (Freud 1963: 178)

Freud asserts that self-denigration in melancholia is analogous to the process of detachment that occurs in mourning. This suggests that both mourning and melancholia are driven by the need to progress from the stage of identification with loss to that of detachment and exclusion. While mourning responds to a conscious loss, the reality of which enables the subject to go on living, melancholia responds to an unconscious loss that must first be converted into a tangible form as ego in order for the process of detachment to occur. Whether the subject experiences the normal process of grief or its pathological counterpart is therefore determined by the comprehensibility of loss.

The structural similarity that Freud finds between mourning and melancholia also suggests that both processes of grief are temporal and follow the general trajectory of incorporation, ambivalence and exclusion. Melancholia appears pathological because the process of grief (specifically, the process of exclusion) takes a detour through the body; it is only after loss has been inscribed on the surface of the body that the subject can overcome it. What I find striking here is the fact that acts of self-harm, which Freud reads as the symptoms of melancholia, also constitute the primary mechanism for detachment. In other words, self-injury not only signifies – by making visible – that the process of grief is taking place, but also produces the body as the site of signification that allows the process to move forward. In melancholia, then, the body provides the perceptual framework that enables the work of grief to occur. Elizabeth Grosz (1994) suggests that the ego is derived from two kinds of surface. She writes, 'On the one hand, it is a projection or representation of the body's "inner" surface of the psychical agencies; on the other hand, it is a projection or representation of the body's "outer surface"' (1994: 37). The work of melancholia becomes visible at the intersection of inner and outer surfaces – at the site where the wound of the mind and the wound of the body meet. This is significant to our understanding of melancholia because it demonstrates what Grosz calls a 'necessary dependence' between psychical interiority and corporeal exteriority (1994: xii). In melancholia corporeal effects signify, and they can signify precisely because the body is always already libidinally invested.

Freud's analysis of grief leaves us with three provocative suggestions. First, while the primary function of grief is to overcome ambivalence over loss by making the reality of loss tangible and ultimately surmountable, in melancholia this process takes a detour through the body. Second, self-punishment can be understood as a bodily expression of grief that is denied on the level of consciousness and reappears on the site of the body. Third, ambivalence over loss first behaves like an open wound (incorporating loss into the ego) and then becomes conscious (and therefore surmountable) through the act of wounding as a means of expelling the other from the self. While processes of grief follow a similar trajectory of accomplishment, melancholia, unlike mourning, provides the unique opportunity to consider how grief can work in and through the surface of the body and in relation to others. Literally and metaphorically, Freud's use of the language of wounds resonates throughout his discussion of grief. Melancholia as a site where the wounds of the mind and body meet attests to the interdependence of psychic and corporeal processes and makes it possible to consider the intersubjective implications of grief.

The melancholy of illness

If, as Freud suggests, mourning responds to the finite occurrence of loss by death, and melancholia to a loss that is unknown, how does grief respond to the possibility of a loss that is neither finite nor unknown? For Freud, the process of grief is driven towards comprehensibility and exclusion and the function of grief is to come to terms with loss by literally severing attachments to it. What are the implications of this process when confronting the illness of a loved person? Can we begin to understand acts of self-injury in light of a melancholy of illness? One of the ethical questions raised by Freud's formulation of grief is how to reconcile what appears as the necessary movement from the incorporation to the exclusion of the other with the fact that in illness the loved person is not gone and cannot be forgotten. Here we are reminded of the ethical dilemma of mourning raised by Derrida, namely, the impossible obligation to interiorize the other within oneself and leave the other, out of respect for his or her difference. In confronting the illness of another, the subject can neither come to terms with loss nor sever attachments to the living. Between the crisis of life and the crisis of death, the melancholy of illness thus appears as a form of suspended grief that both resists and anticipates the possibility of loss of a loved person.

Awakening flesh

Cathy Caruth suggests that the 'oscillation between a *crisis of death* and the correlative *crisis of life*: between the story of the unbearable nature of an event and the story of the unbearable nature of its survival' constitutes the core of traumatic experience (Caruth 1996: 7; emphasis in original). She describes the story of trauma as a 'narrative of belated experience' that both tells of an encounter with death and its endless impact on life. In psychoanalytic theory the term 'trauma', which literally translates as 'wound', is used to refer to a 'wound of the mind' rather than a physical injury to the body. Trauma attests to an event that is 'experienced too soon, too unexpectedly, to be fully known and is therefore not available to consciousness until it imposes itself again, repeatedly, in the nightmares and repetitive actions of the survivor' (Caruth 1996: 4). She argues that trauma functions as a 'double wound' through which a breach of consciousness reappears in acts of self-injury as a repetition of and an awakening to an experience that cannot be assimilated into consciousness, yet cannot be forgotten. This suggests that, in trauma, as in melancholia, the wound of the mind remains hidden until it resurfaces on the site of the body. Here again we see that there is a significant relationship between the impact of the unknown and its psychic and bodily effects. While Freud focuses on injurious acts as a necessary form of detachment through which an unknown loss becomes known, Caruth considers these acts as a symptom of incomprehensibility and a site of crisis that continually returns through the actions of the individual. For Caruth, it is the voice of the wound that awakens us to traumatic experience and bears witness to the 'trauma of the necessity and impossibility of responding to another's death' (1996: 100).

It is for this reason that in trauma we can never get over our losses as entirely as it would seem in mourning. Caruth asserts that the story of trauma, 'as the narrative of a belated experience, far from telling of an escape from reality – the escape from a death, or from its referential force – rather attests to its endless impact on a life' (1996: 7). It is a story of survival that constantly reminds us that the sense of who we are has been altered by the confrontation with loss. Stacey suggests that the experience of 'private and everyday traumas, such as cancer and chemotherapy' can also generate the 'desire for others to bear witness to the impact of the shock' (1997: 16). The repetition of the narrative of illness, like the voice of the wound, 'functions to rehearse that sense of disbelief, but also to return to the moment of impact before the temporal delay occurred' (1997: 16). Stacey observes that the 'horror of diseases such as cancer and HIV and AIDS is precisely that they bring death into life where it has no legitimate place in our culture' (1997: 241). Is the trauma of illness caused by the proximity of death or the inability to return to time before illness when it was possible clearly to separate life and death? Confronting one's own illness or the illness of a loved one forces the subject to both anticipate and resist the possibility of a loss that appears imminent yet unthinkable.

Bonds of love

Returning to the question that both haunts and motivates the writing of this chapter: How did the project with Angela go awry? When I taped five matches to my right arm and lit them, I believed that I was simply 'rhyming' the effects of Angela's chemotherapy injections. How did the desire to produce an inadequate rhyme result in actual wounds to the flesh? Indeed, I had become so consumed by the internal logic of the project that it took me a long time to realize that this action exceeded the limits of safety, and longer still to realize the psychic implications of this act. Peggy Phelan writes that at the 'heart of mimicry is a fear that the match will not hold and "the thing itself" (you, me, love, art) will disappear before we can reproduce it' (1997: 12). Alongside the impulse to mark the inadequacy of every gesture directed toward cancer, to what extent did the obsessive desire to image and imagine illness have to do with a certain fear of disappearance? If, as Freud and Caruth suggest, there is a significant relationship between the incomprehensibility of loss and acts of self-injury, then perhaps I can begin to understand this act of wounding as a bodily expression of grief and of the profound fear of losing Angela.

In her essay 'Art as a Symptom of Not Dying', Claire Pajaczkowska (1995) examines the relationship between art and mortality. She argues against the more traditional impulse to 'turn to art as evidence of human ability to transcend aggression, conflict or destructiveness', toward the possibility of considering 'art as a symptom' of the psychic experience of loss and grief and the 'subsequent search for symbolic equivalence' (1995: 78). She suggests that art, in its ability to facilitate the representation of loss, can function as a sublimation of grief and thus as a significant 'form of work and love'. Within what Jessica Benjamin calls the 'fragile, unenclosed space of intersubjectivity' (1998: 105), Angela and I encountered the generative and difficult possibilities of work and love through our collaborative efforts to perform illness.

The melancholy of race

Since I burned my arm, many aspects of our collaboration have changed. Not only do we ask different questions, but the circumstances have changed too. Angela's cancer has been in remission for a number of years and this wonderful fact has opened a space for each of us to explore some of the related issues on our own. While Angela has gone on to explore representations of health and fitness culture, I have started to use the burning incident as a point of departure for other work. The installation piece *Three on a Match* includes an evening glove made of 90,000 glass beads and steel pins, a beeswax arm with five wicks, and a glove made of 10,000 live matchsticks. In the two-day performance piece *Arm's Length*, I climbed up and down a 25-foot wall on specially fabricated pink scar-like holds using mountain climbing equipment and performed various tasks involving the boiling, slicing and bandaging dozens of eggs. Within this strange taxonomy, eggs begin to rhyme the shape of scars as well as the texture of damaged skin. The most horrifying moment in my own healing process was when the top layers of skin were scrubbed off revealing the absolute whiteness of the smooth new skin below. My ambivalence over this encounter with whiteness on my own body brought me back to the issue of race in interesting ways.

In her recent book, *The Melancholy of Race*, Anne Anlin Cheng (2000) reflects on the 'assimilative and dissimulative effects of race' that continually inform constructions of identity based on loss. She recalls a scene in Maxine Hong Kingston's *Woman Warrior: Memoirs of a Girlhood Among Ghosts* (1975) in which the young Chinese American narrator torments her silent Chinese American classmate in the school lavatory. Grabbing the fatty part of her cheek between her thumb and finger, the narrator squeezes the flesh on her victim's face as she goads her to speak. 'When I let go', the narrator recalls, 'the pink rushed back into my white thumbprint on her skin' (Kingston 1975: 205). Cheng reads this dizzying scene of projection and identification as a moment of racial melancholia in which the white thumbprint of the self on the other appears as the projection of a white ideal that is then flooded with blood as the racial connection between the two Asian American girls (2000: 73–5) Cheng argues that the '*process of racialization itself* functions as the melancholic double-movement of denial and incorporation' (1996: 187; emphasis in original) in which the fear of racial contagion is always coupled with the fantasy of making-the-self-as-other. For Cheng, the 'assimilative failure' of mimicry (almost the same, but not quite) appears not only in colonial

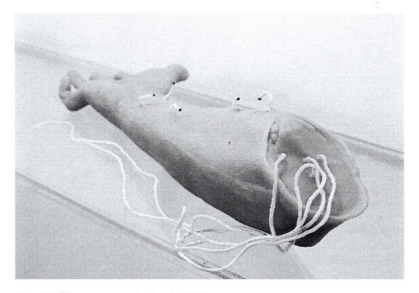

Plate 6.7 Three on a match, detail, 1998
Beeswax, 5 wicks

Tina Takemoto

Plate 6.8 Arm's length
Performance still, NJ, December 1996

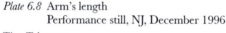
Tina Takemoto

relations between the oppressor and the oppressed, but also in an entire spectrum of inter- and intrasubjective negotiations involving desire and identification. If, as Cheng suggests, the 'malady of doubleness' is the 'melancholy of race', then perhaps for Angela and me this malady of doubleness was the melancholy of race and illness. For within the dizzying scene of our relationship, it became increasingly difficult to untangle the terms of our desire for intimacy and identification against the specter of illness, the fact of our racial difference and the geographical distance between us. Skin as the site of visual rhymes marks the boundaries of our bodies, recalls wounds that will not heal and attests to a love that vows never to forget.

References

Adams, P. (1998) 'Cars and Scars', *New Formations* 35: 60–72.

Anzieu, D. (1989) *The Skin Ego*, trans. C. Turner, New Haven: Yale University Press.

Benjamin, J. (1998) *Shadow of the Other: Intersubjectivity and Gender in Psychoanalysis*, New York: Routledge.

Bhabha, H. K. (1994) 'Of Mimicry and Man: The Ambivalence of Colonial Discourse' in *The Location of Culture*, New York: Routledge.

Caruth, C. (1996) *Unclaimed Experience: Trauma, Narrative, and History*, Baltimore: John Hopkins University Press.

Cheng, A. A. (1996) 'Race and Fantasy in Modern America: Subjective Dissimulation/Racial Assimilation', in J. Reider and L. E. Smith (eds) *Multiculturalism and Representation*, Honolulu: University of Hawaii.

—— (1997) 'The Melancholy of Race', *The Kenyon Review* 19, 1: 49–62.

—— (2000) *The Melancholy of Race: Psychoanalysis, Assimilation and Hidden Grief*, Oxford: Oxford University Press.

Crimp, D. (1990) 'Mourning and Militancy' in R. Ferguson, M. Gever, T. T. Minh-ha and C. West (eds) *Out There: Marginalization and Contemporary Cultures*, New York: New Museum of Contemporary Art/MIT Press.

—— (1993) 'Don't Ask', unpublished lecture, Cornell University.

Derrida, J. (1986) *Memoires: for Paul de Man*, trans. C. Lindsay, *et al.*, New York: Columbia University Press.

Freud, S. (1963) 'Mourning and Melancholia', in *General Psychological Theory: Papers on Metaphysics*, New York: Macmillan.

—— (1971) 'The Psychology of the Dream Processes', in *The Interpretation of Dreams*, trans. J. Strachey, New York: Avon.

Green, C. (2000) 'Doppelgangers and the Third Force: The Artistic Collaborations of Gilbert and George and Marina Abramovic/Ulay' *Art Journal* 59, 2: 36–45.

Grosz, E. (1994) *Volatile Bodies: Toward a Corporeal Feminism*, Bloomington: Indiana University Press.

Irigaray, L. (1985) *This Sex Which Is Not One*, trans. C. Porter, Ithaca: Cornell University Press.

Kingston, M. H. (1975) *Woman Warrior: Memoirs of a Girlhood Among Ghosts*, New York: Vintage.

Morrison, T. (1989) 'Unspeakable Things Unspoken: The Afro-American Presence in American Literature', *Michigan Quarterly Review* 28, 1: 1–35.

Nietzsche, F. (1967) *On the Genealogy of Morals*, trans. W. Kauffmann and R. J. Hollingdale, New York: Vintage.

Pajaczkowska, C. (1995) 'Art as a Sympton of Not Dying', *New Formations* 26: 74–88.

Phelan, P. (1997) *Mourning Sex: Performing Public Memories*, Routledge: London and New York.

Sedgwick, E. K. (1993) 'White Glasses' in *Tendencies*, Durham: Duke University Press.

Stacey, J. (1997) *Teratologies: A Cultural Study of Cancer*, London: Routledge.

7   Carved in skin
Bearing witness to self-harm

Jane Kilby

> In a very simple way, self-mutilation, like self-starvation, is a plea to be witnessed . . .
>
> (Hewitt 1997: 55)

> *This voice is so appalling that even the self speaking cannot stand to hear it. . . . Who can take off their skin and dance around in their bones (Waits 1993), without throwing up? No one I know of.*
>   *This voice is too terrible to contemplate. But we must.*
>
> (McLane 1996: 111; emphasis in original)

Whatever else it may be, self-harm is a naked appeal. The act of self-harm renders skin a deeply eloquent form of testimony, where a plea is made for social recognition. Indeed, the signature cuts and scars of self-harmed skin do nothing less than 'scream out' for this reckoning. It would seem, then, that bearing witness to self-mutilated skin should be only a matter of listening to this 'voice'; a simple response. Yet there is something particularly hard to witness here, something which makes contemplating the testimony of self-cut skin anything but simple. Indeed, it would seem that the act of harming one's own skin by cutting it up and tearing it apart speaks with a 'voice' so sheer that it is virtually impossible for anyone to bear witness to it. Arguably, then, there is something about this 'voice' that defies witnessing, even as it insistently demands it; a not-so-simple response. Thus, I would suggest that the testimony of self-cut skin raises two questions: What is the nature of self-cut skin such that it is difficult to bear witness to? What is the nature of witnessing such that there is a resistance in the testimonial project of self-cut skin? The aim of this chapter is to address these questions.

The language of self-harm: testimony to hidden, silent trauma

In her article 'The Voice on the Skin', Janice McLane argues that for as long as we are subjects, 'we will *say* our lives in order to *have* or *live* our lives' (1996: 107; emphases in original). In other words, without the possibility of speaking, the possibilities of life are delimited. Here, speaking animates life and determines its limits. But if the promise of language fails and speaking cannot sustain life, another 'voice' must be found, especially when faced with the need to testify to the traumatic conditions of life itself. Here, then, wounding one's own skin is another way of speaking of trauma and pain. Indeed, according to McLane, the 'voice' of self-cut skin is a very specific language for gesturing toward childhood trauma, especially childhood sexual abuse, where the act of testifying typically involves using either knives, razor blades or broken glass secretively and ritualistically to cut the skin.[1] Alternative, yet still common, acts of testimony include inflicting blows on the body with the aim of bruising the skin, as well as scalding and burning the skin with, for example, cigarettes and caustic chemicals (Smith, Cox and Saradjian 1998). In all such cases, as indeed with all imperatives to speak of past trauma, it is unclear to what degree the act of self-cutting lies within or beyond conscious control. According to Pembroke, the common reference to 'deliberate self-harm' actually serves to obscure this important ambiguity of intent. Thus, she argues that acts of self-harm can be 'spontaneous and sudden with little awareness or conscious thought' and yet, at times, 'the drive to self-harm may be powerfully constant and unrelenting with a conscious battle raging' (Pembroke 1994: 2).

With regard, then, to the relationship between the disavowed trauma of childhood sexual violation and self-cutting, McLane writes:

> *When hidden pain starts to speak, it will speak silently. Its voice may appear as a cut on the leg, a burn on the arm, skin ripped and scratched repeatedly. There will be no sound, not any, only unfelt and silent pain which makes its appearance in another pain, self-inflicted, and when that second, collateral pain emerges, it will articulate in blood or blisters the open definition you desire, although it may not be in a language you care to see. This, it says, is pain, and this is real in any language you care to speak.*
>
> (McLane 1996: 111; emphasis in original)

Although socially silent, self-harm appears here as a language that articulates past trauma by repeating it in the present of pain. The cutting of skin is thus a way of speaking the past by re-enacting it with a difference: matching pain for trauma. Indeed, here the significance of self-cut skin – its appeal – lies in its own economy of exaggerated and aggressive mimicry. It is a language that communicates the real of past trauma by rendering it more real through a repetition of pain. Arguably, there is a sense in which the pain expressed by cutting one's own skin is, albeit belatedly, the trauma of past violation.

But self-harm also gains its significance because it represents an exaggerated breaking with language: it supplants the promise of language to communicate trauma by rendering the site of pain a language in itself. As self-harm campaigner Louise Pembroke writes of her own practice of self-cutting, when 'I could not find the words to describe it, cutting had become the language to describe the pain, communicating everything I felt' (1994: 35). Again Kim Hewitt writes, 'In an act of self-mutilation gesture replaces language. What cannot be said in words becomes the language of blood and pain' (1997: 58). Unlike notions of 'body language' or 'body talk', which ostensibly refer to non-aggressive and social gestures of the body, the 'voice' of self-cut skin is an extreme substitute for language. Skin deliberately wounded and cut thus speaks violently of the failed promise of language to communicate trauma: it is a rupturing force that tears itself, and its significance, apart from language.

This powerful exposure and redrawing of the social parameters of language carries, however, considerable risks. In a general yet decidedly apt discussion, Judith Butler argues that if subjects speak at the borders of discursive possibility they risk being cast into the realm of the unspeakable, where they become the object of explicitly punitive operations of power. She writes:

> If the subject speaks impossibly, speaks in ways that cannot be regarded as speech or as the speech of a subject, then that speech is discounted and the viability of the subject called into question. The consequence of such an irruption of the unspeakable may range from a sense that one is 'falling apart' to the intervention of the state to secure criminal or psychiatric incarceration.
>
> (Butler 1997: 136)

Here Butler points up the distinct dangers of breaking with language altogether, not the least of which is the erasure of the subject. Indeed, the excessive and idiomatic language of self-harm typically carries this risk, where struggles over the power to name the testimony of self-cut skin serve to reflect the incomprehension witnesses feel toward self-harm and the consequent possibilities of punitive censorship. So there is, for example, a profusion of officially recognised names for self-harm, including: 'deliberate self-injury', 'self-inflicted violence', 'self-attack', 'self-cutting', 'deliberate non-fatal act', and 'symbolic wounding'. But many of these names are subject to dispute on the grounds that they fail to hear the voice of self-cut skin as testimony or that they represent a hostile response to its testimonial appeal. 'Para-suicide' and 'attention seeking' are two terms that are subject to particularly intense contestation. These terms are rejected as substitutes for 'self-harm' for two related reasons. First, 'para-suicide' condenses a reading of self-harm into the sign for a failed act of suicide, when in fact the cutting of one's own skin could be understood as a means of defying death. As one woman writes, '"Attention seeking" and "attempted suicide" are just a couple of the "professional" myths attached to self-harm. Suicide is final. Self-harm is a release from emotional pain and a struggle for survival' (Helen in Pembroke 1994: 23). Second, when self-harm is read as a para-suicidal act of 'attention seeking' (within the context of professional care), self-cutting women emerge as individuals irresponsibly playing with their body surface and flirting with death.

Self-harmers are thus deemed to be playing on/off the moral gravity of skin and death. As a consequence, they are seen as 'time wasters', wasting not only the time of the medical staff – time which could be spent on saving and caring for the lives of the 'legitimately' traumatised – but also their own future life-time. Thus, Pembroke recalls how a nurse, responding to the sight of her self-cut skin, asked: 'Don't you want to get married, have children?' (Pembroke 1994: 41). For

Pembroke, the nurse's enquiry served only to indicate that her life-time, or the life of her skin, was not hers anyway: she should be saving it for an already mapped-out future. Her body and its testimony of cut skin is thus already read (and erased) as the site for the heterosexual (re)production or (re)generation of (family) time. There is no time for her and her skin as such; she is 'not worth it' (Pembroke 1994: 41).

Reading the testimony of self-cut skin as an act that signifies only a desire for attention or the finality of death reduces the complex relationship women survivors of childhood trauma have with their skin and their bodies to an instrumental and calculative narrative of life-time that can be 'spent', 'wasted' and/or 'saved'. More importantly, such a simplification means that life is only ever read as being on the side of life, and death can only be read as being on the side of death. Highly critical of such a teleology, Peggy Phelan argues that while it 'insists that we die once in an expository, teleologically driven future', we can, in fact, die many times in one life-time (1997: 17). Indeed, Phelan goes on to argue that sexual trauma 'is an event of unliving' (1997: 60); it constitutes a hiatus in the structure of life. Similarly, the experience of sexual trauma has been figured as an outliving of the self (Brison 1997). Within the context of self-harm, therefore, hidden and silent trauma is lived precariously at/on the edge of one's skin. So, those who read self-traumatised skin as representing a desire for death and not life negate the experience of living out past trauma. But if, on the other hand, self-harm is read as a testimony to the 'will to survive' pain and trauma, it can be understood as a means of marking the difference between dying in life and death in all its finality, a difference whose border is animated by the effort of cutting skin. As McLane puts it, 'self-mutilation reinstates the boundary between the existence and nonexistence of self' (1996: 112). However, to the degree that the skin border is already rendered animate by social and political discourses, and more specifically here by a prior violating touch, self-harm is a project of re-articulating, if not disrupting, these processes of animation. As a project of re-animation, self-harm reworks the conditions of possibility for the subject at the limits of language. And in so doing, it is a testimony that aims to give a life to skin in a manner that momentarily exceeds its felt state of deathly suspension. By reanimating the skin boundary, the testimony of self-harm serves as a reminder of the line between 'social' and 'literal' death. It serves as a warning that this line should not be crossed, which, in turn, explains the habitual character of self-harm.

Despite appearances to the contrary, then, self-harm serves as a means of articulating experiences of childhood trauma, and in so doing it provides a momentary means of living beyond the deadening touch of trauma. As a result, arguably, it also serves as a technique for self-(re)production. So, where giving testimony in general can be seen to serve as a strategy for survival – 'I testify, therefore I am' – self-harm is an aggressive attempt to substitute and mimic this logic with disturbing exaggeration: 'I cut, therefore I am'. Or, as McLane puts it, 'the feelings caused by the injury make the survivor's existence unavoidably present to herself. She feels, and therefore is' (1996: 113). Thus, where the flow of words and the substantiality of the testimony become the ontological guarantee of being (Felski 1989: 112), it is the flow of blood and the materiality of scarred skin that becomes the guarantee of the existence for the woman who cuts. Here, then, the reciprocity between testifying to past trauma and survival cuts deeply.

Yet this means of producing life is put into question by the dominant reading of self-harm. As I have already noted, women who present themselves at Accident and Emergency departments in the UK with self-cut skin are all too easily read as 'time wasters', and as a result they typically experience degrading and harsh treatment (Pembroke 1994). So, for example, it is not uncommon for women who have deep cuts to their body to turn up at Accident & Emergency departments only to find themselves stitched up with little or no anaesthetic, or to find that the layers of skin tissue have not all been properly sutured, which exposes them to the risk of infection and serious long-term damage (Pembroke 1994). Thus, the political and social struggle for appropriate naming is a very real attempt to ensure that women who speak via the act of cutting skin are not stitched-up as 'just another label and another number' (Marie in Pembroke 1994: 21).

Ultimately, the testimony of cut skin requires the language that it displaces: it requires social and political language for its very own conditions of possibility. Usefully here Phelan argues that skin 'cannot hold all we ask it to contain . . . [since] it lacks the depth, the interiority, we want it to give us' (1997: 41). She goes on to argue that skin cannot be made to bear the weight of our traumatic histories or our faith in its sheer promise of testimony: the 'drama of suffering flesh' exceeds the 'elasticity of skin' (Phelan 1997: 41). So, although skin does have a capacity to bear the weight of trauma and pain, it cannot be made to bear this responsibility alone. Put differently, because self-cut skin is already subject to determined and often punitively presumptive readings, it needs a context and strategy of reading which will work to secure its conditions of possibility. So, for example, Hewitt recognises the need to translate self-harm when she finds that her own body is eating her scarred skin testimony *and* when she discovers that she is not the only woman to have cut up. She writes:

> My scars have flattened over the years. My body is eating the scar tissue away. Several years ago a close friend confessed that she had been cutting herself. As I listened to her I realised for the first time that I wasn't alone. I realised the body has a private landscape without words, and I knew I had to find a language to talk about my scars.
>
> (Hewitt 1997: viii)

By pointing up the fragility of self-cut skin (despite its seeming immutability) and the collective status of this 'cutting voice', Hewitt realises that her 'scars' need a public language which, in turn will open her scars to a general understanding, or at least a general reading; and from there, it is implied, a significance or 'social life' beyond her skin.

This necessity is also hinted at by Naomi Morgenstern (1996) in her article on neoslave testimony. As the distinguishing marks of a traumatic history of slavery, Morgenstern notes thst the scarred skins of black bodies, especially when they mark the back of the body, have to be read in order to signify. As Morgenstern writes 'Scars signify deadness, loss or lack of feeling. The dead flesh of the scar must be read to become meaningful . . . The reading of scars, I want to suggest, is a compelling figure for the process of de-traumatising, or making meaning' (1996: 199, fn.9). Here, scars represent the dead and traumatising weight of history, and for them to signify otherwise they must be read or witnessed. Moreover, by emphasising the place of scars on the back of the body, Morgenstern implies a complete figuration of reading traumatic history. The traumatised carry a trau-matised history they cannot see (they are constitutively blind to it), thus they require another to see it for them. By getting behind the testifying subject, the historical marks of trauma appear before the witness, thus the past is in front of the witness to be read into being. Here, then is a moment in which the future and the past are folded within the present scene of witnessing.

Although Morgenstern is speaking of a very specific history of scarred skin, there is here a general call for the reading of scars, which I am taking as pertinent to the scarred skin left by practices of self-harm. Indeed, uniting them is a desire to open a future for skin that is untouched by trauma. For, paradoxically, the call for reading the skin-traces of self-harm evinces a desire for securing an end to this form of traumatic testimony. In attempting to ensure the possibility of self-harm being read as testimony, there is simultaneously a hope working to establish the conditions for passing beyond the need for self-harm. Hence, McLane writes 'This new possibility would not be the hand holding a razor blade which cuts across the skin, but breath being pushed across the larynx, shaped by mouth and tongue, into a spoken word' (1996: 117). Here, self-harm testimony can be read as articulating a desire for language that can sustain a history of trauma, where the event of 'saying our lives' is a moment of casting '*our body upon air*', not cutting it up (McLane 1996: 108; emphasis in original).

Having said this, it is perhaps somewhat surprising to find that feminist theorists have not taken any particular responsibility for self-harm testimony. For, despite its status as testimony to childhood and sexual traumas, the act of self-harm is rarely read by feminist academics concerned with the relations of language, power and subjectivity. So, while there is a significant feminist literature on anorexia and bulimia (see, for example, Bordo 1993), which can be taken as a closely related form of testimony, there is barely any on self-harm. Can it be then that self-harm disturbs a feminist reading, if not (feminist) readers altogether? And if so, why would the testimony of self-harm trouble a feminist reading, when feminist scholars have not displayed this degree of anxiety when reading the embodied testimony of the anorexic and bulimic? Quite provocatively, Pembroke argues that self-harm confounds readers because it is 'a bit too close to the bone' (1994: 3): the woman who speaks by cutting her own skin threatens to act as a brutally powerful mirror for readers' own painful, if not aggressively compelling, desire to testify to their own traumas. McLane also argues that readers are reluctant to engage with the significance of self-harm testimony because '*no one wants to be reminded of the fact that there are other voices in them speaking, all the time, which might in fact take up residence on their skin*' (1996: 114; emphasis in original).

Here, there is a suggestion that the force of self-harm lies in its threat to expose the fragility and permeability of the reader's own skin boundary. Or that self-harm testimony acquires force with an implied threat of contagion. So, not only is the value of a self-cut skin subject to the force of reading, but the reader also appears here to be subject to the voice of self-harm. In a sense, the reader who would bear witness is also constituted in the encounter with the skin testimony of self-harm. This does not leave the reader devoid of agency as a witness, but, momentarily at least, the reader is inaugurated by the scream of self-harm. It is the sense of shock and experience of dissonance or disjuncture between who the reader is before encountering the testimony of traumatised skin and who they are after reading that serves as its occasion for possibility. Here, the loss of all comprehension becomes the condition of possibility for testimony, since this acute disorientation forces the reader to make a social and political context for both herself and the testimony. Thus, the appeal made by self-harm can be read as nothing more than a willingness to be open to this moment of loss.

The significance of exaggeration, and the exaggerated economy of a naked appeal

In a rare collection of testimonies to self-harm, *Self-Harm: Perspectives from Personal Experience*, there are interspersed among the written testimonies a series of six cartoon-like drawings, numbered 1 to 6 in the original, with the title 'Professional Thought Disorder'. These cartoons constitute Pembroke's own attempt to break the silence over self-cutting, and are offered as a visual testimony to her experiences of psychiatric and medical 'care'. As a medium for translating the testimony of self-harm, the mix of images and words demands a constant reading movement, since the images would have only a vague significance without the words, and the words would have no precise meaning without the images. In short, it requires a doubled or shuttle reading strategy whereby the words must be read within the context of the images and vice versa. Indeed, it is argued, that 'comic' sequential art – which the sketches approximate – are closer than any other form of language to matching the processes of signification. Arguing this point in relation to the use and power of comic testimony, James E. Young argues:

> For unlike a more linear . . . narrative, the commixture of words and images generates a triangulation of meaning – *a kind of three-dimensional narrative* – in the movement between words, images, and the reader's eye. Such a form also recognises that part of any narrative will be this internal register of knowledge – somewhere between words and images – conjured in the mind's movement between itself and the page. Such a mental language may not be reproducible, but it is part of any narrative just the same.
>
> (Young 1998: 672; emphasis in original)

Although the 'commixture' of images and words engenders 'a kind of three-dimensional narrative', this is not unique to its form. Instead, the commixture derives its particular force from its ability to exaggerate the 'mental language' of the reading process itself. Indeed, the force of 'comic' sequential art is understood to derive from its economy of exaggeration, as Nancy Miller puts it: 'accuracy is an effect of exaggeration' (Miller quoted in Young 1998: 698).

I would argue that Pembroke's sketches depend on this logic of exaggeration, and in this they mimic and speak of the economy of significance characterising self-harm. Thus, the drawings gain their signifying power, like self-harm itself, through exaggerated effect. So, for example, the drawings are characterised by an extremely disproportionate use of scale such that the figures of the nurses appear grotesquely large (see Plates 7.1 and 7.2). Read alongside the words of the sketch, this radical disjuncture of scale serves to show, through its excess of irony, the consequences of failed testimony and how great can be the gap following failed attempts to communicate. In addition, the ridiculous smallness of the Pembroke figure represents not only the degree of asymmetry between those who hold power (the nurses) and those who do not (the self-harmers), but also the possibility of slipping from social view. The exaggerations of scale thus work to show, not simply the gap that is opened up by all attempts of testimony, nor simply the extent to which the testimony of the powerless is structurally determined to fail (to fall at the feet of the powerful), but also the risks and dangers that accrue as a result of this gap. Again, the disregard for the self-harming woman is signalled in the sketch by the calculation of time. Thus, it is within a context where 10 minutes becomes the measure of life that the language of self-harm makes sense. Indeed, here it works both as a threat and as means of refusing the (absent) conditions of social possibility (see Plate 7.3).

Yet despite attempts to substantiate and secure her testimony in the presumed immutability of skin, the woman who speaks via self-harm is not free of the sense of alienation that necessarily follows all failed attempts to give testimony. In this instance, however, the effect of alienation is extreme. Pembroke writes:

> My last cycle of self-harm changed. I removed skin completely and required a skin-graft. My skin appeared 'alien' to me, and felt as if something was crawling underneath it. The only way I could relieve the alienation was by tearing it out with my teeth and a blade.
>
> (1994: 40)

Here, the idea that self-harm is a way of animating the possibilities of life summons a deeply troubling significance for the ordinary phrase 'hanging on by the skin of one's teeth'. At this juncture – and with the risk of doing an injustice to Pembroke's testimony of experiencing her skin as alien – 'I cut, therefore I am' mirrors, with a distressing distortion in scale, the difficulties marking all attempts to give testimony. As a way of speaking into being a past trauma and a sense of self, self-harm testimony struggles with the anxiety that it may not capture – within the boundaries of its own form – the felt scale of the first trauma even as it represents a forceful attempt to ensure a correspondence between the trauma and its testimonial form.

Plate 7.1 Professional Thought Disorder Part I (The staff nurse seriously overestimates her intellect)

Louise Roxanne Pembroke

As an expression of the 'will to survive' and as testimony to an antecedent childhood trauma, 'I cut, therefore I am' reproduces the struggle of all testimony projects, albeit with an extreme dimension of violence. The cut-skin testimony of self-harm is a bloody means of seeking the affirmation of an existence denied by trauma. And yet it always risks failing to speak of the traumatic reality which animates its production. Thus, there is always the possibility of profound

Plate 7.2 Professional Thought Disorder Part II (This is a round hole – you will be a round peg)

Louise Roxanne Pembroke

alienation when giving this testimony. No longer an eloquent expression of traumatic experiences, self-harm can become an 'alien' testimony, an object without perceptible relation to the woman testifying. Since personal testimony always involves a risk of possible collapse 'into tribunals of self-castigation' (Mehuron 1994: 171), self-harm, I would argue, risks becoming an endless project of traumatic testimony without even the redemption bestowed by the illusionary and temporary closure offered by a narrative form. Indeed, condemned as such, self-harm is all too often experienced as a forcibly repetitive process that admits of no

Plate 7.3 Professional Thought Disorder Part III (Normalist fascism)
Louise Roxanne Pembroke

transformation. Caught in a potentially 'vicious circle' (Harrison 1995), it is possible that the woman who speaks by cutting her skin will lose herself 'forever in this gestural articulation of violation' (McLane 1996: 117).

The possibility of becoming lost in the testimony of self-harm and the risk of the erasure of self this carries is represented in the fourth sketch, where the figure of Pembroke is partially drawn, with eyes closed (see Plate 7.4). Symbolically disappearing, the figure of Pembroke reflects the status of self-harmers as 'virtually invisible patient[s]'. In addition, the sign 'V.I.P.' – which allows the ironic substi-

Plate 7.4 Professional Thought Disorder Part IV ('You should trust us')
Louise Roxanne Pembroke

tution of 'very important person' – also emphasises the risks of abjection and erasure through its resemblance to the signifier 'R.I.P.' Clearly here, the desire to animate a life through the act of self-cutting brings the spectre of death. But the question of whether death, as opposed to life, is being summoned by the act of self-harm, is, however, denied a definitive answer. This is given symbolic expression in the drawing by affording the speech of the Pembroke figure the status of a 'private thought'. Hence, the 'Well, I wouldn't tell you' symbolises a defiance of the witness's ear, which includes here both the ear of the expert witness and the implied ear of the reader. In a sense, then, neither the doctor nor the reader is given any insight into whether self-harm does signify, in this instance, suicide. But while the use of the 'you' does not operate as an address within the frame of the sketch, it does nevertheless operate formally to interpellate the reader with its defiant and distinctly accusatory address. The reader is both hailed, even accused, within the terms of sketch, and yet symbolically refused 'entry'. Thus, the reader is given no privileged access to the significance of the testimony, yet, at the same time, is implicated in and held responsible for its production.

On the one hand, then, this sketch mimics one of the functions of self-harm testimony, which is the right to determine the terms of access to the significance of self-cutting. Indeed, the significance of self-harm testimony is the attempt to generate meaning privately and secretly, and this demands both recognition and a 'hands off' approach from the reader. In short, self-harm graphically represents a self refusing any approach by others; it is the attempt to author the self without relation, and yet paradoxically this desire only gains possibility if it is given social recognition. Thus, 'my cuts speak for me' (Ross in Pembroke 1994: 14) represents for the authoring hand a desire for a private, exclusive code, a means of reclaiming the self through an intimate, private language: 'my cuts speak for me' as if 'only for me'. Seemingly unlike any other form of testimonial appeal, the language of self-harm conspires to keep the reader at a distance.

The desire for testimony is, however, integral to self-harm. The cuts on the skin can and do speak publicly for the self-harmer. Hence, 'my cuts speak for me' equally carries the significance of social representation; 'they speak on behalf of me', 'they represent me.' Despite a desire for separation and distance, and precisely because it is a largely permanent testimony on the skin surface of the body, the testimony of self-harm does and can 'speak' to others; it does desire the ear of the reader, even if it speaks of this desire for the promise of language in a different idiom. As such, the sketch and self-harm both approximate Doris Sommer's account of 'resistant testimonies', testimonies that 'conjure a walled city that announces No Trespassing at every gate' (1994: 527–8), and yet do so right in the face of the reader. Here empathy is not the rule. This strategy of 'point blank refusal' – or accusatory refusal – does not, however, amount simply to an ethical prohibition on reading or for that matter the suspension of desire for communicating traumatic experience. Sommer writes that resistance 'does not necessarily signal a genuine epistemological impasse; it is enough that the impasse is claimed in this ethico-aesthetic strategy to position the reader within limits' (1994: 524). It is not necessarily a question of forbidden access, but rather a question of approach, encounter and engagement. Indeed, here, it is interesting to note that Sommer figures the relationship between resistant testimonies and readers in physical terms, thus readers are kept at 'arm's length' by resistant testimonies and they 'refuse to run to meet the reader' (1994: 528, 530). Likewise, she describes empathy (as a presumed ethical condition of reading) as an appropriation in the 'guise of an embrace' (1994: 543). In other words, testimony and reading each have a force with which to touch the other.

By their own hand, self-harmers attempt to redraw the lines between testimony, trauma and skin, and in so doing attempt to (re)establish the (violent) agency given the hand in the production of significance. But perhaps more importantly, and as a consequence, self-harmers give flesh to the idea that reading the testimony of self-harm is a question of finding an ethics, and it must be a reading touch capable of sustaining the resistant signature of self-harm testimony. Indeed, the sketches suggest that self-harm is given as a testimony to the very failure of the ear and eye of the reader to sign ethically for its significance.

The terms of the encounter: reading self-harm

As a form of resistant testimony, self-harm asks or requires that readers learn not that they should not prostrate themselves before the testimony in an ethico-political surrender of the rights of access, but rather that they adopt 'a faltering, self-doubting gait too lame for the march of conquest' (Sommer 1994: 530). The ethics of this reading approach lies in the possibility that it opens the ear of the reader to the local sanctions that testimony itself places on appropriative acts of representation, naming and interpretation. Without this ethical approach, I would argue, the reader would miss Pembroke's particular voice and the precise idioms of her speech. Further, if the reader is not 'prepared to listen' to the signature traces of Pembroke's voice, her testimony will always be vulnerable to readings which simply and only hear her acts of self-harm as pathological. Or, conversely, a lack of attentive reading might lead to 'recuperative readings' that see self-harming as *only* a transgressive form of resistance, thus missing precisely the still remaining desire to communicate beyond this.

The failure to achieve correspondence and thus the risk of endless and traumatic re-enactment which lies, as permanent possibility, at the heart of self-harm testimony, acts as an essential reminder to the dangers held by all testimony projects. Self-harm reveals, in a particularly graphic way, that the project of testimony is never simply an ideal form for bringing unspoken trauma and traumatised subjects into existence. However, it is also because self-harm cannot faithfully reproduce, or completely match, the painful experiences of childhood abuse that it offers a chance for transformation. Again McLane writes:

> *To express pain, you must feel it, and move as the pain tells you to move. You may do that by standing a little away, holding yourself at arm's length. For the self-mutilator, this is the length of the arm from shoulder to wounded skin, making a circuit of safety, of pain, of lack of pain, of punishment, of solitude, of connection. A circuit of arm, knife, skin, wound, mind which expresses and denies, reproduces and transcends, is and is not the original trauma which prompts it.*

> (McLane 1996: 115; emphasis in original)

Ultimately, it is the interval opened up by the fact that self-harm testimony reproduces and transcends the original trauma that serves as the occasion for possible future release, and it is here that the reader can make all the difference. It is here that the reader can either compound the traumas of the past and their contemporary speaking, thus closing the gap between the traumatic testimony and the original trauma. Or, it is here that the reader can work to secure and further establish the difference between the trauma of self-harm and the trauma of childhood sexual trauma, thus widening the gap for transformative possibility.

As testimony, self-harm appears as that which holds the possibility of life, and it is precisely for this reason that the reading of such testimony becomes a profound question of a *just* reading. Indeed, sketch five (Plate 7.5) raises with particular

Plate 7.5 Professional Thought Disorder Part V (Respecting a person's distress)
Louise Roxanne Pembroke

graphic force the question of ethical readings by offering 'us' the significance of Pembroke's testimony in her 'own words' at the very same time as it offers us the incredibly violent 'reading' of the doctors: 'So what were you trying to do dear . . . cut your tit off?'. Pembroke thus challenges the reader of the sketched testimony to do justice to it, and, by implication, to do justice to the testimony of self-harm, by exaggerating what a reading response can look like. To do justice to self-harm testimony is understood here as a reading capable of sustaining the possibility of the testimony, not foreclosing that possibility with the force of reading. Indeed, the very future possibility of the testimony and its significance is made a function of an ethical, non-coercive reading. And just in case 'we' are still under any illusions as to the ethical significance of reading, the last sketch (Plate 7.6) shows the figure of Pembroke laying prostrate on a hospital bed after a suicide attempt, closer to death than in all the other sketches. Significantly, for the first time, Pembroke is drawn alone, prostrate and to a different scale. In this sketch, Pembroke's image fills and dominates the scene in a way that it has not done previously. Consequently, the sketch's subtitle – 'I hear you' – serves as an ironic statement, since within the terms of the sketch, it cannot assume the status of (reported) speech. Yet because it is written between speech marks, the 'I hear you' is left suspended as a reported (or rumoured) promise. The question is whether the reader will assume responsibility for it. Suspended as such, 'I hear you' loses its irony and becomes instead a deadly serious speech act to be made by a witness. By hailing the reader in this way, Pembroke disrupts the boundaries of her testimony and acknowledges that the 'success' of any testimony depends on its relation to the reader and whether they will cite in response the speech act: 'I hear you'.

   This sketch also serves to caution the reader who might say 'I hear you' too quickly, too emphatically. As I have said above, the reader is left – in the face of the lone and deathly figure – to reproduce the scene by saying 'I hear you', where the uptake by the reader represents a difference, altering the deathly scene. Thus, the reader saying 'I hear you' might understand Pembroke's act to be the right ethical response because she reads the scene as deathly. But in addition to be being drawn to a larger scale, the figure has a greater context, with fuller and more complete details than in any of the other sketches. And with her eye looking directly out of the frame, there are dimensions of life represented in the figure that are also not found in any of the other sketches. So, which scene is the reader reproducing by saying 'I hear you'? Or alternatively, which scene is being fore-closed? Sometimes, it will be possible to say that the reader is reproducing both, and that they do not need to be read as mutually exclusive. This constitutes one reading decision. But sometimes the reader will have to decide which scene to reproduce. Either way, the reader cannot assume that she is necessarily doing the right thing. This is a reading without sanction, then, which is to say that it is a groundless reading, a reading which refuses the displacement of responsibility effected by the claim that 'I am doing this *in* her name, *in* her words, *in* her image'. It requires that the reader accept that '*I* am doing this reading for the possibility of her name, of her words, of her image'.

Plate 7.6 Professional Thought Disorder Part VI ('I hear you')
Louise Roxanne Pembroke

So far, I have read the sketches in the order in which they appear in the book's pages. In accordance with this ordering, the sketch I have just read is the last one in the book. On a closer reading, however, I noticed that the roman numerals marking the sketches from one to six did not follow this sequence exactly. Instead, sketches five and six had been reversed, leaving me as a reader with no way of knowing which ending Pembroke 'meant' for her testimony. To what extent would my reading of Pembroke's testimony change if I read the fifth sketch as the last one? Does my narrative reading of the testimony do an injustice to Pembroke's testimony onced this mixed ordering has been acknowledged?

These are not trivial questions. The lack of closure refutes a simple licence for witnessing, indeed it makes such reading a difficult task. For as Maurice Blanchot argues, reading testimony is fraught because testimony 'is empty – at bottom it doesn't exist; you have to cross an abyss, and if you do not jump, you do not comprehend' (1986: 10). Here, even the testimony of skin is empty in the sense that it does not have a significance of its own and can only make sense if the reader is willing to risk the decision to jump, and whether testimony is alive or dead hangs in the balance of that decision. But, importantly, the enabling fantasy or faith is that the reader can get across: it is the possibility that we can do justice to self-cut skin that becomes the occasion for its testimony. Aptly here, Morgenstern writes that 'it is only in its moments of wilful optimism . . . that the precariousness of testimony itself seems to disappear' (1996: 117). Self-harm is a naked testimony risking itself for a reading, and even though it cannot secure it, it appeals, nevertheless, for a careful leap of witnessing. Its status of animation is always in a critical condition.

Note

1 It is important to note that self-harm can be understood more generally as a form of post-traumatic distress syndrome which will signal other known and unknown histories of trauma. For a small, yet important, activist and feminist literature on self-harm, see Arnold 1994, 1995; Babiker and Arnold 1997; Harrison 1995, 1997; Johnstone 1997; McLane 1996; Parker and Lindsay 1996; Pembroke 1994; Smith, Cox and Saradjian 1998.

References

Arnold, L. (1994) *Women and Self-Injury Booklet Series*, Nos. 1–3, Bristol: Bristol Crisis Service for Women.
—— (1995) *Women and Self-injury: A Survey of 76 Women*, Bristol: Bristol Crisis Service for Women.
Babiker, G. and Arnold, L. (1997) *The Language of Injury: Comprehending Self-Mutilation*, Leicester: BPS Books.
Blanchot, M. (1986) *The Writing of the Disaster*, trans. A. Smock, Lincoln, NA and London: University of Nebraska Press.
Bordo, S. (1993) *Unbearable Weight: Feminism, Western Culture and the Body*, Berkeley: University of California Press.
Brison, S. (1997) 'Outliving Oneself: Trauma, Memory, and Personal Identity', in D. T. Meyers (ed.) *Feminists Rethink the Self*, Oxford: Westview Press.
Butler, J. (1997) *Excitable Speech: A Politics of the Performative*, New York: Routledge.
Felski, R. (1989) *Beyond Feminist Aesthetics: Feminist Literature and Social Change*, Cambridge, MA: Harvard University Press.
Harrison, D. (1995) *Vicious Circles*, London: Good Practices in Mental Health.
—— (1997) 'Cutting the Ties', *Feminism and Psychology*, 7, 3: 438–40.
Hewitt, K. (1997) *Mutilating the Body: Identity in Blood and Ink*, Bowling Green, Ohio: Bowling Green State University Popular Press.

142   *Jane Kilby*

Johnstone, L. (1997) 'Self-injury and the Psychiatric Response', *Feminism and Psychology*, 7, 3: 421–6.

McLane, J. (1996) 'The Voice on the Skin: Self-Mutilation and Merleau-Ponty's Theory of Language', *Hypatia*, 11, 4: 107–19.

Mehuron, K. (1994) 'The Ethics of Reminiscence: Reading Autobiography', in A. B. Dallery and S. H. Watson with E. M. Bower (eds) *Transitions in Continental Philosophy*, Albany: State University of New York Press.

Morgenstern, N. (1996) 'Mother's Milk and Sister's Blood: Trauma and the Neoslave Narrative', *differences: A Journal of Feminist Cultured Studies* 8, 2: 107–26.

Parker, K. and Lindsay, H. (1996) *Women and Self-Injury Booklet Series*, No. 4, Bristol: Bristol Crisis Service for Women.

Pembroke, L. R. (ed.) (1994) *Self-Harm: Perspectives from Personal Experience*, London: Survivors Speak Out.

Phelan, P. (1997) *Mourning Sex: Performing Public Memories*, London and New York: Routledge.

Smith, G., Cox, D. and Saradjian, J. (1998) *Women and Self-Harm: Understanding, Coping, and Healing from Self-Mutilation*, London and New York: Routledge.

Sommer, D. (1994) 'Resistant Texts and Incompetent Readers', *Poetics Today* 15, 4 : 523–51.

Young, J. E. (1998) 'The Holocaust as Vicarious Past: Art Spiegelman's *Maus* and the Afterimages of History', *Critical Review* 24: 666–99.

8   Three touches to the skin and one look

Sartre and Beauvoir on desire and embodiment

Penelope Deutscher

Skin is rarely discussed in Jean-Paul Sartre's *Being and Nothingness*. Encounters he depicts between subjects and others are visual and aural, more than they are tactile. His description of the encounter between torturer and tortured victim includes no description of the victim's being as hands or instruments of pain lay into his flesh, nor of the torturer in tactile contact with the victim. Instead, the encounter is used to depict the torturer's vulnerability to being rendered a being-for-others as he becomes aware of the gaze of the victim (Sartre 1966: 525–7). In *Nausea*, the contact with the world is a repeated example of the horror of the world, our encounter with its brute being and contingency. In *Being and Nothingness*, tactile encounters with the in-itself (my hand engulfed in honey, for example) are again depicted in negative terms and serve as a metaphor for how the for-itself is threatened with engulfment by the in-itself (Sartre 1966: 775).

An unusually tactile encounter between self and other is that depicted between sexual partners, when Sartre narrates the strategy that, in his view, motivates the caress. To desire, writes Sartre, is first to be reduced to one's own body:

> I *feel* my skin and my muscles and my breath, and I feel them not in order to transcend them *toward* something as in emotion or appetite . . . but as a *passion* by which I am engaged in the world and in danger in the world . . . The being which desires is consciousness *making itself body*.
>
> (Sartre 1966: 505; emphases in original)

Desire is narrated by Sartre as a strategy, part of our impossible but constant struggle to appropriate the other's freedom. I wish to grasp the other's freedom, but I can only grasp the other's body. Desire is a wily ruse to incarnate a body with consciousness and then possess it:

> It is now that I *make myself desire*. Desire is an attitude aiming at enchantment. Since I can grasp the Other only in [his/her] objective facticity, the problem is to ensnare [his/her] freedom within this facticity. It is necessary that [s/he] be 'caught' in it as the cream is caught up by a person skimming milk. So the Other's For-Itself must come to play on the surface of [his/her] body; and

> by touching this body I should finally touch the Other's free subjectivity. This
> is the true meaning of the word *possession*.
>
> (Sartre 1966: 511–12; emphases in original)

The meeting of two desiring bodies is theorised as a complicated game of
entrapment. In this context, Sartre declares that desire is anything but a
meeting of two skins. He writes, 'We know well the deceptiveness of that famous
expression, "The contact of two epidermises"' (Sartre 1966: 506): As he puts it:

> It is in this sense that the caress is an appropriation of the Other's body. It is
> evident that if caresses were only a stroking or brushing of the surface,
> there could be no relation between them . . . they would remain on the
> surface like looks and could not *appropriate* the Other for me . . . the caress is
> not a simple stroking; it is a *shaping*. In caressing the Other I cause [his/her]
> flesh to be born beneath my caress, under my fingers.
>
> (Sartre 1966: 506–7; emphasis in original)

In addition to being one of Sartre's rare descriptions of a touch to the skin by the
other, this is one of Sartre's very few discussions of the erotic in *Being and Nothingness*. It occurs in the context of a philosophical framework according to which our
encounters with others are governed by our desire to entrap their consciousnesses,
while not reducing them to controlled objects whose perspective on us could no
longer have any value.

Simone de Beauvoir's philosophical ability is often seen as being limited to
a faithful appropriation of Sartrean existentialism to analyse the condition
of women. It is partly for this reason that she is rarely included in histories of
twentieth-century French phenomenology. But, as several recent studies on
Beauvoir have noted, she articulates a concept of eros quite distinct from that of
Sartre. The specificity and breadth of the concept of eros or desire in Beauvoir's
work has been the object of study of a number of recent commentators, notably
Debra Bergoffen in her *The Philosophy of Simone de Beauvoir* (1997). Eva Lundgren-
Gothlin has argued, for example, that Beauvoir aligns herself far more with
Hegel's account of reciprocal recognition (a concept rejected by Sartre) than with
Sartre's account of inevitable agonistic and appropriative relations between sub-
jects in which reciprocal recognition is impossible (1996: 211–12).

Fragments in *The Second Sex* and elsewhere articulate an ideal of non-
appropriative, reciprocal erotic relations between lovers which constitute an
important alternative to Sartre's analyses of desire. Beauvoir hoped for a 'full and
happy flowering of feminine eroticism' (1988: 421) and argued that this could
only be achieved by establishing a relation of reciprocity with one's partner:

> Under such conditions the lovers can enjoy a common pleasure, in the fash-
> ion suitable for each, the partners each feeling the pleasure as being his or her
> own but as having its source in the other. The verbs to give and to receive
> exchange meanings; joy is gratitude, pleasure is affection. Under a concrete

and carnal form there is reciprocal recognition of the self and of the other in the keenest awareness of the other and of the self. Some women say they feel the masculine sex organ in them as part of their own bodies; some men say that they *are* the women they penetrate. These are evidently inexact expressions, for the dimension, the relation of the *other* still exists; but the fact is that alterity no longer has a hostile implication, and indeed this sense of the union of really separate bodies is what gives its emotional appeal to the sexual act; and it is the more overwhelming as the two beings, who together in passion assert and deny their boundaries, are similar and yet unlike. This unlikeness, which too often isolates them, becomes the source of enchantment when they do unite.

(Beauvoir 1988: 422; emphases in original, translation modified)

Consider the different notion of the tactile that occurs in this passage. Touching the skin of the other is not simply an example of the constant drive to appropriate the other. Instead, it is a context for subjects to enjoy a complex reciprocity, in the simultaneous assertion and undermining of bodily and subjective boundaries. A theorisation of the other as both same and different (and affirmed as this paradox) arises from Beauvoir's work, but not from that of Sartre. To touch the skin of the other, to experience one's own and the other's desire, is a complex recognition both of similitude (in so far as I can experience desire at once and at one with my partner) and difference (for I can never assume that the other experiences desire as I do). The touch is at once a moment of greatest proximity and greatest distance, and is affirmed as such – as *enchanting* – in Beauvoir's sexual imaginary.[1]

Elsewhere, Beauvoir also de-emphasises the central nature of self–other relations and sexual encounters in her discussions of eros: eros is located in my capacity to be troubled, surprised or charmed by the world and its objects. Beauvoir thus articulates a rich sensuous world and its pleasant and shocking sensations, seen in her many delighted descriptions of the fresh air when hiking, the feeling of the ground against her feet, the richness of a cocktail. In Sartre's work, also, desire is located more broadly than in self–other sexual relations. He describes the caress of objects ('gritty, smooth, tepid, greasy, rough, *etc.*') the discovery of 'something like a *flesh* of objects':

My shirt rubs against my skin, and I feel it . . . the warmth of air, the breath of the wind, the rays of sunshine, *etc.*,: all are present to me in a certain way, as posited upon me without distance and revealing my flesh by means of their flesh. From this point of view desire is not only the clogging of a consciousness by its facticity; it is correlatively the ensnarement of a body by the world.

(Sartre 1966: 509)

But, as seen in this passage, objects are largely threatening; they ensnare us, just as, in Sartre's narrative, my strategy to appropriate an other by incarnating their flesh will fail as I become ensnared in my own torpid desire. In Beauvoir's work, the other, and the alterity of objects, is often troubling. But in contrast to Sartre,

Beauvoir often valorises this kind of troubling of my own parameters by others and by the world. It is a kind of troubling which she takes to be one of the most valuable facets of human existence, pleasurable or not. It is not subordinated in her work to strategies of appropriation of others or of the world.

One thing shared by Sartre and Beauvoir is their rejection of the tactile encounter as a simple physical contact of the epidermis with objects or others. For both, the touch of the skin does not remain on the surface. It is the locus of a subjective project of relation to the world, and illustrates how physiological and psychological domains cannot be separated. For both, the touch occurs as part of a subject's making itself body. For Sartre, the touch of a skin against an object or an other occurs as part of a constant project to appropriate the world, its things and the consciousness of others. Making oneself body is seen as the necessary cost of this drive to appropriate. For Beauvoir, the touch occurs as part of a being in the world which thrills to disturbance, being unsettled or tantalised by objects and others. The touch represents a making oneself body, with the aim of being surprised by, rather than possessing, objects and others.

Erotic bodies lost and found I

Beauvoir is sometimes seen as devaluing female bodies, and as valuing contexts in which women transcend female embodiment so as to live as free and equal subjects, asserting themselves in active projects. This view is partly due to the very negative account she gives in *The Second Sex* of the facts of female biology, in addition to sections describing sexual initiation as traumatic for women and menopause as a relief which can free women from the sexual obligations of marriage. But she protests the denial to women of sexual liberty and considers the 1940s depiction of women's poor relation to sex to express a sometimes harsh reality which is due only to socially, economically and existentially impoverished female lives. There is no doubt that Beauvoir values as an ideal that women have a full experience of sexuality and a positive relationship to feminine embodiment.

One notices in much of Beauvoir's autobiographical work the positive significance of having a body, the particularly strong association that occurs between embodiment, erotics and a positively rendered sexuality. Beauvoir writes that her affair with Claude Lanzmann 'freed me from my age' at a time when there are 'the first warnings of physical decline' (1965: 285). It is joyfully described: 'I had rediscovered a body' (Beauvoir 1965: 280; translation modified). Associated with the depiction of old age as the loss of her body is the loss specifically of desire, of imagination, luminous horizons, the deprivation of the pleasures of the body. The loss of the body, according to the formulation offered at the conclusion of *Force of Circumstance*, is 'never feeling any new desires: they wither before they can be born' (Beauvoir 1965: 657). For this reason, at her most extreme she describes old age as a 'mutilation' of herself, and also as a loss of her body: 'In spite of everything, it's strange not to be a body any more' (Beauvoir 1965: 657).

What does seem clear is that when desire remains, one still has what Beauvoir wants to define as a body; when desire is lost, one has lost it. It is not simply that a good embodiment is that to which we can be oblivious whereas a bad embodiment is that which we are returned to or troubled by, which is the common interpretation of *The Second Sex*.[2] In the light of both Bergoffen's interpretation, and much of Beauvoir's work on old age, it can be argued that, even in *The Second Sex*, a good body is a sexual, desiring, imaginative and surprised body. While it is true that the feminine body is portrayed as largely deprived of that kind of existence, Beauvoir laments that feminine existence has in this sense been deprived of 'the body'. She is also clear that this deprivation is the result of an inseparable synthesis of biological, social, physiological, psychological and economic factors. What reinforces this interpretation are the positive ideals for erotic relations depicted in the work and brought to the fore by Bergoffen.

Whereas Sartre incorporates erotic experience into an agonism in which we attempt to retain subjective control both over the other and over our own body, and a concept of appropriative conflict between subjects is seen in his account of love, sex and desire, Beauvoir uses her emphasis on the erotic to develop concepts of complementarity and reciprocity, and does not devalue a body which is troublesome in its desires. Bergoffen rightly emphasises Beauvoir's important intervention in this regard, whereby a disruptive body may be the most subjectively valuable body, particularly because an erotic encounter involves being subjectively and physically troubled by the difference of the other. This is the locus of a crucial exchange with the other-qua-other in proximity to me. It is not associated with humiliation or annihilation, and it does not inevitably place me in a combative or warlike relationship.

This interpretation of Beauvoir refigures her as having offered an unrecognised alternative to Sartre, Sade and others. Given that Beauvoir is often seen as a philosopher who devalues feminine embodiment, it is important to assess the extent to which this is not the case. The erotic is the context for Beauvoir to rethink what is valuable in self–other relations. The erotic becomes an ideal for my having a troubled engagement with the difference of the other. I agree with Bergoffen that focusing on the erotic is a way of highlighting Beauvoir's originality and independence as a philosopher in this regard.

A first attempt to compare Beauvoir and Sartre, in terms of their positions on embodiment, then, might go as follows. For Sartre, our making ourself a body is a necessary aspect of our project to appropriate the world and others, but it is in many ways a necessary evil. I risk being overwhelmed by the world of objects and others I hope to know, penetrate and appropriate. Furthermore, a body of which I am overly conscious is in many ways an undesirable body. A 'good' body is an invisible body of which I am not directly conscious as I engage in activities in the world. Sartre's tendency is to devalue bodies of which I become overly conscious. For example, he describes the way in which, when I put on trousers, my leg may be touched, but this occurs only in a 'surpassing' of my body towards the action I am engaged in. 'I am present to it without its *being me* and without my *being it*' (Sartre 1966: 403; emphasis in original). A need to attend to the touch of my leg is likely to occur only in an interruption of the projects and activities I am trying to pursue – for example, if my leg hurts, or becomes entangled in my trousers.

Far more than Sartre, Beauvoir values embodied subjectivity. A full and active sexual life is valued by her, and represents having a body. The loss of this life is experienced as catastrophic. And, as Bergoffen reminds us:

> It is important to be clear here. Beauvoir's turn to the erotic is crucial not because it validates the sexed and sexual body . . . but because it [does so] . . . in accordance with the criteria of generosity and the gift, and according to the body understood as an ambiguous phenomenological intentionality.
>
> (Bergoffen 1997: 202)

Beauvoir values the particular relation to the other, theorised in terms of simultaneous sameness and difference, and simultaneous confirmation and disruption of my subjective and bodily boundaries, which erotic embodiment represents. To lose this possibility, then, would be to lose what she consider to be both the fundamental, most valuable human possibility of relating to the world and to the other.

All this said, what might we conclude from the fact that Beauvoir's lengthy work, *Old Age*, is the object of just five pages of discussion in Bergoffen's reconstruction of Beauvoir as philosopher of erotic ethics? It is not that the work has nothing to offer Bergoffen's interpretation, for she comments that the erotic is best described in that work (Bergoffen 1997: 186).[3] Nevertheless, I think Beauvoir's work on old age can be particularly troublesome for theories which would validate Beauvoir's notion of erotic embodiment against the Sartrian model. To think through Beauvoir as a philosopher of erotics and embodiment, I think one should spend more time with her material on old age. I will indicate some directions for additional focus on this material.

I suggested that we compare, as emblems of the different approaches to eros of Sartre and Beauvoir, their two different accounts of tactile encounters with lovers. But focusing on Beauvoir's emphasis on the erotic encounter with a lover leads, I have argued, to her discussions of old age. Some of her most vivid material on the importance of this encounter is associated with her memorable anxiety about its loss, a threat she attributes to the coming of age. But Beauvoir's material on old age is complex. Toril Moi has offered a critical reading of her autobiographical writing in this area:

> For Beauvoir, death evokes the spectre of non-existence, whereas old age is above all associated with the loss of sexual attractiveness, and therefore – according to her beliefs – the loss of love.
>
> (Moi 1994: 237)

Focusing on her autobiographical accounts of old age, Moi does not discuss her theoretical work in this area, and so barely mentions *Old Age*. However, even Beauvoir's autobiographical material is nuanced by some very sensitive writing on the subject, in which she discusses the old age of Sartre and also of her mother.

So I want now to locate a very different moment in Beauvoir's reflections on eros and touch, which could also be compared with Sartre's caress. This time, the subjects are not lovers, and a subject will be caressed not by a human but by a metal tube. Even more than Beauvoir's account of the lovers' contact, it is this account which best incarnates differences between her account of eros and that of Sartre. To the touch of lovers, I want to compare a different description of the touch of skin. In *A Very Easy Death*, Beauvoir is describing her dying mother's last days in hospital, with advanced and agonising intestinal cancer:

> What touched our hearts that day was the way she noticed the slightest agreeable sensation: it was as though, at the age of seventy-eight, she were waking afresh to the miracle of living. While the nurse was settling her pillows the metal of a tube touched her thigh – 'It's cool! How pleasant'. She breathed in the smell of eau-de-Cologne and talcum powder – 'How good it smells'.
>
> (Beauvoir 1969: 44)

In suggesting this particular comparison, I hope to open up a discussion of Beauvoir's contribution to a philosophy of eros, which focuses not on her work on gender, but on her work on old age.

In her theoretical work *Old Age*, Beauvoir reminds us of many in the third age who do live active, conventionally sexual lives. But she does not consider those who believe they are 'too old' to be in bad faith. Instead, she explains such attitudes in terms of a complex nexus of social and physiological factors which arises from the fact that old age is 'the other'. Lived experience of old age is 'conditioned by society's ideological and practical attitudes' (Beauvoir 1977: 15, translation modified). What appear to us as the physiological facts of old age are always already in synthesis with historical meanings: the social and economic situation of the subject; the social and economic status of women and the aged; the social interpretation of aged and feminine embodiment; the individual response (defiant or not) to those forces, and so on:

> one never lives in a state of nature: in one's old age, as at every age, one's status is imposed by the society to which we belong . . . It is an abstraction, as we know today, to study the physiological and psychological aspects separately . . . the psychic life of an individual can only be understood in the light of one's existential situation. . . . [which] affects one's physical organism and the converse applies.
>
> (Beauvoir 1977: 15; translation modified)

Beauvoir is highly sympathetic to those who experience old age as representing real physical limits to human existence. Her novella 'The Age of Discretion' depicts the narrator's dawning realisation that it need not be bad faith to attribute to old age lost desire, lost energy, lost motivation for action, lost intellectual creativity, lost physical strength or physical deterioration. This is an important departure from Sartre's account of all subjects as radically free, and so inauthentic in so far as they might deny that freedom. Instead, 'The Age of Discretion' depicts old age as physically limiting. Meanwhile, *Old Age* argues that we cannot isolate physical facts from other factors. From this perspective, those subjects who do experience old age as the inevitable loss of eros are doubtless, according to Beauvoir, the product of the complex nexus of social attitudes, psychological and physiological factors evoked in the work. The work does not pass judgement on different modes of experiencing old age, and is in this regard far more neutral than *The Second Sex*.

In her own case, at a certain, autobiographically depicted moment of her life, Beauvoir believes that her old age represents the withering of new desires before they are born, and the end of her own erotic life.[4] But this autobiographical depiction is rendered complex by other depictions: for example, those of many aged subjects for whom this is not true are discussed in *Old Age*, and in the depiction of her mother, who in her last months is described in *A Very Easy Death* as rediscovering sensual pleasure. This leads to one of Beauvoir's best, if briefest, accounts of erotic life. It departs from discussions of the erotic which are limited to an account of overtly sexual or penetrative encounters between subjects. It departs from Sartre's account of an appropriative relation with others and things, instead depicting as erotic an ability to be delighted with the new. Having theorised this kind of phenomenological intentionality, one not limited to self–other relations, Beauvoir's account of eros is also no longer limited to descriptions of young, sexually active adults. Instead, this is a concept of subjective life that pertains to subjects theorisable at all ages and breaks from a noticeably age-limited account of subjectivity in Sartre's work.

However, we should now turn to the 'on the other hand' of Beauvoir's writing on old age. Old age is not inevitably a loss of the erotic body. But, where it is so, it seems the loss of the erotic body is the loss of 'the body' for Beauvoir (the loss of what Beauvoir deems 'the body'). What becomes clear in this material is the lengths to which Beauvoir goes to save a positive depiction of the body. Becoming sexual, active, imaginative and desiring is to become embodied, to 'gain one's body'. Losing these aspects of embodiment is to lose the body (for example, in the mid-life sexual neglect she describes in her mother's life (Beauvoir 1969: 32–3) or where this may occur in sickness or old age). Beauvoir so wants to install a positive representation of embodiment that the loss of a valorised, active, sexual body is represented as the loss of the body itself. Of forms of embodiment less valued by Beauvoir (older, slower, less desiring, ill), Beauvoir does not say: this is what becomes of the body, but, this is the loss of the body. Far from Beauvoir devaluing embodiment, it might be said that she sacrifices everything in order to retain the conception of valorised, active erotic embodiment that is so valuable to her.

And of course, this is at the same time exactly the problem. Bergoffen offers an interpretation which recuperates Beauvoir from the view that she 'devalues embodiment' and constructs her as a philosopher who specifically opposed negative depictions of a troubling body, such as Sartre's descriptions of sexual encounters or Sade's linking of 'the flesh with vileness, old age, filth and bad odours' (Bergoffen 1997: 123). These were negative connotations of embodiment

Beauvoir specifically wanted to avoid, and in the context of the philosophical frameworks she was rejecting, we can sympathise. All of her effort goes, therefore – as Bergoffen points out – towards evoking the possibility of a positive erotic embodiment as engagement with the other. In this, she offers a far more astute reading than those who have focused only on the negative portrayal of feminine embodiment in *The Second Sex*. But, perceiving that this is what Beauvoir manages to save, perhaps Bergoffen is wrong to downplay what is also sacrificed here. Refusing to associate embodiment with 'vileness, old age, filth and bad odours', Beauvoir significantly fails to offer an account of old age, filth and bad odours as also crucial, inevitable to human embodiment. It is not that she fails to give an account of old age, filth or bad odours. Exactly what was shocking about her account of Sartre's death, moving about her mother's death and strong in *Old Age*, is this description. Beauvoir is unable to give an account of these domains as embodiment, precisely at the point at which she would say that there is no longer the erotic.

Beauvoir's work on old age does, I have suggested, allow a reconsideration of the idea that female embodiment is simply devalued in *The Second Sex*. The importance of the erotic in her autobiographical and later work inspires us to return to the earlier work and pay closer attention to the importance, for Beauvoir, of a positive sexuality and erotic relation for women. What is negative about the constant and isolated repetition of housework is the absence of the new, the absence of an erotic relation to the world. What is negative about some women's experiences of sexuality is that social conventions can deprive women of the positive relationship to eros that Beauvoir values. Still, some of the most troubling aspects of *The Second Sex* remain the wholly negative accounts of menstruation and pregnancy, breastfeeding, and so on. And it is noticeable that, while a dying body retains the potential of eros in its pleasure at the touch of cool metal, a woman's bleeding body is certainly not affirmed by Beauvoir as erotic and, as has often been noted, neither is a pregnant body.[5]

What then is the erotic for Beauvoir? Bergoffen defines it as an ethics of protecting the other's strangeness (1997: 50). Although it is the locus for the theorisation of a positive engagement with the other as troubling, Bergoffen points out that it concerns not only self–other relations, or relations between individuals; it also emerges from my encounter with the world, revealed to me as a 'world of desire'. Here, Bergoffen tries to evoke the sorts of experiences of the otherness of the world which exhilarate Beauvoir, as a revelation of 'the warm face of the otherness of being' (1997: 203). The erotic body is defined as 'existing outside of its imaged limits' rather than as 'enclosed', as 'open towards otherness', or 'permeable, penetrable, vulnerable' (Bergoffen 1997: 205). Readers have sometimes commented that Beauvoir seems often to express a desire for control of the body, and a fear of a 'gaping' body. I don't read in Bergoffen's position a disagreement, but rather a perception that Beauvoir does not simply devalue a troubling and threatening world that renders me vulnerable. Instead, she frequently revels in the trouble and risk this represents.

If an erotic world is a world we are able continually to experience as 'new'

(Bergoffen 1997: 189) in an ethics which can be defined as 'protecting the other's strangeness' (Bergoffen 1997: 50), then this is consistent with the idea that for Beauvoir the body is no longer erotic at the point at which one has lost the ability to 'create luminous horizons' for oneself, at the point at which one's imagination has taken leave of us, when there is no longer the 'new'. For this reason, although in Beauvoir's work the erotic is a means of identifying a particular kind of relation between two individuals, in which we are drawn beyond our limits, it is also a means of identifying an erotic relation to the world. Beauvoir's dying mother's pleasure at the cool touch of metal and the scent of cologne provides a particularly good example of Beauvoir's concept of a positive erotic body.

I return, then, to the formulation according to which an aged body is not necessarily a non-erotic body, a strong thematic in Beauvoir's work. However, what is doubtless the case is that an erotic body is a positive body, and a non-erotic body is not only negative but represents disembodiment *par excellence*. I don't find it accidental that Bergoffen stops the analysis short of a full discussion of Beauvoir's material relating to old age while also commenting that this material offers us the best example of how the concept of the erotic is not restricted to sexual relations between individuals. For the material on old age draws our attention to the point at which Beauvoir's ability to offer a concept of the subject as always already embodied also stops short. It is the very analysis of an erotic body which is supposed to reveal in Beauvoir's work the success of her break with Cartesian dualism.

Bergoffen reminds us of Leder's argument whereby Descartes was able to

separate mind from body because he [took for granted a] structure of bodily disappearance . . . the lived body as a self-effacing and 'disappearing' reality [which] hides itself when all goes well and calls ourself to our attention when it dysfunctions as in illness, pain, fatigue.

(cited in Bergoffen 1997: 32)

By contrast, Beauvoir's non-separation of mind and body is supposed to be evident in her theorisation of an erotic subjectivity valuably troubled by a world of alterity, sensuously encountered, which renders it vulnerable to the new. The lived body is an appearing, rather than a disappearing, reality. The problem is that the formulation from Leder is reversed here, but not really overcome. Rather than disappearing when all goes well, in Beauvoir's model the body appears when all goes well. Rather than calling itself to our attention when all goes badly, the Beauvoirian body is lost. But precisely what this does not do is break with the formulations of a dualist model. A subject who is still conceived as separate from it gains and then loses her body with the waxing and waning of the erotic.

I suggested in opening that two key moments in the Sartrean and Beauvoirian analyses of eros are to be found in their fragmentary depictions of the touch of skin. In Sartre's account, my touching of the other's flesh is the moment where Sartre clarifies that his concept of desire is fundamentally appropriative. I touch the other's flesh with hidden and self-serving intent, and my strategy is to possess the other's consciousness. The pleasurable touch of my skin by the world should disrupt this model, but for Sartre, it is also subordinated to an account of a consciousness whose aim is to avoid at all costs being overwhelmed by a sensuous other, or by a sensuous tactile world of objects. In Beauvoir's work, I have suggested that the moment of the sensuous pleasure of an old and dying woman in the touch of skin by metal is similarly emblematic of an overall model of embodiment and desire which is entirely different. Beauvoir's concern is not to prevent at all costs the collapse of consciousness into the flesh. Instead, it is when the pleasures of the flesh are no longer available to us that the most valuable aspect of consciousness and human existence are considered lost. Her fear is not to succumb to the body, but to lose the body. And yet, I have also suggested that the lingering dualism which many have argued haunts Sartre, in his anxious account of an in-itself which threatens to overwhelm the for-itself, is not entirely avoided by Beauvoir. The symptoms of this are multiple: there is the model of a female subject who gains and loses her body. While embodiment is positive in Beauvoir, as opposed to its negative connotations in Sartre's work, the implication that the subject can be conceptualised as separate from its body is inescapable. This is complicated by the fact that Beauvoir considers the erotic the most crucial and valuable aspect of human consciousness. There is also the exclusion of certain aspects of embodiment from this positively valued eros. There may be an excessive romance in the location of tactile pleasures in an agonised death. But tactile pleasures, and novelty and surprise certainly remain crucial to the eros that is in turn crucial to positive embodiment and crucial to Beauvoir's account of human existence. This is a sequence of associations which does exclude the theorisation of some aspects of embodiment as critical to human subjectivity: some experiences of old age, of decaying or bleeding bodies, of pain, disease or dying bodies, which may be more difficult to conceptualise in terms of the erotic.

In a more recent book on this subject, *Connecting Gender and Aging*, the editors suggest that 'aging potentially liberates older women from the restrictions placed upon them by family, conventional gender role and their portrayal by others as sex-objects' (Arber and Ginn 1995: 177). The editors also comment,

> Despite the combined effects of ageism and sexism in cultural attitudes towards older women, the chapters in this book demonstrate how older women may be developing a more authentic identity and orientation, especially following widowhood, when they are no longer constrained to fulfill gendered role obligations expected within marriage.
>
> (Arber and Ginn 1995: 174)

This may seem far from Beauvoir's views, but in fact, and as early as 1949, Beauvoir had written of old age as follows:

> It is in the autumn and the winter of life that woman is freed from her chains; she takes advantage of her age to escape the burdens that weigh on her; she knows her husband too well to let him intimidate her any longer, she eludes

> his embraces, at his side she organizes a life of her own . . . She can also permit herself defiance of fashion and of 'what people will say'; she is freed from social obligations, dieting and the care of her beauty.
>
> (Beauvoir 1988: 595)

Beauvoir's books on gender and ageing should have been an important reference for Arber and Ginn,[6] because in passages like this Beauvoir analyses such attitudes rather than reiterating them. She takes them to be the indication of a particularly impoverished feminine existence, and argues that liberty should not be located in a transcending of normal gender expectations which old age might seem to represent. She goes on to describe this phenomenon of apparent newly found freedom as one from which women rarely benefit. Old age is not valorised in western societies. Meanwhile, norms of feminine subjectivity are more associated with youth than those of male subjectivity. Because one does not live in a bell jar, isolated in one's subjectivity from societal attitudes, the possibilities of an authentic existence are hindered, not by old age but by societal attitudes towards old age, which are inseparable from the facts of one's physiological and psychological existence. So the belief that one has finally been liberated from the conventions of femininity can, she argues, result in the tendency to lament that one is not needed, or to live by proxy through one's children, or to be lonely, regretful, frustrated or bored. The problem lies not, of course, with women, but with societal norms which do not cease to affect subjective life even when the combination of ageism and sexism leads to aged women no longer being seen as women.

The suggestion – made most recently by Arber and Ginn in an optimistic spirit (1995: 177) but criticised by Beauvoir – that women may find freedom only once they transcend being seen as women is a disturbing one. To repeat a much-used formulation: Does this not reconsolidate a perception that the problem with women is that they are women? Is this an implicit reiteration of the ideal of becoming a gender-neutral subject? Should we not instead hope that possibilities arise for women more broadly, rather than only for those women understood as having transcended youth and gender? Freedom, to remain with Beauvoir's language, should be associated with femininity, not with its transcendence. Beauvoir's own point is that women's positive experience of such freedom can only be inhibited, and rendered deeply ambivalent, if it occurs in a context of continuing social validation of youthful femininity.

It is interesting here to note the return of a problem that also arises in Beauvoir's own work. While we may give this positive or negative connotations, women are being depicted repeatedly as gaining and losing their bodies. While, for Beauvoir, we saw that an aged body is not necessarily a non-erotic body, we also saw that she views the erotic body as a positive body and the non-erotic body, not only as negative but as representing disembodiment *par excellence*. And this is not without its relationship to the implication, devalorised in *The Second Sex* but optimistically discussed by the editors of *Connecting Gender and Aging*, that old age represents the potential for freedom from the conventions of feminine embodiment, from demands made on women at a bodily level. For in both cases, is the suggestion not that a woman is, after all, something different from her body?

As we have seen, while Beauvoir's exceptionally positive depiction of 'having a body' breaks with those of her peers such as Sartre, it also leads to considerable problems in her work, in so far as the body comes to be represented autobiographically as that which we can gain, and lose.[7] Autobiographically, though less so theoretically, Beauvoir's work on old age will return her to dualist accounts of a body as that from which we are distinct. I want to consider one final example in this regard, the material discussed by Toril Moi in *Simone de Beauvoir* (1994).

Two different accounts of touching skins have so far offered key contexts for assessing Beauvoir's distinctness from Sartre, although the accounts themselves are problematic. I am going to end this chapter with a third and final account of skin. Again, I consider it to be emblematic, and it enables us to ask what happens to the specificity of the Beauvoirian model in these autobiographical depictions of her own age. It is an account, not of touched skin, but of skin that is seen.

Erotic bodies lost and found II

We have already seen that Beauvoir offers a horrified depiction of her own aged embodiment. Her depiction of the loss of youthful beauty is agonised. This leads to a description of her aged body, in which her living of aged skin is negative to the point where she simply seems to be consolidating conventions about physical beauty and youth:

> My seventy-second birthday is now . . . close . . . To convince myself of this, I have but to stand and face my mirror . . . I often stop, flabbergasted, at the sight of this incredible thing that serves me as a face. I understand La Castiglione, who had every mirror smashed. . . . I loathe my appearance now: the eyebrows slipping down toward the eyes, the bags underneath, the excessive fullness of the cheeks, and that air of sadness around the mouth that wrinkles often bring.
>
> (Beauvoir 1965: 656)

At such moments, and despite the absence of moralism in *Old Age* about how an individual experiences old age, the reader may find herself wishing, perversely, to condemn the 'bad faith' of Beauvoir and recall her to an ethics of radical freedom. Beauvoir focuses abjectly on her aging skin. She depicts many physical changes, in particular a loss of energy. But when she comes to depict her skin, she is confronted with a problem of being for others which is subordinated to the visual: the sense of oneself as subjected to the visual assessment of an other. She is subordinated to viewing herself as she would appear to an other.

As before, it is particularly in the context of Beauvoir's comments on skin that the specificity, and also the limitations, of her model become clear. It is a common and ageist supposition that an ageing body has a limited or neutral erotic life. Discussing her mother, Beauvoir sees the way in which an ageing body may have a particular, erotic relation to the world, and may focus pleasure on touch. By contrast, discussing herself, Beauvoir returns to the most conventional accounts of ageing, in which ageing is subordinated primarily to visual perceptions.

Discussing her mother, Beauvoir gives an account of her mother's indifference to the gaze of the other.

> Maman had an open hospital nightdress on and she did not mind that her wrinkled belly, criss-crossed with tiny lines, and her bald pubis showed. 'I no longer have any shame,' she observed in a surprised voice. 'You are perfectly right not to have any,' I said. But I turned away and gazed fixedly into the garden.
>
> (Beauvoir 1969: 18)

By contrast, Beauvoir discovers a heightened subordination to the gaze of the other as she ages. Her earlier indifference to her appearance was, she now discovers, a product of complacency that she was young and attractive (Beauvoir 1965: 656). She becomes conspicuous as a being for others as her skin ages. We should be hearing about the touches of the world, and of others which still startle her body. But instead, we hear about Beauvoir's horror about how she looks. Having contrasted depictions of encounters with the other as primarily a 'look' with those depicted in terms of touch, we might argue that the problem with Beauvoir's account here is that it depicts a skin looked at rather than a skin touched. Looking is associated with objectification and, in recounting this, Beauvoir suppresses the way in which the domain of touch is open to diverse possibilities of subjective, bodily experience and pleasures.

This returns us to the outset of this chapter, where we noticed the rarity of tactile metaphors in Sartre's work. Instead, his self–other encounters are dominated by visual, and to a lesser extent aural, encounters, in which the greatest risk I run is that of objectification.

Beauvoir's horrified account of her ageing body is problematic for a variety of reasons. We notice the absence of accounts of tactile encounters with objects and the world that continue to delight us in old age. This account reinforces, violently, cultural views about ageing. It loses sight of the irony Beauvoir elsewhere expresses about subjects unable to accept living in time, and depicts her own subjection to the conventional associations between femininity, youth and beauty that she had analysed – with some undertones of derision – in *The Second Sex*:

> She has gambled much more heavily than man on the sexual values she possesses; to hold onto her husband and assure herself of his protection, and in most cases to keep her job, it is necessary for her to be attractive, to please (qu'elle plaise); she is allowed no hold on the world save through the mediation of some man. What is to become of her when she no longer has any hold on him? This is what she asks herself anxiously while she looks on helpless at the degeneration of this fleshly object she mistakes for herself. She puts up a battle. But hair-dye, skin treatments, plastic surgery, will never do more

than prolong her dying youth. Perhaps she can at least deceive her mirror. But when the first hints come of that fated and irreversible process which is to destroy the whole edifice built up during puberty, she feels the fatal touch of death itself.

(Beauvoir 1988: 588, translation modified)

Of course, Beauvoir's negative response to her own ageing should be placed in the context of Western devaluations of ageing, those same devaluations she analyses so comprehensively in *Old Age*. But the matter is complicated. Beauvoir's account of femininity must similarly be placed in the context of Western devaluations of femininity, yet she still finds a positive politics in the possibility of women affirming their freedom and ability to live a full and active erotic life, as well, of course, as seeking economic and personal independence. Similarly, Beauvoir writes about these same kinds of possibilities in the theoretical work *Old Age*. Analysing the Western devaluation of ageing, we still expect Beauvoir to embrace a politics which affirms the possibility of ageing subjects living an erotic life, and that certainly is widely discussed in her theoretical writing and fiction and also in much of her autobiographical work. But at one point, suddenly subordinated to the vengeance of the visual, Beauvoir can only describe a loss of autonomous subjectivity and a loss of erotic possibilities. This cannot be explained in terms of the social depiction of ageing, because the point of her philosophical framework is to locate the possibilities for freedom and independence in the context of such social forces. And we have seen that Beauvoir's autobiographical depictions are more than capable of departing from the model shared with Sartre in which our existential life is dominated by the competing forces of objectification and being objectified. I have argued that Beauvoir's model is most able to depart from that model when she writes about the phenomenology of tactile pleasure: the stroking of the skin by the world, its objects and others.

Notes

1 Debra Bergoffen also emphasises the importance of touch in Beauvoir's account of eros (1997: 34–5, 163).
2 I am not suggesting that an author's later work inevitably clarifies what the author was saying in earlier work. But in the same way that a new critical interpretation can help us look anew at common interpretations of a well-known work, other work by the same author can allow the same process.
3 Among the reasons proposed are that, in Beauvoir's analysis, as with women, the denial of full subjectivity is connected to the social denial or restriction of 'erotic possibilities'. Second, despite Beauvoir's frequent attribution of sexual relationships and erotic desire to the aged, the work also valuably highlights that the erotic for Beauvoir is 'not necessarily linked to the explicit sexual relationship' (Bergoffen 1997: 188).
4 The relevant passages occur in *Force of Circumstance* (Beauvoir 1965: 656–7). A longer discussion of these themes is to be found in Deutscher 1999. As Moi points out, autobiography published subsequent to *Force of Circumstance* does not bear out Beauvoir's earlier belief that eros has permanently left her life (Moi 1994: 242). See Beauvoir 1987.
5 I take the opportunity to thank the Institute for Women's Studies, Lancaster University,

for an extremely helpful discussion session following a seminar presentation of this argument in 1998.

6 Neither Beauvoir nor *The Second Sex* or *Old Age* appear in the index of this thirteen-chapter recent anthology of scholars working on gender and ageing, nor in its twenty-page bibliography of work in the field.

7 This leads to another interesting exchange between Beauvoir's autobiographical and her theoretical material on old age, also discussed in Deutscher 1999 at greater length. It might be said that problems occur less in her theoretical work *Old Age* than in her autobiographical work on her own old age. If so, this raises the question of the extent to which we should attribute ethical and philosophical significance to the autobiographical material and read it with her theoretical material on the same themes. Karen Vintges (1996) has argued that the role of the autobiographical accounts of Beauvoir's life is to offer an exemplary account of femininity lived in freedom. For this reason, Vintges argues that Beauvoir's autobiographical material should be interpreted in tandem with her theoretical material. But this is not an argument which could be proposed in relation to Beauvoir's autobiographical accounts of old age. This material (which Vintges does not consider) must be differently assessed, for it cannot be considered as depicting an exemplary account of old age – on the contrary. Is it easier to mount arguments about the intersection of theoretical and biographical material when their themes concord, than when they do not?

References

Arber, S. and Ginn, J. (1995) *Connecting Gender and Ageing: A Sociological Approach*, Buckingham and Philadelphia: Open University Press.

Beauvoir, S. de (1965) *Force of Circumstance*, trans. R. Howard, London: André Deutsch and Weidenfeld & Nicolson.

—— (1969) *A Very Easy Death*, trans. P. O'Brian, Harmondsworth: Penguin.

—— (1977) *Old Age*, trans. P. O'Brian, Harmondsworth: Penguin.

—— (1984) 'The Age of Discretion' in *The Woman Destroyed*, trans. P. O'Brian, London: HarperCollins.

—— (1987) *All Said and Done*, trans. Patrick O'Brian, Harmondsworth: Penguin.

—— (1988) *The Second Sex*, trans. H. M. Parshley, London: Picador.

Bergoffen, D. (1997) *The Philosophy of Simone de Beauvoir: Gendered Phenomenologies, Erotic Generosities*, Albany: State University of New York Press.

Deutscher, P. (1997) *Yielding Gender: Feminism, Deconstruction and the History of Philosophy*, London: Routledge.

—— (1999) 'Bodies, Lost and Found: Simone de Beauvoir from *The Second Sex* to *Old Age*', *Radical Philosophy* 96: 6–16.

Fullbrook, K. and Fullbrook, E. (1994) *Simone de Beauvoir: The Remaking of an Intellectual Legend*, New York: Basic Books.

Gatens, M. (1991) *Feminism and Philosophy: Perspectives on Difference and Equality*, Bloomington: Indiana University Press.

Jardine, A. (1986) 'Death Sentences: Writing Couples and Ideology' in *The Female Body in Western Culture*, Cambridge, MA: Harvard University Press.

Kruks, S. (1990) *Situation and Human Existence, Freedom, Subjectivity and Society*, London: Unwin Hyman.

Leder, D. (1990) *The Absent Body*, Chicago: University of Chicago Press.

Le Doeuff, M. (1991) *Hipparchia's Choice: An Essay Concerning Women, Philosophy, etc.*, trans. T. Selous, Oxford: Blackwell.

Lundgren-Gothlin, E. (1996) *Sex and Existence: Simone de Beauvoir's 'The Second Sex'*, trans. L. Schenck, London: Athlone.

Marks, E. (1973) *Simone de Beauvoir: Encounters with Death*, New Brunswick, NJ: Rutgers University Press.

Moi, T. (1994) *Simone de Beauvoir: The Making of an Intellectual Woman*, Oxford: Blackwell.

Sandford, S. (1998) 'Writing as a Man: Levinas and the Phenomenology of Eros', *Radical Philosophy* 87: 6–17.

Sartre, J.-P. (1966) *Being and Nothingness: A Phenomenological Essay on Ontology*, trans. H. E. Barnes, New York: Washington Square Press.

Vintges, K. (1996) *Philosophy as Passion: The Thinking of Simone de Beauvoir*, Bloomington: Indiana University Press.

9 'You are there, like my skin'

Reconfiguring relational economies[1]

Margrit Shildrick

The question of difference, and of what is at stake in the relational economies of self and other, has been taken up in feminist thought as possibly the most urgent and critical focus of postconventional theory[2] in general. In these reflections on monstrous corporeality, both as a category and in some specific instances – particularly that of conjoined twins – I want to problematise the issue of the normative subject as it is marked by the closed skin boundaries of the body. What concerns me here is the epistemological, ontological and indeed ethical status of those organic beings whose difference is always/already apparent at the surface. In what follows, the reality or otherwise of the bodies to which I refer is not at issue.[3] To the extent that all bodies are phantasmatic, what matters is not any empirical claim to anatomical certainty, but the production of a morphological imaginary. And once the normative standard of ordered and sealed bodiliness, against which monstrosity is measured, is understood as an impossible ideal in itself – as something to be achieved rather than as a given – then it makes good sense to take the incoherence of the monstrous as the starting point. I shall be looking, then, at the issue of monstrosity as a manifestation of the always already unstable corpus, and as a difference that defies distinction.

It is notable that the opening up, in recent postmodernist philosophy, of monstrous corporeality to a discursive analysis finds strong resonances within feminist scholarship. As a figure, the monster may be read most fruitfully alongside, and supplemental to, the already familiar conjunction of matter and mother through which feminism stages a critique of the dominant forms of western discourse. All those conditions – mother/matter/monster – are both excessive to, and yet, as feminism has come to recognise, embedded unacknowledged in the structuration of the logos. And it is the very move of excavating that structural function that disrupts and throws into doubt the modernist phantasy – for no such figure exists – of a stable, autonomous and singular human subject as the centre of the logos; of a self that is foundational without being embodied; and of a body whose morphological integrity is so unquestioned that it may be forgotten, transcended. Above all, it is the corporeal ambiguity and fluidity, the troublesome lack of fixed definition, the refusal to be either one thing or the other, that marks the monstrous as a site of disruption. What is at stake is the fundamental closure of both subjects and bodies that characterises and propels western discourse, most particularly in its modernist form. And as the most visible boundary of all, the skin is both the limit of the embodied self and the site of potentially transgressive psychic investments.

The focus in this chapter on the phenomenon of conjoined twins, for whom the organ of the skin is of particular significance, points up the more general disturbance that problematises, as I have put it elsewhere, 'not only the protection of one's own body from encroachments, but a denial of the leakiness between one's self and others' (1997: 178). The implicit danger of such an approach – which must be acknowledged lest it play out the very ethical erasure that I am contesting – is that the specificity of any single instance should be betrayed by reference to a generalised category of monstrosity. But in so far as my task is to deconstruct the strategies of a morphological imaginary that covers over the differences within and across terms whilst universalising the differences between terms, then it is a risk that can be negotiated. Moreover, the greater violence would be to assume that the particularity of the other is within our grasp, that the place of the other is fully accountable from the 'outside'. The issue, then, is one not only of contesting the epistemological and ontological boundaries of bodies of knowledge and bodies of matter, but of reconfiguring the ethics of relationship.

Despite the multiple histories of thinking subjectivity, the underlying question of what it is to be a subject, and to experience oneself and the world as such, is most usually addressed in one of two opposing ways. In the dominant Cartesian mind/body model, the body may be bracketed out, as though it were of no concern. According to a more phenomenological approach, selfhood is seen as inseparable from material being-in-the-world. Yet, despite the nature of embodiment being a fundamental component, the phenomenological perspective assumes, none the less, a 'normal' model of corporeal development and fails to theorise adequately the grossly disordered body. But what if the focus were on the 'abnormal', on the visibly monstrous? Just as feminist phenomenologists have challenged the assumption of a gender-neutral, ageless and universalised body as the centre of lived experience, so too we may gain further insights by theorising non-normative morphology, not as a failure of form but as an-other way of being. I am not suggesting that the phenomenological approach has not already figured prominently in staging the ontological and epistemological consequences of corporeal anomalies, be they the result of illness, trauma, or congenital disorders, but rather that the integrated and fully functioning body remains throughout an implicit standard. And where the existence of monstrosity serves to define by comparison and opposition the delimited corporeality and secure subjectivity of the majority, it is important to realise that the standard is not normal but normative.

Within conventional western discourse, to be a self is above all to be distinguished from the other, to be ordered and discrete, secure *within* the well-defined boundaries of the body rather than actually being the body. We live, as sovereign selves, within our own skins, where to imagine inhabiting the body of another would be a special kind of madness, or to find our own bodies shared by another would constitute an invasion. In short, though the *integration* of mind and body may be undermined by a western discourse of transcendent subjectivity, there are few doubts as to which minds and bodies go together. And though self-identity may always and necessarily be a case of misrecognition in the Lacanian sense, it is precisely the mapping of the boundaries between both singular selves and singular bodies that authorises our being in the world as subjects. Where early infants are unable to recognise the distinctions between self and other, or between inside and outside, the mirror stage inaugurates the ego as 'both a map of the body's surface and a reflection of the image of the other's body' (Grosz 1994: 38). It is the point at which a subject becomes distinguished from its objects. My concern, then, is to uncover the extent to which the western notion of the sovereign self, and of the bounded body, is, in general, both guaranteed and contested by those who do not, indeed cannot, unproblematically occupy the embodied subject position. It is not my claim that every form of the monstrous effects the same counter-logic, but that all demand a rethinking of the strategies by which the self is secured.

For all that dominant modernist discourse privileges a putative split between mind and body that casts doubt on the ontological status of the body, the result has not been disengagement from questions of corporeal being. Contra Descartes, we are obsessed with our bodies. But it is not of course normative morphology that engages the greatest attention, but those bodily forms – like conjoined twinning – which most clearly challenge the distinctions both between mind and body and between body and body. Against an ideal of bodily closure that relies on the singular, the unified and the replicable, monstrosity, in the form of either excess, lack or displacement, offers a gross insult. For the most part, inevitably, such monstrosity is manifest as surface phenomena in which the skin itself as putative boundary of the self's clean and proper body – to use Kristeva's phrase – may be compromised both in form and structure. The significance of that skin is, as always, not simply organic but also psychic. One need only look at the many representations of the Monster of Cracow – a sixteenth-century favourite displaying both excess and displacement – to appreciate how violently monstrosity might breach the borders of humanity. The human-born infant is beset not only with manifold excrescences which burst through the surface membrane, but by an inhuman mix of fur, horn, skin and scale. Moreover, the deformities constitute a multiplicity of additional orifices; the creature is described as having apes' faces instead of breasts, dogs' heads at both elbows and knees, and cats' eyes under the navel (Bateman 1581). The emphasis on the points of exchange between inner and outer marks the creature's monstrosity as a matter of being as much as of appearance. Its contaminatory potential is clear.

Now, lest we suppose that the Monster of Cracow is simply a semi-mythological construct that stands in contradistinction to the 'natural' possibilities of the human body, we should reflect that although its narration undoubtedly served a political purpose in the context of sixteenth-century Europe, that *techne* plays a part in the construction of all monsters, indeed all bodies. As Haraway reminds us: 'Biology is discourse, not the living world itself' (1992: 298). What I am disputing, then, is the givenness of any body, the sense of a foundational and certain form which then may be compared to an ideal template. It is not simply that the developing body is always dynamic, but that bodies, rather than being material and graspable from the start are, as Butler outlines (1993), materialised through a set of discursive practices. The so-called normal and natural body, and particularly its smooth and closed up surface, is then an achievement, a model of the proper in which everything is in its place and the chaotic aspects of the natural are banished. As Bakhtin puts it: 'That which protrudes, bulges, sprouts or branches off . . . is eliminated, hidden, or moderated. All orifices of the body are closed. The basis of the image is the individual, strictly limited mass, the impenetrable façade' (1984: 320). In short, the normal body is materialised through a set of reiterative practices that speak to the instability and leakiness of the singular standard.

In contrast, at the very simplest level, the monster resists the values associated with what we choose to call normality and becomes instead a focus of normative anxiety. But rather than being simply an instance of otherness, it reminds us of what must be abjected from the self's clean and proper body. Even the Monster of Cracow's gross violation of external order, its suturing together of surfaces that should remain apart, cannot disguise its claim on the human. It remains a figure of both horror and fascination. As Kristeva (1982) makes clear, the abject is never completely externalised. It is, then, the failure of the monster to occupy only the place of the other that betrays the fragility of the distinctions by which the human subject is fixed and maintained as fully present to itself and autonomous. In collapsing the boundaries between self and other, monsters constitute an undecidable absent presence at the heart of the human being. Alongside their external manifestation, they leave also a trace embedded within, that, in Derridean terms, operates as the signifier not of difference but of *différance*. What is at stake throughout is the risk of indifferentiation.

With that in mind, I want to turn now to a consideration of conjoined twins, who have been a source of fascination and unease throughout the socio-history of teratology, as is evident in diverse archival texts, such as the 'monster books' of the early modern period or the historical proceedings of the Royal Society. The manifestation of the body which is not one demands specific epistemological and ontological reflection, in which the issue of the boundaries of subjecthood is particularly acute. Unlike human–animal hybrid embodiment, which leaves room for a wholly exclusionary approach, the incidence of corporeal doubling in which both bodies are visibly human is highly disruptive of western notions of individual agency and personal identity. The significance of morphology, and the relationship between the body and the subject, is put centre-stage by the wide variety of forms that conjoined twins may take. Given the ideal of wholly independently embodied personhood, the simplest are those, like the nineteenth-century 'Siamese' twins, Chang and Eng, whose bodies appear relatively self-complete externally albeit joined by fleshy material and shared circulation. The anomaly of conjunction is overridden in these cases by the common-sense judgement that in all other respects such twins *are* two autonomous beings, and indeed Chang and

Eng were each accorded full social and legal identity. None the less, despite such strategies of normalisation, an ambivalence remained. Was their unmodified corporeal excessiveness only skin deep, or were they freaks[4] who existed only as a unit?

Unlike the Monster of Cracow, or other similar figures of the early modern period, the disturbance at the level of the skin does not, for conjoined twins, necessarily signal an inner transgression of normative humanity. Indeed, the perception that separation is in the best interests of conjoined twins rests on the prior assumption that two separate persons with distinct identities have, as it were, become trapped in a single morphology. As surgical intervention has become possible in practice, the issue is taken as settled in principle, and subject only to technical feasibility, as though there is nothing at stake except an inappropriate body. It is as though the body were merely instrumental and the shared organ of the skin – which is the minimum condition of conjunction – bore no relation to the 'real' persons beneath. But such an account misses not only the complexity of perception as it is mediated by the skin, but the psychic investments of body image and the phenomenological sense of being-in-the-world, in which corporeal extension is indivisible from subjecthood and identity. It is the privileging of singularity and autonomy so evident in western discourse and the value accorded bodily self-determination which combine to erase any consideration that there might be other ways of being, or that a different morphology might ground other relational economies. What is primarily at stake here is the conceptual separation between subject and object in which property in one's own body is the ground of selfhood. As Luce Irigaray puts it: 'Property, ownership, and self-definition are the attributes of the father's production. . . . To be. To own. To be one's own' (1985a: 300).

To critique the separations demanded by a masculinist logos is one thing, but the question of the psychic separation – as Irigaray herself makes clear – is rather more complex. It is not, then, that I am suggesting that conjoined twins should not be seen as two persons, but rather that the question of identity is not so easily settled. The (mis)recognition of the Lacanian mirror stage is in a sense the permanent condition of such twins, the evident difference being that in that moment they may refuse identity in its symbolic sense and choose identification. There is plenty of evidence that monozygotic twins in general habitually blur the boundaries between one and the other – simultaneously thinking the same thoughts, making the same choices, speaking together as one. It should not be surprising that conjoined twins, who must share experiential being, do not make the separations that are commonly taken for granted. And yet in non-autobiographical accounts of conjoined twins, both modern historical and contemporary, the one consistent factor that overrides differences in morphology is the persistent reiteration that beneath the skin they are essentially separate. So deeply is the ideal of corporeal and mental autonomy written into the western understanding of what it is to be a person that there is scarcely any suggestion that conjoined twins could function as a merged unit.

But might there be a quite different way of understanding the significance of concorporate bodies, and more specifically the co-extensivity of the skin? Along-side the understanding of the skin as no more than a containing sac for both physical and psychical apparatus, a unifying envelope for the self, and a protective barrier between that self and a potentially threatening outside, the skin is also a primary organ of communication (Anzieu 1989). From the moment of birth, the skin is an extraordinarily sensitive surface which both registers sense impressions of the external world and transmits information as to the baby's own state of being. But as a psychoanalytic reading makes clear, for the early infant there is no distinction between inside and outside marked by the epidermal membrane, but rather a co-extensivity with the mother in which they seemingly share a common skin. As Anzieu puts it:

> This common skin ensures direct communication between the two partners, reciprocal empathy and an adhesive identification: it is a unique screen which comes to resonate with the sensations, mental images and vital rhythms of the two.
>
> (Anzieu 1989: 62–3)

The task for the developing infant is then to move beyond that corporeal and psychical indifferentiation to a state where what is experienced at the surface of the skin serves to constitute a separate and increasingly self-aware ego. And as the interval between self and other is established, so too the intermediary function of the skin loses ground, or perhaps more accurately is conceptually overlooked.

It has seemed to many feminist theorists, none the less, that the emphasis on the detachment of the specular at the expense of the immediacy of touch is a characterisitic of a masculinist logos rather than an adequate image of relational economies. The turn, then, to both Merleau-Ponty and Irigaray seems to me to offer a way forward, particularly in Irigaray's recognition that touch is the sub-stratum of all the senses. Despite very different theoretical agendas, each is concerned to mark the tactile as that which not simply precedes, but more accurately defers, the separation of the subject from its objects (Irigaray 1991: 108; Merleau-Ponty 1962). As Merleau-Ponty puts it: 'Tactile experience ... adheres to the surface of our body; we cannot unfold it before us and it never quite becomes an object' (1962: 316). Moreover, touch is always reversible in that the hand that touches is also touched, and that double sensation is especially evident in the contact between two animate surfaces. The subject accordingly is in a mutually constitutive relationship with its objects, intertwined one with the other through touch. And yet, for Merleau-Ponty, a form of hierarchy remains in that the revers-ibility is never the indeterminacy of merging: 'I am always on the side of my body' (1968: 148). And although Merleau-Ponty analyses at some length the tactility between one's own two hands or lips, he does not, I think, offer an account that satisfies my own questions about conjoined twins. The irreducible flip that he proposes between the active and passive is premised on the image of one hand *reaching out* to touch the other, not on two surfaces that are always already touching.

I turn then to Irigaray, who specifically displaces Merleau-Ponty's active hand with her own image of two hands touching as though in prayer (Irigaray 1993) for an account more adequate to concorporation. For Irigaray, it is the issue of a specifically feminine desire that is addressed through the image of bodily contact, not necessarily as an anatomical event, but in the imaginary. None the less, her evocation of feminine morphology as concorporate – 'the birth that is never accomplished, the body never created once and for all, the form never definitively completed' (1985b: 217) – is highly pertinent in the present context. For the body Irigaray proposes, the issue of the cut is displaced, just as it might be for conjoined twins in an alternative cultural discourse. In stark contrast to the normative insistence on the independent and proper body sealed into singularity by its own skin, Irigarayan corporeality is positive precisely in so far as it is mediated by touch, by mucus, by the mingling of blood. The masculinist economy of subject and object finds no place here: 'Everything is exchanged, yet there are no transactions. Between us, there are no proprietors, no purchasers, no determinable objects, no prices. Our bodies are nourished by our mutual pleasure' (1985b: 213). It is an image that indeed suggests an-other mode, not of being, but rather of becoming. Can we then make sense of Irigaray's image in the context of actual bodies as they are lived?

The case of the Irish conjoined twins, Katie and Eilish Holton, whose early childhood and subsequent separation features in two television documentaries, suggests that we can. Given the nature of their particular morphology, it is perhaps more accurate to describe them as concorporate rather than conjoined. The twins' body is merged from the upper thoracic area giving them just two legs and two functioning arms – with two other residual upper limb stumps having been already excised in the expectation of future separation surgery. There are separate hearts and lungs, but all other organs are single. What is at stake throughout, for both the parents and the medical team, is how best to balance the risk of separation – and it is made clear that the twins' degree of concorporation exceeds any in which surgical intervention has been previously attempted – with the normative desire that each should have a functionally autonomous existence. The issue of corporeal normalisation is, however, clearly distinct from a more complex and contradictory understanding of what would constitute normality in the specific case of the twins. For the parents, Katie and Eilish already operate as two 'normal' children, having individual personalities which they do much to encourage; while for his part, the consultant surgeon stresses that he cannot promise the twins a 'normal' life if they are separated. The characteristic western split between mind and body is mirrored in the assumption of an existential normality that is merely obstructed by the abnormal morphology of the children. Under the skin, it is asserted, they are certainly two. The voiceover suggestion that 'although we value individuality, they might not value it. They might prefer togetherness' (*Katie and Eilish: Siamese Twins* 1993) is, then, both a disturbing glimpse of other ways of being, and a reminder of what the normative regime of individuality must repudiate.

It is not, I think, that there is any recognition that the concorporation of the twins might speak to new forms of embodied subjectivity, but rather that the ideal of the autonomous subject is contested by the twins' concurrent and co-operative intentionality. Their successful negotiation of their environment largely depends on their acting as one, even in such small matters as unscrewing a bottle. None the less, the sense that being-in-the-world might imbricate with body and environment is not explored; to those who must decide their future, the discrete subjectivities of the twins is already given and simply awaiting release from the fleshy bondage of their shared skin suit. Despite the very evident pleasure that Katie and Eilish take in their mutual and reversible touch – they are shown stroking each other's faces – the trope of liberation from the body is a common motif in narratives of conjoined twins. Although both parents and doctors are sensitive to the implicitly ethical question of potentially disrupting the twins' current contentment, their more major concern is with the material risks of surgery. The decision to go ahead is taken, the initial procedure being to implant expanders under the skin which will artificially extend its surface area. Rather than itself suffering the cut, the skin is seen as no more than the manipulable covering-over for the wound to come. Following the operation the now-separated Katie swiftly dies, while for Eilish final success depends on the resealing of her body and the recontainment of her self.

The point of turning to this often very moving narrative is not so much to critique the practice of heroic medicine represented by the surgeon's knife – for in this case the participants, whether detached professionals or closest family, are all properly caring and reflective – but to illustrate the power of ontological anxiety. Against the corporeal excessiveness of Katie and Eilish, the attempt to reconstruct their bodies speaks eloquently to the notions of closure and containment assumed to be at the heart of being. What is finally unacceptable about the twins is not the degree of their disability – and indeed it is unclear that a successful outcome would have increased function – but the ambiguity of their concorporation. For all the discursive efforts to normalise their life in terms of assigning dual individuality, it remains undecidable whether they are one or two. In contrast, the conventional understanding of the only proper form of subjectivity requires a clarity of boundaries between self and other, an affective and effective autonomy that is fully realised only by singular embodiment sealed by the skin. Despite the death of Katie, then, the father of the twins is constrained to justify the operation by remarking on the surviving twin's enhanced quality of life after separation: 'She's free of being joined to another human-being' (*Eilish: Life Without Katie* 1995). Yet what are we to make of the separation in the light of Freud's remark that 'the ego is first and foremost a bodily ego' (1923: 26), that is, the psychic location of introjected sensation – touching and being touched – at the surface of the skin? In fashioning Eilish's body so that she may comply with normative ideals, she is supposedly realised as an intelligible subject, and a body that matters. The impossibility of the ideal is made clear, however, in the acknowledgment that for Eilish, body modification must be continued throughout life: her prosthetic leg and body harness must be periodically replaced to ensure scopic normalisation. It is ironic that although no-one seems able to articulate the wider significance of Eilish's phenomenological disruption, the doctor worries that in losing her first prosthesis she will think some part of her is being taken away. For her own part Eilish renames her new leg 'Katie', in recognition of the absent presence of her highly tactile self/other.

The phenomenological specificity of concorporate being-in-the-world is not addressed by any adult in the films, except perhaps in the psychologist's half recognition that Katie is still incorporated into the life of her surviving twin. At night, Eilish gets what she calls her 'Katie kisses', but even that observation is normalised in that the ritual happens 'in a healthy way, not in any way that is holding Eilish back' (*Eilish: Life without Katie* 1995). That implicit rewriting of concorporation as obstructive is reiterated in an interchange in the second documentary between Eilish and her sisters. When asked what she remembers of her twin, Eilish directly echoes Irigaray's words – 'I carry you with me everywhere. . . . You are there, like my skin' (1985b: 216) – in her own reply: 'She used to bring me round everywhere'. But the poignancy of the moment is swiftly interrupted by an older sibling who declares: 'Eilish couldn't go wherever she wanted'. What matters to the family is that Eilish should be well-adjusted, and indeed, despite the four months spent in hospital post-operatively during which she was described as traumatised, she does appear happy and talkative in the second documentary shot over the next two years. For her parents, her social and physical recovery is clearly a matter of relief, but it is evident too that, for Eilish herself, the splitting of her (subject) body has produced an effect somewhat akin to the phenomenon of the phantom limb. As Merleau-Ponty explains it, to experience such a phantom is to remain open to the presence of what is lost. The wound that Eilish endures, unacknowledged, is as much psychical as material, a severe disruption to the unified, albeit imaginary, body map that founds the ego.[5] When Teresa, the elder sister, says of Katie, 'She had freckles', the response from Eilish is both confused and defiant: 'So did I, so do I, [pushes Teresa], I still do' (*Eilish: Life without Katie* 1995). Katie both is and isn't there, a shifting body memory and continued inscription on the flesh of her twin.

What this narrative emphasises is the persistence of a dominant post-Enlightenment discourse in which our psychic investment in the corporeal is covered over by the illusion that the body is merely instrumental, a source only of impediment or advantage to the subject. The clarity of corporeal boundaries is what grounds existential and moral personhood, while the meeting with the other is premised on bodily self-determination and property rights in one's own body. The conjunction of two consciousnesses is characterised primarily in terms of a meeting of self and other, properly mediated by contact or by the calculation of individual best interests. Yet, as Susan Cataldi notes, the reality of physical contact tells another story:

> the experienced ambiguities, the doublings and reversibilities of touch confuse the sharp distinctions philosophers try to draw between what is 'internal' and what is 'external'. Through our flesh and thanks to tactility, we are always already 'outside' of our 'selves'.

> (Cataldi 1993: 126)

And where the skin is literally co-extensive, as for conjoined twins, the other is also the self – a transgressive and indeterminate state in which corporeal, ontological and ultimately ethical boundaries are distorted and dissolved. If the hand that held the knife were that of the concorporate body itself, where, we might ask, would it cut to establish self and other?[6] None the less, what separation surgery attempts – aside from cases where it is medically indicated to preserve life – is a reconstitution of autonomous subjecthood as the only proper way of being in the world. As Clark and Myser put it, the assumption is 'that conjoined life, precisely because of its imagined phenomenological unintelligibility, must be intolerable' (1996: 351). And, one might add, intolerable to society rather than to the twins themselves. There is no sense here that corporeality might constitute the subject, only that a somehow foundational subject – or rather two – is thwarted by a monstrous body.

I want finally to mention very briefly some other forms of concorporation which seem to erase any possibility, theoretical or material, of an interval between self and other.[7] It is not simply that the organ of the skin fails to differentiate one body from another, but that the embodiment seems to speak to incorporation rather than concorporation. One specific form is called parasitic twinning, where the very naming – parasitic – speaks of a putative insult to an ideal of bodily self-determination; the other concerns the incidence of supernumerary heads on singular bodies. In both, the ideal of a clean and proper body is visibly disordered by what appears to be an eruption from within bursting through the skin, that, as with other types of conjoined twins, with their shared blood, bowels and fecal matter, mobilises the uncanniness of the abject. Such anomolies are clearly rare but by no means unique, and as neonatal death is not a necessary consequence, they too raise questions as to the closure and integrity of the self. In parasitic twins, of whom the seventeenth-century Coloredo brothers are the best-documented example, one body may be fully endowed with mental and motor capacity, while the second may show physical affect but no evidence of rational thought (Turner 1697, Pt 2, Ch. 7: 8). The resulting confusion as to where the boundaries of the self lie, or even if an other exists as such, is even greater in the case of supernumerary heads. The phenomenom is well illustrated by the so-called Bengali boy of the eighteenth century whose second head grew upside down and back-to-front on the top of the child's scalp. In life, the 'bodyless' head had well-formed facial features, ears, growing hair, and separate affect, while postmortem examination revealed that 'the two brains were [. .]. separate and distinct, having a complete partition between them' (Home 1790). Although at the time the occurrence generated little discussion regarding the boundaries of the self, but became instead the object of a biomedical controversy concerning the process of evolutionary development, I want to return to questions of personal identity.

If the issue of subjectivity or identity is at very least problematised in the indistinct corporeality of those conjoined twins with two relatively well-formed bodies, both internal and external, or more remarkably where two heads append the same body, then it is radically challenged by such incomplete instances of doubling as those considered above. In her essay entitled 'Freaks', Elizabeth Grosz remarks: 'it is no longer clear that there are two identities, even if the bodily functions of the parasitic twin occur independently of the will or awareness of the other. In such cases, is there one subject or two?' (1991: 34). That question clearly haunts the historical accounts of the cases I have mentioned. Although independent affect occurs in both 'parasitic' sites, what marks a difference between the two cases is that whereas the Coloredos are always referred to as two distinct persons, and indeed, according to report, each was baptised, the Bengali boy is already singular. Although surgical intervention was not a possibility in either case, a discursive normalisation of the excessive subject has taken place. And yet it is only in the insistence that monstrosity is radically other – the exceptional case that secures the normative standard – that the similar construction of all subject bodies as singular is obscured. Whether through Irigaray's play on the originary mother-matter, which continues to ground female-to-female relationships but is repudiated in the male, or as the inherent instability of corporeality in its always incomplete process of abjection, it remains the case that regimes of normalisation must be constantly reiterated to defer the slippage of an excessive embodiment that threatens always to overwhelm. As Grosz puts it:

> the stability of the unified body image . . . must be continually renewed, not through the subject's conscious efforts but through its ability to conceive of itself as a subject and to separate itself from its objects and others to be able to undertake wilful action.
>
> (Grosz 1994: 43–4)

So what type of subjectivity or identity could fit such a range of differences, and how does the monstrous corporeality of my examples imbricate with the sense of self? Where Elizabeth Grosz (1991) posits a continuum of identity – ranging from the autonomous, self-complete and individuated subject, which modernist western discourse assumes as the standard for all, to a non-differentiated, quasi-collective subject in which the symbolic moment of distinction between self and other is endlessly deferred – I am inclined to caution. The desire for full self-presence is, I think, never realised, and results only in a phantasmatic structure of subjectivity. As I understand it, monsters both define the limits of the singular embodied subject and reflect our own ultimately insecure and unstable identities. And it is the move forcibly to impose the norm of one body/one mind, the move to erase difference either by exclusion or by processes of normalisation, that underlines the instability of the ideal. Where monsters blatantly blur the parameters of being, they invoke in us all – and this seems particularly true of the doubling of twinned bodies – both a nostalgia for identification and the horror of incorporation. They demonstrate that the relation between self and other, as with body and body, is chiasmatic, precisely in so far as corporeality and subjectivity – body and mind – are themselves folded back into each other, overflowing, enmeshed and mutually constitutive.

Though the cut to the flesh may hope to avert the overtly transgressive, its very practice alerts us to the crisis at the boundaries of the body which is never one. As the in-between, as *différance*, what the monstrous shows us is that neither the one nor the two is proof against the deconstruction of closure. Promise and risk lie equally in the move beyond/before the one that determines ontological and corporeal unity, or the two that mark difference as opposition, and relationship as the quasi-contractual exchange between autonomous beings. And it is in the openings of touch that 'our bodies overstep their bounds; our flesh is in flux' (Cataldi 1993: 126). The space of tactile interaction is never a static given, but what Cataldi calls 'the embodied space of copresent implication' (1993: 126). There is here no suggestion that the contact between bodies signals indifferentiation, for that lies only in the lost pre-subjectal plenitude of undifferentiated infant/maternal corporeality, which as Irigaray herself makes clear must be left behind. It is rather that the subject–object relation might be rewritten as the contiguity, as even a certain undecidability, between subjects. What matters, I think, is that the contact, the touch that mediates, should remain fluid and open.

Once the surface of our bodies is understood not as a protective envelope that defines and unifies our limits, but as an organ of physical and psychical interchange, then the (monstrous) other is always there, 'like my skin'. And it is the necessarily incomplete abjection of monstrosity – both as the other within and as the other who claims us – that guards against the successful closure of what Derrida has called 'an illegitimately delimited subject' (1991: 108). In that sense I read monstrous corporeality as potentially figuring not just the site of a reconceived ontology but of a new form of ethics. To relinquish the determinacy of the bounded body is to open up the possibility of reconfiguring relational economies that privilege neither the one nor the two. Instead of an 'anaesthetic' ethic that works by separation and division, there is licence for Irigaray's vision: 'The internal and external horizon of my skin interpenetrating with yours wears away their edges, their limits, their solidity. Creating another space outside my framework. An opening of openness' (1992: 59). It is a space where the double relation between the normal and the monstrous does not hold; a space that no one of us can fully occupy. As such, it mobilises an ethical economy in which our specificities, rather than haunted by, are in communion with, the differences between, and internal to, us all.

Notes

1 Some parts of this paper, with a somewhat different focus, have already appeared in 'This Body Which Is Not One: Dealing with Differences' (Shildrick 1999).
2 I am using the term 'postconventional' to signal a whole range of discourses, including the phenomenological, that contest the paradigms of modernity without necessarily being assimilable to postmodernism, even as that cannot be reduced to a single form.
3 I make no attempt, either, to reconstruct the specificity of their socio-historical significance. Given a belief that all readings of past 'evidence' are constructs in and of the present, what is illuminated are our own preoccupations.
4 Like many other conjoined twins of the nineteenth and early twentieth centuries, and others with congenital corporeal disorders, Chang and Eng frequently featured in the

so-called freak shows of the period. The commercial 'showing' of such monstrous bodies in Europe at least has a history going back many centuries.
5 In psychoanalytic terms, the mirroring process (both literal and metaphorical), by which the infant comes to see itself as separate and distinct, allows accession to a self-image of corporeal unity that covers over the reality of the fragmentary and unco-ordinated motor experiences of the child (Lacan 1977). As an ego ideal, however, the resultant body map is precarious, having 'a psychical interior, which requires continual stabilization, and a corporeal exterior, which remains labile, open to many meanings' (Grosz 1994: 8).
6 I am grateful to Janet Price for posing this question.
7 A fuller account is given in Shildrick (1999).

References

Anzieu, D. (1989) *The Skin Ego*, New Haven: Yale University Press.
Bakhtin, M. (1984) *Rabelais and His World*, trans. H. Iswolsky, Bloomington: Indiana University Press.
Bateman, S. (1581) *The Doome Warning All Men to the Iudgemente*, Ralphe Nubery.
Butler, J. (1993) *Bodies that Matter: On the Discursive Limits of 'Sex'*, London: Routledge.
Cataldi, S. L. (1993) *Emotion, Depth, and Flesh: A Study of Sensitive Space*, New York: State University of New York Press.
Clark, D. L. and Myser, C. (1996) 'Being Humaned: Medical Documentaries and the Hyperrealisation of Conjoined Twins' in R. G. Thomson (ed.) *Freakery: Cultural Spectacles of the Extraordinary Body*, New York: New York University Press.
Derrida, Jacques (1991) ' "Eating Well", or the Calculation of the Subject: An Interview with Jacques Derrida' in E. Cadava, P. Connor and J-L. Nancy (eds) *Who Comes after the Subject?* London: Routledge.
Freud, S. (1923) 'The Ego and the Id' in J. Strachey (ed.) (1953–66) *The Standard Edition of the Complete Works of Sigmund Freud*, Vol. 17: 217–52, London: Hogarth Press.
Grosz, Elizabeth (1991) 'Freaks', *Social Semiotics* 1, 2: 22–38.
—— (1994) *Volatile Bodies: Toward a Corporeal Feminism*, Bloomington: Indiana University Press.
Haraway, D. (1992) 'The Promises of Monsters: A Regenerative Politics for Inappropriate/d 'Others' in L. Grossberg, C. Nelson and P. A. Treichler (eds), *Cultural Studies*, London: Routledge.
Home, E. (1790) 'An Account of a Child with a Double Head', *Philosophical Transactions of the Royal Society*, 80: 296–305.
Irigaray, L. (1985a) *Speculum of the Other Woman*, trans. G. Gill, New York: Cornell University Press.
—— (1985b) *This Sex Which Is Not One*, trans. C. Porter, New York: Cornell University Press.
—— (1991) 'The Limits of the Transference' in M. Whitford (ed.) *The Irigaray Reader*. Oxford: Blackwell.
—— (1992) *Elemental Passions*, trans. J. Collie and J. Still, London: Athlone.
—— (1993) *An Ethics of Sexual Difference*, trans. C. Burke and G. Gill, New York: Cornell University Press.
Kristeva, J. (1982) *Powers of Horror. An Essay on Abjection*, New York: Columbia University Press.
Lacan, J. (1977) 'The Mirror Stage as Formative of the Function of the I' in *Ecrits: A Selection*, trans. A. Sheridan, New York: W. W. Norton.

Merleau-Ponty, M. (1962) *Phenomenology of Perception*, trans. C. Smith, London: Routledge and Kegan Paul.

—— (1968) *The Visible and the Invisible*, Evanston, IL: Northwestern University Press.

Shildrick, M. (1997) *Leaky Bodies and Boundaries: Feminism, Postmodernism and (Bio)ethics*, London: Routledge.

—— (1999) 'This Body which is Not One: Dealing with Differences', *Body & Society* 5, 23: 77–92.

Turner, W. (1697) *A Compleat History of the most Remarkable Providences*, London: John Dunton.

Yorkshire Television (1993) *Katie and Eilish: Siamese Twins*, Network First.

—— (1995) *Eilish: Life Without Katie*, Network First.

Part III

Skin sites

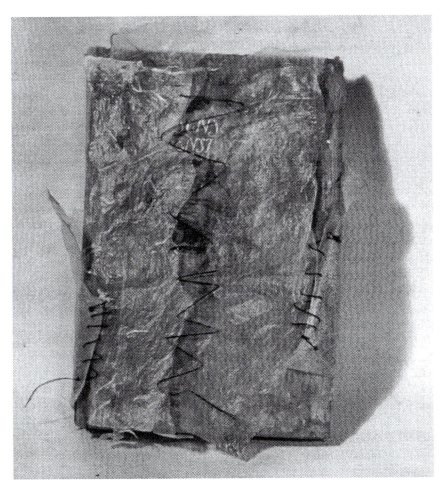

Frontispiece 3 'Book of Skin'
Reworked book with skin, hair, wax and thread
From installation *Writ(e) of Habeus Corpus*, 8 inches × 4 inches
Susan McKenna and Elizabeth Hynes

10 Inscribing identity[1]

Skin as country in the Central Desert

Jennifer Biddle

The title of this chapter is in fact a misnomer. For to speak of 'inscribing identity' is to evoke the figure of the text: page, surface, stylus, mark. It is to posit a medium in advance, prior, as it were, to the act of inscribing, whether this be blank page, canvas or skin, for there must, after all, be some *thing* upon which inscription writes.

Judith Butler (1990: 129–31) and Mascia-Lee and Sharpe (1992: 147) argue that the metaphor of culture as corporeal 'inscription' is particularly dominant in the wake of Foucault's conceptualization of the body as written on by historically-specific discursive regimes and technologies. This inscriptive model, however, is problematic because it assumes the existence of an ontologically prior, pre-cultural and thus natural medium (body or surface of skin). Not only does this make the work of culture literally superficial – on the 'surface' of an already assumed stable, unified, and natural 'thing' – but it posits culture as inherently distinct from this pre-given 'natural' material. As one recent article entitled 'Written in the Flesh' puts it: 'the human body is man's first worked on object' (Falk 1995: 99). Here, the universal projection of what is a Euro-centric conceptualization of the body as text is clear. 'The human body' is assumed to be at once singular in form, discrete and unified ('the'), 'human' (as opposed to animal, and thus a distinct species), 'body' (as opposed to non-body, and thus subject as opposed to object), and already existent, thus natural (as opposed to cultural).

Not arbitrarily, this body is also modelled as male. As Moira Gatens (1991) has argued, the idea of 'the human body' – a single body which metonymically represents all bodies – is the direct result of nineteenth-century liberalism. The explicit exclusion of women's (and other) bodies, interests and activities was necessary for the constitution of the 'body politic', a constitutive membership of bodies pre-defined by their capacities for certain kinds of reason, action, speech, ethics. This required that 'the' body was freed from the 'wills or desires' in Hobbesian terms (Gatens 1991: 84) of reproduction, domestic work and other activities which might detract from this dream of equality; a dream of the ultimate interchangeability between assumed self-same male bodies. As Gatens (1991: 83) puts it: 'Man is the model and it is his body which is taken for the human body'. In short, 'the human body' is predicated upon the necessary exclusion of any other kind of body.

This assumption of the so-called 'human body' lends itself inevitably to the tendency found in so many works on 'body decorations of the world', where a certain 'variations-on-a-theme' approach is taken to the presentation of bodily 'adornments' cross culturally, with such titles as *The Body Decorated* (Ebin 1979), *The Decorated Body* (Brain 1978) or, for a really complex variation, *Decorated Skin* (Groning 1997). In these kinds of pseudo-structuralist approaches, differentiation is only a matter of type. And indeed it is equally the form of a typology which is found in contemporary post-structural theorists who adopt this cross-cultural comparative perspective, such as Falk (1995) and Lingis (1978, 1983), who contrast 'primitive' bodily inscriptions with 'modern' or 'western' inscriptions. This schematization is perhaps particularly disturbing given the kinds of critiques that have been leveled against the totalizing, binaristically derived category of the 'primitive'. For of course, as Shelly Errington (1994), Marianna Torgovnick (1990) and others have argued, 'primitivism' has only arisen in relation to colonialism and serves to legitimate its projects. The lumping together of the majority of the world's cultural practices, and keeping them as distinct (and virtually distant) from a very small part of 'modern' or 'contemporary' culture, that is, small and specific parts of Europe and its ex-colonies (an equally imaginary 'space' at that, as unified and generalized in its supposedly shared practices as that of the 'primitive'), has no necessary descriptive cogency. Rather, the category of 'the primitive' stands here, as elsewhere, as a way of producing a distinctiveness it purports to describe,[2] producing an assured, absolute, even abjected identity against which the 'modern' or 'civilized' can be defined. Not only politically and conceptually suspicious, this kind of schematization fails to offer any close analysis of what so-called 'primitive' inscriptions might actually be like or what they might actually do in terms of the societies from which they derive.

It is against these kinds of tendencies that this chapter is written. Rather than assuming that 'skin' provides a natural surface for cultural elaboration, or that discrete, individual bodies pre-exist the social, I argue 'skin' itself may well be involved in the production of the very distinction we call 'human'. That is, 'skin' is very much the 'stuff' of culture. The very boundary 'we' so-called 'modern western subjects' understand the 'skin' as providing – that is, 'skin' as a material, external cover for a stable, self-identified and self-identical subjectivity – is not a universally held understanding. Indeed, as I explore below, 'skin', in the Warlpiri Aboriginal context, provides the medium through which women regularly can and do transform into the object world: 'become' landscape, country, other species. This fundamentally challenges and disrupts notions of 'the human body' and, in turn, it refigures the role of 'skin' inscription from the superficial to the constitutive in the production of cultural identities and differences.

But I get ahead of myself. I first need to describe something of the culture, the particular practices of which I want to speak. And I need to do so in some detail, for it is only in and through concrete terms that culture operates. By virtue of the constraints imposed by a chapter such as this, I am obliged to generalize far more than I would like. Where possible, I have indicated further references for the reader to pursue should they wish to do so.

Who are Warlpiri?

The inscriptive practices I analyse belong to a group of Australian Aborigines who call themselves Warlpiri. There are approximately 3,000 Warlpiri living in remote communities and outstations to the north and west of Alice Springs in the Tanami Desert. Warlpiri are perhaps best known internationally for their acrylic 'Dreaming' paintings, which have attracted considerable attention since the 1980s from art curators, collectors, journalists, film makers and anthropologists alike. The success of these paintings has had no small effect locally. As Dussart (1997: 186) points out, income from art production is now the second-largest source of income for Warlpiri.

The signs and symbols employed in acrylic paintings form the basis of this analysis. These signs derive from the ritual domain: in the case of women's paintings, from ceremonial body inscriptions called *yawulyu*, and for men, from ceremonial ground inscriptions and ritual object design.[3] As I have argued elsewhere (Biddle 1996), this same visual system is utilized not only in ritual contexts but now in more secular ways too. Almost like print literacy, this visual system is used not only to produce and reproduce more sacred knowledges, but also to communicate 'new' information and ideas.

These inscriptive signs and symbols are called *kuruwarri* – a complex term meaning mark, trace, ancestral presence and/or essence, and birthmark or freckle. *Kuruwarri* are said to be the marks made, left over, by Ancestors as they roamed the same country as Warlpiri do (where they still have access to traditional countries) – camping, hunting, fighting, defecating – creating the landscape, flora, fauna, weather and people as they are today, during the time of what Warlpiri call *Jukurrpa* or The Dreaming.

As Nancy Munn (1971) has argued, *kuruwarri* carries with it a notion of 'imprint'. The defining characteristics of country are understood to be products of Ancestral imprintation, what Munn has described as a 'transformation' of Ancestral bodily 'subjective' experiences into the fixed 'objective' features of the landscape. These so-called sites of Ancestral bodily 'transformation' are usually marked by name – the constellation of the verbal and the visual here as elsewhere create a fixed experiential realm for day-to-day inhabiting. These sites also hold precise affiliations and identifications, as well as powerful and potentially dangerous forces. Even if disengaged from the body of the Ancestor, these forms, features, marks, places continue to retain Ancestral presence. Hence the constitutive force, power and effects associated with the putting of *kuruwarri* by *Yapa*[4] include rejuvenating the country or a species; controlling fertility; regulating social relations and relatedness; causing illness and healing.

But *kuruwarri* also means 'birthmark, freckle' – a much overlooked aspect of the meaning of these marks. The emphasis on country, the concomitant interpretation of acrylic paintings as 'maps of country', has resulted in an understanding of that as the only possible referent, the over-determined signified, of *kuruwarri* signs being the literal cartographic country itself. This results, no doubt, from the protracted and equally over-determined history of Warlpiri–European relations, that is, the result of ongoing struggles over land rights, royalty negotiations, Native Title.[5] And it is not insignificant that acrylic paintings have been used as evidence in land hearings. Central Desert women regularly performed *yawulyu* at early hearings to great effect, orchestrating the way in which the Land Rights Acts were interpreted (to have maternally-linked kin included in notions of primary 'owner'), as Hamilton (forthcoming) has argued.

What gets overlooked in this context, however (and what compels my argument here), is that *kuruwarri* are embodied traces and imprints. Indeed, they provide a necessary material intercorporeal means for linking Ancestral bodies to *Yapa* bodies in crucial ways. It is not only in the country itself that Ancestral presence resides, but these presences (located in certain sites and affiliated with certain species) can enter women's wombs, cause conception and, in turn, leave birthmarks, freckles and other identifying traits of specific kinds of subjectivity upon individuated Warlpiri (see Meggitt 1962: 270–80). Hence the term *kuruwarri* also refers to corporeal imprintation. The fleshly traces of birthmarks and freckles are indicative of how 'skin' is literally, materially, the same 'substance' as country in that it is equally a medium in which Ancestral traces reside.

While I draw here on the work of Munn (1971, 1986), my account differs substantially from hers. I maintain that it is not only Ancestors who transform into country but, indeed, that *Yapa* themselves, in occupying a literally analogous relation to and with Ancestors, also 'become' country, species, place, in and through 'skin'. Munn opposes 'subject' and 'object'; but such oppositional logic is itself challenged by the haptic and phenomenological productivities of 'skin'. In so far as it is possible to speak of an objectified 'landscape' or 'country', I want to suggest that this materiality is the result of the productive, performative, pedagogic repetitions made by and through contemporary bodies; work which I locate here as dependent necessarily upon the 'skin' of women.

In other words, it is not what *kuruwarri* signs mean that I am interested in here. Munn's greatest influence has been in contributing to the dominant interpretative framework for these signs as 'iconography'. 'Iconographic' keys now accompany the majority of acrylic paintings as they make their way from Desert communities to the galleries of London, Paris and New York – a direct result of Munn's first major study in this area *Walbiri Iconography* (1986). But this kind of 'iconographic' deduction is illusory. While Warlpiri claim the country speaks, it does so only to those who are authorized by complex kinship, gender, age and other social restrictions, what Eric Michaels (1985) describes as differentiations between the 'right to speak, the right to know, and the right to hear'. Elsewhere I have identified this restricted economy as a great 'coup' of Central and Western Desert paintings – they purport to a meaning which cannot ultimately be possessed – as precisely what makes them desirable to a European audience seeking an indisputable 'Aboriginal' authenticity (Biddle 1991).

Rather than yet another analysis of what these signs mean, I want to explore what has not been explored to date, that is, *how* these inscriptions are made. What do they make, what work do they perform, in the ways they are put and re-put?[6] What does this tell us about 'skin' and its productive capacities in the Warlpiri context? How may this kind of analysis work to rethink our conceptualizations of 'skin', of culture, of the potentialities of the so-called 'human body'?

How is *kuruwarri* inscribed?

The body is not a 'natural' surface (nor is the ground a 'natural' text)

It is of no small significance that the supposed 'surface' or 'background' to be inscribed in the case of *kuruwarri* inscription onto body or canvas never simply proceeds, despite the fact that, at least as 'our' logic would have it, the skin of the body, the surface of the canvas, already exist as potential 'surfaces'. But for *Yapa*, a prior act of producing a 'surface' – and a very particular kind of 'surface' – is first enacted.

In *yawulyu* (women's ceremonial Dreaming ritual) the breasts and upper shoulders are first rubbed, coated with oil (emu fat if it is available, or more likely, cooking oil, baby oil or butter). The skin 'surface' is covered, coated in its entirety, by hands dipped in oil, once, twice and again, prior to any application of ochre designs.

Plate 10.1 *Kirda* and *Kurdungurlu* prepared for *Purlapa-Wiri Yawulyu*, Circular Quay, Sydney, September 1997
Picture, from left, *Kirda* (with *Ngapa Jukurrpa*): Jennifer Nampijinpa Biddle, Topsy Nangala Ross and *Kurdungurlu* (with *Ngatijirri Jukurrpa*): Judy Napaljarri Walker. Other *Kirda* present at this performance (not pictured): Rosie Napurrurla Tasman, Molly Napurrurla Tasman, Kumanjayi Nampijinpa Patrick and Joanne Nangala Wesley. Other *Kurdungurlu* present at this performance (not pictured): Alice Napaljarri Kelly, Lily Nungarrayi Hargraves, Kajingarra Napangardi Granites and Myra Nungarrayi Patrick.

A certain erasure of any previous inscription(s) thus necessarily occurs in the creation of this inscribable surface. Nancy Munn describes the smoothing and clearing of the ground between 'scenes' in the narratives of women's secular sand stories as 'erasure' (1986: 69). That is, the creation of one surface – its rendering as a markable surface – means to do away with, to erase, another. Each and every act of inscription proceeds, as it were, from scratch. The activities of Ancestors who initially roamed an unmarked, unmade landscape are here literally recreated by the conditions of contemporary inscription. *Jukurrpa* – the Dreaming – is not something that happened once and for all in some absolute past but is repeated, recreated, re-made continuously, indeed, one could argue that the condition of *Jukurrpa* – its constitutive repeatable form – is in fact structured by, to borrow Derrida's (1990) framework, iterability. That is, signification is already inherently multiple: repeated, necessarily repeatable. Despite the insistence on the immutable, timeless nature of *Jukurrpa* (the Dreaming, the Law), the imperative to repeat these inscriptions by *Yapa* must, arguably, be compelled by what is an instability ultimately in the constitutive terms of the Law. As Judith Butler has argued in relation to gender (1993) and homophobia (1997), the repetitious nature of the discourses on these subjects reveal, contrary to expectation, the very fragile nature of their constitutions. Why else the necessity to repeat if not to combat instability?

Canvas for acrylic painting is likewise rendered, worked over, prior to inscription by coating the surface of the canvas in its entirety. Brown is the preferred colour for this blanketing background when available, but the stock at the local shop, individual preferences and, more recently, the community-based artists association Warnayaka Arts Centre all allow for orange, blue, green and red figuring. Annette Hamilton (forthcoming: 8) argues that this preference for brown is modeled on 'skin' colour. And/or it may derive from an association with the 'ground'. The term for brown in Warlpiri is *walya walya*, a duplicated form of the term *walya* meaning 'ground'. As I argue here, however, a clear distinction between the two, ground and skin, is not ultimately sustainable, precisely because the two are rendered commensurate in and through and by inscription.

'Ground' itself is similarly treated. Prior to ceremonies, not only are stones and sticks which may hurt the feet carefully removed but the site is brushed, raked, smoothed over, bulldozed even, if the event is a large one – gestures that simultaneously erase and renew. Warlpiri use a particular word for this process: *maparni*. The *Warlpiri Dictionary* (*Verbs*: 24) defines *maparni* thus: 'to anoint [with oil (JARA)], paint, grease (with fat/oil), smear, rub on, rub with'. The notion that *maparni* means 'to anoint' seems particularly apt in the case of *kuruwarri* inscription, in so far as it implies a sacred or religious act which transforms the profane into the sacred. And it is precisely this kind of transformation that is achieved in and through *maparni*; through anointing, a simultaneous erasure and renewal of a site is rendered receptive to the inscription of *kuruwarri*.

The imprintation: inscription proceeds in not on a surface

Not unlike the pencil or pen (but unlike the computer screen I now work on), Warlpiri styluses literally drag the mark behind them, the way a finger or stick is dragged through the dirt and leaves a trace in its wake. There is a friction between stylus and surface. Something happens *between* implement and surface.

In *yawulyu*, a flattened stick bound at one end with cotton thread, knitting wool or hair-string is used to apply ochre to skin. The stick (*watiya*) is literally dragged through the oil. So too in *kuruwarri* application to canvas, the paint mark follows behind the movement of the finger or paintbrush.[7] In other words, the *kuruwarri* sign is understood not only as an imprintational trace, but it is literally produced as one. These are not so much visual or aesthetic signs as they are literal marks. And I think here of Derrida's (1976, 1990) and now others' (Boone and Mignolo 1994) emphasis on the gramme, the graph, the glyph, the appreciation of writing *as inscription* – an appreciation that allows me to focus on writing as a material phenomenology. Writing not as representation, not as that which refers, defers, to speech, sound or word, but rather as a force itself with effects: an inscription that inscribes, an imprintation that produces, marks that make. The very attention Warlpiri give to surface suggests a profound sensitivity to the conditions of the productivity of writing in its properly semiotic sense. A debt to the difference between 'background' and 'mark', between ground and stick, between oil and ochre, between absence and presence – these are differences necessary for writing; these are the differences necessary for the constitution of meaning itself. This very debt to difference, this debt to and detour via something else for the production of meaning, is precisely what is occluded in Western metaphysics generally and in notions of writing particularly, according to Derrida (1976, 1985 and 1990); a debt Warlpiri, in contrast, appear actively to acknowledge.

The shimmering: between one thing and another

This sense of *kuruwarri* as material imprintation is further evinced in how the *kuruwarri* are themselves inscribed prior to any other marking. *Kuruwarri* signs are put and re-put. The thick indelible lines – half circle, line, shape – will be painted and re-painted. Ochre will be dragged and re-dragged on breast; paint will be applied, thick and dark on canvas, once, twice, again.

This reiteration, this tracing and retracing, will literally continue in the ensuing 'outlining' of the *kuruwarri*. For the design structure – if one can call it that – in both *yawulyu* and much acrylic painting practice takes the form of tracing the *kuruwarri*. In *yawulyu*, this takes place through contrasting colours of ochre being traced in lines around the original *kuruwarri*, twice, maybe three, four times.

The impression is almost that *kuruwarri* are the spaces left over from tracing. For in *yawulyu*, the red ochre of the *kuruwarri* mixes with oiled colour of the skin such that what one 'sees' is not the *kuruwarri* so much as the white ochre traces. This effect is particularly evident when *yawulyu* is inscribed on non-*Yapa* skin, on White skin, where the opposite effect occurs; where what one 'sees' instead is precisely the ochre *kuruwarri*, as evinced in the photograph of *Purlapa Wiri Yawulyu*. The very shape of the *kuruwarri* on *Yapa* skin, however, its apprehension as a figure, is manifest only in, through and by the trace that surrounds it. Literally analogous to the signs of Ancestral presence in the landscape, the trace is the determinative; indeed, it is the only form through which such manifestations of presence are 'seen'.

Canvas production follows a similar pattern. Again, white is consistently used for the initial outlining here.[8] Rather than a notion of these additional lines and/ or dots as 'semantically empty' fillers, as Michaels describes their function (1994: 156) , or as an aesthetic background 'to make it look nice', as Senn suggests (1991: 124), I argue that these lines and dots represent a crucial reiteration of the *kuruwarri*. Important constitutive effects are produced through this reiteration.

What is evinced here, it seems to me, is the 'staging of an appearance-as-disappearance', to borrow a phrase from Roland Barthes (1975: 10). For what is most crucial – the virtual signs of Ancestral presence – disappear as they appear only in repetition. At a crude level, this seems to me to augment the very way in which country itself is only known in and through the repetitions – the marks, rituals, songs, stories – that *Yapa* tell of it, rendering a landscape, a place as known through such cultural 'tellings'. As de Certeau (1988) and Casey (1996) argue, there is no landscape, no known sense of place, no existential lived environment which is not narrativized, which is not organized, arranged, made meaningful by such cultural discourses.

But this 'appearance-as-disappearance' manifests in terms more compelling yet. For there is an imperative in this movement, in this vacillating, oscillating, at once appearing and disappearing *kuruwarri*. This doubling 3-D effect, this vibrancy, this tremulousness of the text, is perhaps the most remarked upon characteristic of Central Desert Painting. The seemingly 'alive' nature of the canvases, the sense of movement, of animation, the mesmerizing quality of the work, creates, as Barbara Glowczewski has put it, 'a movement which . . . invites us to penetrate the texture of the canvas' (1991: 120). This effect is, I would like to argue, the point of the workings discussed above. For the efficacy of *kuruwarri* marks depends precisely upon this ebullient potentiality, a simultaneous animating of body and country. Warlpiri call this vibrancy, this 3-D effect, 'shimmering', according to Dussart (1997). 'Shimmering', in her account, helps both to clarify the design and ensure its spiritual potency (Dussart 1997: 192). It is important to stress that this potency is not simply available in these *kuruwarri* signs themselves (as has been previously interpreted); they must be rendered in precise ways to become efficacious, to become performative, in and through the kind of work I've described here. The 'latent law' of *Jukurrpa*, of The Dreaming, as Michael Jackson has put it (1998: 132), must be 'reanimated' to be effective.

Barbara Glowczewski claims that in *yawulyu*, the aim is to outline the design until the background becomes saturated, so that the *kuruwarri*, the Ancestral force, enters the body and 'feeds' the woman. The rhythmic, repetitious marking and re-marking literally press the *kuruwarri* mark in. One could also here speak of the pressing, penetrative, putting-on of the repetitious 'dots' in acrylic painting as enacting a similar effect. In *yawulyu*, what was previously outside is brought inside, traced round the breasts, up around the collarbone and shoulder blades, down the breast again. But equally, what is 'inside' is brought 'out'. Penetration effects emergence – the movement is bi-directional – and it is this that creates the quivering, the shimmering, the nervous liveliness of texture.

What specifically is repeated is the movement from what Warlpiri call *kanunju* (what is secret, 'underneath' or 'below' – where Ancestors now reside having once emerged to walk the landscape and where, in most cases, they have returned to rest) to *kankarlu* (what is in the world as it is seen and known 'above' and in the 'public' domain). In and through the performance of a given *yawulyu*, Ancestral presence manifests itself: it is brought *kankarlu*, above and into the present.

In short, a certain embodied expression of Ancestral presence is effected: one 'becomes' ancestor, 'becomes' country. I prefer the term 'becoming' here to Munn's notion of 'transformation', because the latter assumes an already distinct-ive mode of existence whereas in fact, one's constitutive being is always already attenuated in distinctive ways to what is understood as 'sentient', as Stanner (1965) describes the human-like qualities that country, flora, fauna express. That is, the rendering of the body commensurate with country is not a one-way pro-cess. For the aim of *yawulyu* is, after all, the care of country – as part of a larger series of what have been described as generalized 'increase' ceremonies (Dussart 1988, Peterson 1970)[9] in which the livening-up of country – rejuvenating, revital-ising, 'feeding' certain places, species and persons accordingly – occurs. This rejuvenating potential of ceremony is perhaps particularly crucial in a context where country is no longer literally inhabited; where acrylic painting, *yawulyu* and/or other ritual performances constitute the only kind of 'care'. Re-creation of country in the contemporary context includes an essential pedagogic function: the teaching about country which is no longer inhabited to children who have no other access to country outside these manifest presentations of it (see, for example, Warlukurlangu Artists: 1987).

I do not mean to suggest that this rendering of the body commensurate with country is limited to ceremonial or explicit inscriptive contexts. A more general mutual and reciprocally defining set of relations typifies the contemporary habi-tus. As Franca Tamisari (1998) has argued for Yolgnu, a day-to-day 'following in the footprints of the Ancestors' provides the model for how the lived-world is habitually occupied. Naomi Smith (1997) has argued a similar case for Wik. A certain haptic sensibility works to align certain contemporary Aboriginal bodies akin with that of Ancestors. One does not, for instance, 'tell' a *Jukurrpa*, a Dream-ing narrative, in Warlpiri. The verb form is *yimi-purrami*, 'to follow', implying that the speaker is not so much 'telling' but literally 'following' an already established account. *Yapa* travel the same regions, camp in the same places, perform, where they can, the same activities as Ancestors themselves.

We might think of this in terms of *Yapa* living an already intercorporeal, an already syncretic, open relationship to and with Ancestral bodies in their varying manifestations. If there is no body as such, as Diprose (1998, 1994), Weiss (1999) and Grosz (1994) argue, but only ways of being bodily in culturally and situationally specific terms, then 'becoming' country becomes thinkable in a very literal sense.[10] If *Yapa* 'become in relation to country' (and I think here of both senses of 'becoming', as 'coming into being' and as 'suit, befit'), it is because their own bodies are not produced as bounded, bordered, discrete. If one can speak, in Merleau-Ponty's terms (1964), of a cultural 'corporeal schema' – what Diprose defines as a 'set of habits, gestures and conducts formed over time in relation to other bodies' (1994: 105) – one would have to argue that for *Yapa*, this schema is formed, necessarily, in relation to Ancestral bodies. What makes up, what makes for, the potentiality of such a corporeality imbibes, embraces, opens out to, and equally introjects Ancestral habits, sentiments, sensibilities. The surface of the body, somatically rendered the same as the surface of the country, allows for this intercorporeal exchange, this inter-changeability by making the two *almost* identical. And I stress the almost here, for the one is never completely reducible to the other. There can be reciprocity – exchange *between* Ancestor and *Yapa* – because there is alterity – someone *else* to exchange with. What lies between the two – 'skin' – is not so much a border as a certain bridging potentiality. This intercorporeality makes for what *Yapa* describe when witnessing a particularly good *yawulyu*: they don't say, for example, that Napurrurla is performing or enacting a particularly convincing *Ngurlu* or *Kurlukuku Jukurrpa* (Mulga Seed and/or Diamond Dove Dreaming) – as we might speak of an actor's successful 'portrayal' or 'depiction' – but indeed, *Yapa* say that she really is 'that one now, that *kurlukuku*, that Diamond Dove'.

A different 'epidermal schema'?

There is a final, further sense in which 'skin' in the Warlpiri context operates to augment a radically variant bodily potentiality, at least in principle, and which brings me back to where this chapter began. I want to ask: To what extent does this ideal of 'the human body' allow for variation and in what terms? For Warlpiri possess what are called in English (for there is no single generic Warlpiri term for this classificatory system) 'skin'. 'Skins' are what anthropologists might describe as classificatory socio-centric names which indicate corporate membership in patrilineal moiety-based subsections. To translate: 'skins' identify specific kinds of relatedness to others.[11] They provide a crucial abbreviated and stable form for the expression of complex kinship-based 'ownership' and 'management' of country, Dreaming, ceremony and design. They are the form through which 'ownership' and 'relatedness' are established in Land Rights hearings; the form in which 'ownership' of country and Dreaming 'design' is given in the (translated) 'stories' that accompany acrylic paintings; they are the form in which Warlpiri distinctiveness is described more generally to non-Warlpiri outsiders (as, for example, in Ross 1987). Ancestors possess the same 'skins' as *Yapa*. 'Skins' now form part of the 'proper' name of *Yapa*, as in the artists Clifford Possum *Tjapaltjarri*, Michael *Jagamara* Nelson, Lorna *Napurrurla* Fencer.

As I have discussed elsewhere at length (Biddle: 2000), there is something crucial, constitutive even, in this differentiating and thus identifying inclusion of the 'skin' in the otherwise European-identified 'proper' name. The inclusion of 'skin' produces a mark differentiating Aboriginal identity from non-Aboriginal. That is, 'skins' serve not only culturally internal identificatory purposes, but external purposes as well. Indeed, the two purposes conjoin: 'skin' literally fits the terms of both. For the adoption of 'skins' by Warlpiri occurred during the very period when Warlpiri first came into contact with Europeans, around 1930, according to Meggitt (1962: 165–8), who argues that 'skins' were readily adopted by *Yapa* because they coincided with traditional kinship structures and forms. But they were also adopted, I'd like to suggest, at a time when in fact 'skin' itself was for the first time 'seen', by both outsiders and *Yapa* in turn, to be the operative marker of difference. It was precisely on the basis of 'skin' – that is, on racially identified terms of difference – that colonization was enacted. The systematic techniques of displacement, removal, surveillance and subjugation perpetrated upon the bodies of *Yapa* were enacted through the evaluative and differentiating terms of 'skin'. Warlpiri 'skin' terms conjoin, repeat and become again in relation to colonial expectations.

What I wonder is this: Is the insistence upon figuring identity in terms of an epidermiologically identified schema – 'skin' – not driven by a context thoroughly saturated already with 'skin', a context structured by the supposedly immutable differences of race, and its embodied colonial practices of racism? Linda Alcoff (1999) has recently argued that race itself needs to be understood phenomenologically. 'Race' posits affectively oriented, affectively generative, differences between bodies. 'Racialized' experiences and expressions (even if discursively constituted, even if culturally constructed) produce certain corporeal gestalts – perceptual, somatic, existential. That is, 'race' may be experienced as natural, located as it is in bodily experiences and expression, as Iris Young's (1990a) work suggests. In short, if 'race' in its bodily location of difference has been and continues to be a predominant colonial and post-colonial marker and maker of differences, and in turn, identities, then is it so surprising that the very same site of such difference – 'skin' itself – should be so critically repositioned by *Yapa* in the contemporary context?

The existential reality of those who have been subject to the effects of such differential bodily regimes demonstrates the lived consequences of colonial classifications. In this sense, Warlpiri have been particularly 'good' colonial subjects. For their world is ontologically bifurcated by the effects of this 'epidermal schema', mimicking as it does the very apartheid-like conditions and structures of not only remote communities but the greater conditions of post-colonial Australia – where class, education, income, deaths in custody, the Stolen Generation, Mabo are now some of the salient discursive markers of this same lived legacy. It seems that not all bodies are equal after all. At the local level, these differential understandings of bodily experience, expectation and intention are the requisite terms of trade. What is *Yapa-kurlangu* – what belongs to 'us mob' Warlpiri, to Blackfellas, insiders, human beings, as opposed to what is *Kardiya-kurlangu* – belonging to outsiders, to Whitefellas, non-human even – extends indefinitely. Rigorous and exacting appreciations of food, fashion, housing, cars, emotions, sexual conduct, illnesses, ways of playing football, making and drinking tea – there is nothing experientially, no way of doing or being, which does not belong to one category or the other. The terms of lived existence are expressed in terms of black and white.

It seems to me that there is a critically productive repetition at work in the kinds of insistence upon a skin-based, skin-figured identity that *Yapa* currently evoke, in the sense Homi K. Bhabha (1994) has suggested. What is revealed in this repetitious insistence upon 'skin' is the 'narcissistic' and 'paranoid' terms of the colonizers who, in attempting to create mimetically similar subjects in and through colonial reform, nevertheless ensure that difference remains between themselves and the colonized. Bhabha writes of the only ever 'partially' reformed, 'partially' resembling colonized subjects who simultaneously mime and menace the colonial desire for a reformed colonized subject who is 'almost the same but not quite' (1994: 86), or rather, 'almost the same but not white' (1994: 89). In this sense, the mirror Warlpiri hold up is by no means cloudy. What is revealed is the categorical terms of White Australia's colonial offering: so-called common 'humanity' is refused.

But what is equally revealed in and through this insistent repetition are the problems inherent in the more recent attempt to rectify the colonial past. I refer here to the callings for certain liberal rights-based models of subjectivity and sovereignty – ones increasingly utilized in arguments for recognition of Native and Indigenous Land Rights here in Australia (see Pritchard 1998), as the United Nations recent reprimand of Australia for its treatment of Aborigines indicates (see 'Rough Justice at UN Hearing on Native Title', *Sydney Morning Herald* 19 March 1999: 15). This model, in its call for international 'human rights' for Aborigines, may, in another sense, do away again with what it was, what it is, that Warlpiri ask for. Von Sturmer figures this simply: what 'blackfellas say ... [is] "recognise us, recognise us" (1995: 101). And it is precisely this recognition that has been, that continues to be, refused. Aboriginal 'forms of being', von Sturmer claims (1995: 102) are disallowed. For it is not the extension of 'humanity' or 'human rights' as 'human beings' that is being asked for here. Warlpiri 'skin' terms instead insist that 'we' are not 'all human'; 'we' are not all 'just people'. The proffering of so-called 'humanity' – a self-same equality – may efface the very difference(s) upon which Warlpiri identity rests.

For *Yapa* bodies, it seems to me, challenge even the more radical refigurings of the so-called 'human body', such as Merleau-Ponty's, given their potentiality to materially embrace not only other bodies but so-called 'things' – flora, fauna, country itself – in their constitutive 'becomings'. Moreover, not just anybody can 'become' just any kind or part of the country. That is, there may in fact be more than one cultural 'corporeal schema' operating for *Yapa*. Only already differentiated bodies – bodies differentiated by subsection or 'skin' and, in turn, authorized through the proper accumulation of experience, knowledge and ritual – can 'become' already differentiated country. In other words, there may be more like sixteen (the number of gendered subsections or 'skins') differing corporeal schemas operating, which radically refigures even the kinds of critiques of a singular cultural corporal schema that have been made on the basis of gender

(Diprose 1998; 1994; Grosz 1994; Young 1990b; Weiss 1999) and 'race' (Weiss 1999; Young 1990a). In short, the insistence, the demand *Yapa* currently make,[12] is for the recognition of a difference that is not simply 'skin deep'.

Notes

1 I would like to thank the Carlyle Greenwell Bequest of the Department of Anthropology, University of Sydney; the Australian Institute for Aboriginal and Torres Strait Island Studies (AIATSIS); and Macquarie University for grants supporting this research. Jane Sloan and Jack Marshall offered important editorial advice. I also need to thank my *Yapa* family and friends for their tireless and inspired teachings. I hope they can continue to countenance the grandiose nature of my interpretations. The ideas expressed in this paper are my own.

2 My formulation here is close to that of Judith Butler (1993: 2), who writes of discourse which 'produces the effects that it names'. I am indebted to Butler for her stressing the often overlooked, and crucial, aspect of Derrida's (1982, 1990) re-conceptualization of the sign – what he might call *différance*, – that is, the constitutive, material effects of signification itself.

3 Unfortunately in a chapter of this length, I cannot discuss the complex and crucial issues of sexual difference(s) in *kuruwarri* form and content. See Munn (1973), Bell (1981), Dussart (1988, 1997) and Watson (1997) for further discussion.

4 I use the term *Yapa* here, for it is the term Warlpiri use to refer to themselves. *Yapa* means Warlpiri, Aborigines, insiders, Blackfella, human beings. It is often contrasted with, defined by, its other, *Kardiya*, that is, non-Warlpiri, non-Aboriginal, outsiders, Whitefella, and perhaps non-human. These terms, as I discuss in conclusion, refer to far more than merely categories of person.

5 For readers who are not familiar with the current Australian legislation regarding indigenous Australian land rights: in 1992, an historic judgment was passed down by the High Court, now refered to simply by the last name of original claimant, 'Mabo', in which the hitherto legislative state of Australia as *Terra Nullius*, that is, legally un-owned by any other group (and hence, claimable and claimed as Crown property) was overruled. Aboriginal, or 'native title', was thus introduced into the Australian legal system, instigating the rights of Aboriginal peoples to make claims of entitlement, based on an acknowledgment of their prior occupancy. A further High Court decision in 1999, 'Wik', which held that pastoral leases do not extinguish native title, enlarged the areas in which claims could be made. However, the resultant uncertainty, and the administrative complexities which have resulted from the implementation of native title, have created a conundrum of legal and political problems which in no way ensure land-entitlement for the majority of Aboriginal peoples.

6 For the purpose of this chapter, I am limiting my discussion to women's *kuruwarri* production, focusing on a comparison between women's *yawulyu* inscriptions and acrylic paintings (see the paintings by Lajamanu men in Ryan (1989), however, for many formal similarities). More specifically yet, I focus here on a marked tendency in the *yawulyu* 'styles' and in turn, acrylic painting 'styles' practised in Lajamanu in the early 1990s (1989–1992 specifically), a tendency which, while still predominant in the majority of paintings from this region, also now shows some variations, with the works of Lorna Napurrurla Fencer and Gloria and Kathleen Petyarre, for example, influenced perhaps by the most famous of all painters from the Central Desert, that old lady Kngwarreye from Utopia (who passed away last year, and hence, whose name is now taboo), who arguably, first, formally and consistently, did away with this *kuruwarri*/outline empatternment altogether.

7 Unlike in European painting practices where the paintbrush might, for example, 'wash' a background with watercolour paint on paper or 'dab' paint onto canvas, the putting

of *kuruwarri* marks is distinguished by this kind of dragging, tracing movement. This technique is particularly marked in its difference from the 'dotting' techniques which 'puts' dot after dot on the canvas (with the end of a wooden skewer or match) following the outline the *kuruwarri* provides in the traditions I describe here.

8 This use of white, and the use of dots, may represent a certain standardization in form that has developed since the inception of acrylic painting in Lajamanu. While it is hard to generalize, a large number of canvases now follow this formula where dotting follows, as tracing the shape of the *kuruwarri* (at least initially) out to edges of canvas (cf. paintings in Brody 1984, Ryan 1989, Sutton 1989 and HALT 1991). This 'standardiza-tion' may represent a movement towards stabilizing a certain code or 'script', resultant from certain associations between writing and painting, arguments I have pursued at length elsewhere (Biddle 1996).

9 As Bell (1981) discusses, women's ceremonies were historically misrepresented by eth-nographers influenced by gender conceptualizations of their era. *Yawulyu* was relegated to the 'profane' and not considered to be of the same status as the 'sacred' nature of men's ceremonies. These problematic conceptualizations have been more recently reshaped by feminist ethnographers, who find that *yawulyu*, like men's 'increase' cere-monies, celebrates specifically female-identified characters and activities in the Dream-ing, in site-specific terms. See Bell (1981, 1983), Hamilton (1986, forthcoming) and Dussart (1988, 1997) for further discussion.

10 According to Merleau-Ponty (1962, 1964), corporeality is not a private individual experience or expression, nor is it determined by the muscular skeletal conceptions that physiology and biology afford us. Rather, bodily potentiality derives from a literal sharing in the bodies of others – what Gail Weiss (1999) calls corporeality as 'intercor-poreality'. In this modelling, we literally inhabit the bodies of others through activities, intentions, habits which are shared reciprocally and mutually dispersed among seem-ingly disparate bodies with a given culture. This arises from an irresolution ultimately of a primary syncreticism between the body of the infant and its mother's, where one system, one shared bodily schema, initially constitutes the infant's mode of experience. We learn of the world through initially enacting other's intentions, intentions which become our own, only of course, never quite, for we remain indebted to and dependent upon the bodies of others to mutually mirror and reciprocally define our own sense of identity throughout life. A bodily openness and inter-changeability with others typifies what Diprose (1998) calls the 'ambiguity of existence' because self-identity remains other-defined; it is not achieved in some once-and-for-all final state, but is refigured, redefined, even undone, by and through continuous intercorporeal exchanges with others around us.

11 Crucially, 'skin' classifies according to what Warlpiri call *kirda*, or 'owners', as opposed to *kurdungurlu*, or 'managers'. Such distinctions are also now used to describe the regula-tion of marriage 'choices', participatory rights in ceremonies, and other crucial cultural issues. See Nash (1982), Laughren (1982) and Meggitt (1962) for further discussion of the *kirda/kurdungurlu* distinction and other aspects of Warlpiri kinship.

12 *Yawulyu* is currently performed far more often than it ever was in the past, as the women themselves acknowledge. Contrary to expectation, this is not a healthy sign. Aboriginal ceremonies are in fact performed when there is a need to establish cohesion, to rectify certain social relations, when something is amiss. This is also the point of my argument here: something is amiss.

References

Alcoff, L. M. (1999) 'Towards a Phenomenology of Racial Embodiment', *Radical Philosophy* 95: 15–26.

Anderson, C. and Dussart, F. (1989) 'Dreamings in Acrylic: Western Desert Art', in

P. Sutton (ed.) *Dreamings: The Art of Aboriginal Australia*, South Yarra: Viking in association with the Asia Societies Gallery.

Barthes, R. (1975) *The Pleasure of the Text*, trans. R. Miller, New York: Hill and Wang.

Bell, D. (1981) 'Women's Business is Hard Work: Central Australian Aboriginal Women's Love Ritual', *Signs* 7, 2: 314–37.

—— (1983) *Daughters of the Dreaming*, Melbourne: McPhee Gribble.

Bhabha, H. K. (1994) *The Location of Culture*, London and New York: Routledge.

Biddle, J. (1991) 'Dot, Circle, Difference: Translating Central Desert Paintings', in R. Diprose and R. Ferrell (eds) *Cartographies: Poststructualism and the Mapping of Bodies and Spaces*, North Sydney: Allen and Unwin.

—— (1993) 'The Anthropologist's Body or What it Means to Break Your Neck in the Field', *The Australian Journal of Anthropology* 4, 3: 184–97.

—— (1996) 'When Not Writing is Writing', *Australian Aboriginal Studies* 1: 21–33.

—— (1997) 'Shame', *Australian Feminist Studies* 12, 26: 227–40.

—— (2000) 'Writing without Ink: Literacy, Methodology and Cultural Difference' in A. Lee and C. Poynton (eds) *Culture and Text*, Sydney: Allen and Unwin.

Brain, R. (1978) *The Decorated Body*, New York: Harper and Row.

Boone, E. H. and Mignolo, W. D. (eds) (1994) *Writing without Words: Alternative Literacies in Mesoamerica and the Andes*, Durham, NJ and London: Duke University Press.

Brody, A. (1984) *The Face of the Centre: Papunya Tula Paintings 1971–1984*, Melbourne: National Gallery of Victoria.

Butler, J. (1990) *Gender Trouble: Feminism and the Subversion of Identity*, New York: Routledge.

—— (1993) *Bodies That Matter: On the Discursive Limits of 'Sex'*, New York and London: Routledge.

—— (1997) *The Psychic Life of Power: Theories in Subjection*, Stanford: Stanford University Press.

Casey, E. S. (1996) 'How to Get from Space to Place in a Fairly Short Stretch of Time: Phenomenological Prolegomena', in S. Feld and K. Basso (eds.) *Sense of Place*, Santa Fe: School of American Research Press.

De Certeau, M. (1988) *The Practice of Everyday Life*, trans. S. Rendall, Berkeley: University of California Press.

Derrida, J. (1976) *Of Grammatology*, trans. G. C. Spivak, Baltimore: Johns Hopkins University Press.

—— (1982) 'Différance' in *Margins of Philosophy*, trans. A. Bass, Chicago: University of Chicago Press.

—— (1985) 'Roundtable on Translation' in C. V. McDonald, (ed.), *The Ear of the Other: Otobiography, Transference, Translation*, trans. P. Kamuf, New York: Schocken Books.

—— (1990) *Limited Inc.*, trans. S. Weber and J. Mehlman, Evanston, IL: Northwestern University Press.

Diprose, R. (1994) *The Bodies of Women: Ethics, Embodiment and Sexual Difference*, London and New York: Routledge.

—— (1998) 'Generosity: Between Love and Desire', *Hypatia* 13, 1: 1–23.

Dussart, F. (1988) 'Warlpiri Women's Yawulyu Ceremonies: A Forum for Socialisation and Innovation', unpublished Ph.D. Thesis, Department of Anthropology, Australian National University.

—— (1997) 'A Body Painting in Translation' in M. Banks and H. Morphy, (eds) *Rethinking Visual Anthropology*, New Haven and London: Yale University Press.

Ebin, V. (1978) *The Body Decorated*, London: Thames and Hudson.

Errington, S. (1994) 'What Became Authentic Primitive Art?', *Cultural Anthropology* 9, 2: 201–26.

Falk, P. (1995) 'Written in the Flesh', *Body and Society* 1, 1: 95–105.

Fanon, F. (1967) *Black Skins, White Mask*, trans. C. L. Markmann, New York: Grove Press.

Gatens, M. (1991) *Feminism and Philosophy: Perspectives on Difference and Equality*, Cambridge: Polity Press.

Glowczewski, B. (1991) 'Between Two Images' in *Yapa: Peintres Aborigenes de Balgo et Lajamanu*, Paris: Baudoin lebon éditeur.

Groning, C. (1997) *Decorated Skin*, London: Thames and Hudson.

Grosz, E. (1994) *Volatile Bodies: Toward a Corporeal Feminism*, Bloomington: Indiana University Press.

HALT (Healthy Aboriginal Life Team) (1991) *Anangu Way*, Alice Springs: Ngananpa Health Clinic.

Hamilton, A. (1986) 'Daughters of the Imaginary', *Canberra Anthropology* 9, 2: 1–25.

—— (forthcoming) 'Gender, Aesthetics, Performance' in S. Kleinert and M. Neale (eds) *Oxford Companion to Aboriginal Art and Culture*, Melbourne: Oxford University Press.

Jackson, M. (1998) *Minima Ethnographica: Intersubjectivity and the Anthropological Project*, Chicago and London: The University of Chicago Press.

Laughren, M. (1982) 'Warlpiri Kinship Structure' in J. Heath, F. Merlan and A. Rumsey (eds) *Languages of Kinship in Aboriginal Australia*, Oceania Linguistic Monographs, No. 24, Sydney: University of Sydney.

Lingis, A. (1978) 'Savages', *Semiotexte* 3, 2: 96–112.

—— (1983) *Excesses: Eros and Culture*, Albany: State University of New York Press.

Mascia-Lees, F. and Sharpe, P. (1992) 'The Marked and the Un(re)Marked: Tattoo and Gender in Theory and Narrative' in F. Mascia-Lees and P. Sharpe (eds) *Tattoo, Torture, Mutiliation, and Adornment: The Denaturalization of the Body in Culture and Text*, New York: State University of New York Press.

Meggitt, M. J. (1962) *Desert People: A Study of the Walbiri Aborigines of Central Australia*, North Ryde: Angus and Robertson.

Merleau-Ponty, M. (1964) 'The Child's Relations with Others' in J. Edie (ed.) *The Primacy of Perception and Other Essays on Phenomenological Psychology, and Philosophy of Art, History and Politics*, Evanston, IL: Northwestern University Press.

—— (1989/1962) *Phenomenology of Perception*, trans. Colin Smith, London and New Jersey: Routledge and The Humanities Press.

Michaels, E. (1985) 'Constraints on Knowledge in an Economy of Oral Information', *Current Anthropology* 26: 505–10.

—— (1994) *Bad Aboriginal Art: Media, Tradition and Technological Horizons*, St. Leonards: Allen and Unwin.

Munn, N. D. (1971) 'The Transformation of Subjects into Objects in Walbiri and Pitjant-jatjara Myth' in R. M. Berndt (ed.) *Australian Aboriginal Anthropology*, Nedlands: University of Western Australia Press.

—— (1986/1973) *Walbiri Iconography: Graphic Representation and Cultural Symbolism in a Central Australian Society*, Chicago: The University of Chicago Press.

Nash, D. (1982) 'An Etymological Note on Warlpiri *Kurdungurlu*', in J. Heath, F. Merlan and A. Rumsey (eds) *Languages of Kinship in Aboriginal Australia*, Oceania Linguistic Monographs, No. 24, Sydney: University of Sydney.

Peterson, N. (1970) 'Buluwandi: A Central Australian Ceremony for the Resolution of Conflict' in R. M. Berndt (ed.) *Australian Aboriginal Anthropology*, Perth: University of Western Australia Press.

Pritchard, S. (1998) 'International Law Standards and their Relevance in Australia' in

G. Nettheim (ed.) *Native Title: Facts, Fallacies and the Future*, Sydney: University of New South Wales Press.

Ross, T. N. (1987) 'The People and their Home' in Warlukurlangu Artists *Kuruwarri: Yuendumu Doors*, Canberra: Australian Institute of Aboriginal Studies.

Ryan, J. (1989) *Mythscapes: Aboriginal Art of the Desert*, Melbourne: National Gallery of Victoria.

—— (1990) *Paint Up Big: Warlpiri Women's Art of Lajamanu*, Melbourne: National Gallery of Victoria.

Senn, C. (1991) 'Lajamanu Art', in B. Glowczewski *Yapa: Peintres Aborigènes de Balgo et Lajamanu*, Paris: Baudion lebon éditeur.

Smith, N. (1997) 'Body, Land and Performance of Identity in Wik Dance', unpublished Honours Thesis, Department of Anthropology, Macquarie University.

Stanner, W. E. H. (1984/1965) 'Religion, Totemism and Symbolism' in M. Charlesworth, H. Morphy, D. Bell and K. Maddock (eds) *Religion in Aboriginal Australia*, St. Lucia: University of Queensland Press.

Sutton, P. (ed.) (1989) *Dreamings: The Art of Aboriginal Australia*, South Yarra and New York: Viking in association with the Asia Societies Gallery.

Tamisari, F. (1998) 'Body, Vision, Movement: In the Footprints of the Ancestors', *Oceania* 68, 4: 249–70.

Torgovnick, M. (1990) *Gone Primitive: Savage Intellects, Modern Lives*, Chicago and London: The University of Chicago Press.

von Sturmer, J. (1987) 'Aboriginal Singing and Notions of Power' in M. Clunies Ross, T. Donaldson and S. Wild (eds) *Songs of Central Australia*, Oceania Monograph, 32, Sydney: University of Sydney.

—— (1995) '"R stands for . . . ": An Extract from a Mabo Diary', *The Australian Journal of Anthropology* 6, 1–2: 101–16.

Warlpiri Lexicography Group (1986) *Warlpiri–English Dictionaries*, Centre for Cognitive Science, Cambridge: Massachusetts Institute of Technology.

Warlukurlangu Artists (1987) *Kuruwarri: Yuendumu Doors*, Canberra: Australian Institute of Aboriginal Studies.

Watson, C. (1997) 'Re-embodying Sand Drawing and Re-evaluating the Status of the Camp: The Practice and Iconography of Women's Public Sand Drawing in Balgo, WA', *The Australian Journal of Anthropology* 8, 1: 104–24.

Weiss, G. (1999) *Body Images: Embodiment as Intercorporeality*, New York: Routledge.

Young, I. M. (1990a) 'The Scaling of Bodies and the Politics of Identity' in *Justice and The Politics of Difference*, Princeton: Princeton University Press.

—— (1990b) 'Throwing Like a Girl: A Phenomenology of Feminine Body Comportment, Motility and Spatiality', in *Throwing Like a Girl and Other Essays*, Indiana: Indiana University Press.

11 'My furladies'

The fabric of a nation

Chantal Nadeau

This chapter is about women and fur, or in my rendition, *furladies*. If the history of Canada is literally mapped, if not tainted, by fur trade chronicles, travelling accounts and economic studies of the influence of the fur trade on the development of the country, a meagre body of work has considered the very sexual beaver ties and stitches that inform the relationships between women, fur and the nation. This project proposes to unfold the cultural and political links between fur and women, beaver and *furladies*, in the gendering and sexualising of the national space(s).

My approach fleshes out how both national and postcolonial enterprises are historically infatuated with the culture of the beaver. Central to my analysis is the notion of *furladies*, a term that fleshes out the multiple crossings between sexuality and national/ism in Canada, and blurs the boundaries between the political, economic and sexual value of the 'beaver' in the establishment of Canadian identity. In this way, the notion of furladies addresses sexualised national narratives in which the beaver is more than a trading commodity, a token of value for the fur business, or a symbol of British and French colonial enterprises, but also refers to women as producers of the national economy.

The absence of women from studies of fur and the genealogy of the nation is even more remarkable as Canada is the land of the beaver and owes its foundation to the penetration of the beaver trade/trail by European traders. I cannot take credit for such a statement; the famous Canadianist Harold Innis made it in his landmark study written in 1930 *The Fur Trade in Canada: An Introduction to Canadian Economic History* (1956).[1] As instructive as Innis's study is for a close look at the origins of Canada – most notably as a fascinating erotic taxonomy of fur geography from which I have learned that the richness of beaver (fur) is a question of northerly attitudes and exposure – it discards a fundamental and obvious dimension of the politics of the fur trade and national formation: the centrality of sexuality, of a sexual economy of beaver fur in the fabrication of the nation. This chapter offers a close look at how the long neglected question of the beaver, as an exchange value for female sex/uality, is indissociable from a national history so infatuated with colonial and postcolonial beaver fever. In the second part of the chapter, I will use the 1950s' Canadian fur musical review, *My Fur Lady*, as a strategic trading post to explore how certain cultural formations weave together the complex threads between women, nation and fur.

In refusing to disassociate the sensuality of skin and the raw materiality/physicality of fur, my analysis favours a critical reconsideration of the cultural and political formations that mark the 'authentic Canadian beaver' as both an emblem of national unity and a marker of national sexual economy. The notion of *furladies* not only marks the encounter between women and fur, but also encapsulates the many tender ties that exist between skin and fur. In this sense, the gesture of (dis)articulating the boundaries between women, fur and nation relies on a very simple assertion: without skin there is no fur. And without the 'beaver' there is no trade, there is no capital movement, there is no crossings of national borders, there is no memory, no nation. Henceforth, I argue that the beaver economy, drawing upon the interfaces of skin, flesh and fur, is what keeps the 'business' of the nation going, wonderfully echoing the Hudson's Bay Company's motto *Pro Pelle Cutem* [a skin for a skin's worth]. In fact, references to the beaver in the cultural economy of Canada go beyond the colonial/animal imagery of the beaver to include the sexual and racial commodification and subjection of women to the more popularised manifestations of national discourses. In other words, as in the process of skinning the beaver pelt to gather the felt in the fabrication of beaver hats,[2] the role of women in the fur cultural enterprise in Canada is entrenched in the very act of skinning the fur to get to the skin. In this sense, the furladies are not limited to the size of their fur coats. The furladies themselves form the fabric of the nation, to echo the Fur Council of Canada's slogan.[3] Focusing on furladies rather than fur coats allows me to move from the (obvious) evidence of the fabric to address the active roles occupied by women in the maintenance of domestic continuity and the renewal of national resources, including skin. In many fashions, the furladies embody the sensational value of female skin in the nationalisation of natural resources.

Beaver tales

Fur provides a unique texture for questioning the key points that knit together the fabric of the nation, not only in terms of fashion, but also in the ways in which Canadian national land, as well as American historical narratives of progress, have been stitched by Furladies. In the encounter between skin and pelts, fur forms the foundations of a culture of the 'authentic Canadian beaver', within which are entrenched both the aesthetic dimensions of fur and the market of skin. This double articulation between economy and sexuality begs a series of questions regarding the ways that nation, sex/uality and identity intersect: How profitable has the beaver been for the nation? How busy have the fur ladies/beavers been in the construction of a national economy? How is the representation of women as agents negotiated in a culture and a market where the expressive value of fur involves shadowing the traces of skin?

As part of my argument that without skin there is no fur, I want to reassert the importance of sexuality in relation to questions of nation. Along the same lines, one of the key aims of my research on fur and ladies is to seek a reconciliation of the contradictions between the ubiquity of women in furs in the production of national imagery and popularised displays of the nation, and their marginalisation from the modes of political and economic formations of the beaver country. If a sexual edge easily emanates from popular locuses of representation and consumption of such cultural phenomena as tourist campaigns, the fashion industry, official commemorative imagery and even anti-fur rhetoric, the process of sexualisation of these events within the nation and postcolonial space is yet to be explored on a theoretical level. While most feminist work addresses the centrality of gender and its bodily expressions in the process of defining the conditions of subalternity and agency for women under the national/postcolonial moment, very little attention is given to sexuality as central to the organisation and the development of the colonial and postcolonial enterprises. By sexuality here I mean less sexual identity per se, than the ways that the production and the commodification of the postcolonial enterprise – as well as the national moment – is sexualised.

This becomes all the more apparent when one considers that the most readily available popular image associated with women and fur in Canada – and still today with the revival of the fur industry – has been that of an animal, that of the beaver; sexuality, race and class is here confused. The modes of production of fur imagery, even contemporary ones, consistently feature and position women – as both subject and material (skin) – as the real fur. Even if the perfect match between beaver and women originated historically from the very first moments of the fur trade, countless political events and cultural representations since then have certainly reinforced the symbiotic encounter between skin and fur. Though this symbiotic encounter has been a dominant aspect of the twentieth-century redeployment of a sexual economy of fur, the 1950s constitute a unique conjuncture in the (cultural and economic) close encounters between skin and fur. The excessive and conservative modes that made fur and skin the very fabric of the nation were exacerbated by the convergence of the booming post-war fur economy with an unprecedented political debate about national identity that raged at the time due to the Massey Commission (as I will discuss in the second part of this chapter). *My Fur Lady* came at a time when fur was once again flying from coast to coast, as a symbol both of colonial reminiscence and national renaissance.

As a key illustration of the tensions between sensuality and sexuality, domesticity and international pretensions, the fur advertising campaigns designed by major fur retailers during the 1950s offer rich narratives of the intimacies between skin and fur, documenting the range of strategies used by the fur trade to expose and display the intimacies between women, beasts and the land. For instance, this 1950 advertisement promoting the new beaver collection of Montreal fur manufacturers Arpin-Gendron Limited glitters among dozens of other ads in the fiftieth anniversary issue of the *Canadian Fur Review* (Plate 11.1). Sensually entitled 'Natural Beaver: Choisy', the advertisement features a brunette model, femme fatale yet definitely classy. Glamorously gazing at the camera, the model is all fur,

Figure 11.1 'Natural beaver', Choisy campaign, Arpin & Gendron Limited, 1950

as much as the beaver coat she is wearing is all skin. One cannot help but see two Canadian beavers in this image, reunited in a troubling yet vivid representation of the intimate association between women and fur for the vitality of the national trade market. Model and coat hit the catwalk of the 1950 Canadian Fur Industry fashion show, introduced to the buyers by the following blurb:

> Full-length coat of Canadian beaver. The luxurious beauty of Canadian beaver, lavishly styled into a magnificent coat! The flared back falls in four deep folds, emphasising the markings of the skins. The club collar can be worn straight up – or turned down in the casual manner. The deep sleeves are cut in the new spiral pattern.[4]

As the blurb and the image powerfully evoke, this advertisement celebrates how women – white and native in particular – have been traditionally presented, if not displayed, as quaint cultural vignettes for the colonial and national fur trade. The fact that the advertisement appeared in the fiftieth anniversary issue of the Canadian Fur Council album, when the post-war fur industry was in complete economical and cultural transition is all the more telling; no matter how 'modern' the trade fancied itself, its foundations were still embedded in the inescapable display of the fur coat as a natural extension of female skin. This constant crossing between skin and fur leads me to consider the sexual economy of furladies, not only in terms of the flatness of display, but also as a mediated and trademark national body, through the production of corporate culture in relation to fur.[5]

The representation and association between women and fur is thereby strongly entrenched in the production and representation of postcolonial ties as promiscuous ones. In skinning and re-dressing the furladies, I question how women participate in the process of circulation of commodities, goods and the culture of national production. If, historically, the fur trade has been presented as an exclusively male-controlled activity (Innis 1956; Newman 1985, 1987; Mackay 1948), one cannot deny the role of women (European, Inuit, Native and Canadian) in the production of fur as the *national skin*. As Innis points out, '[t]he history of Canada has been profoundly influenced by the habits of an animal which very fittingly occupies a prominent place on her coat of arms' (1956: 3). The notion of furladies represents a specific embodiment of the intersections of nationalism and sexuality, illustrating the connections between discourses of Canadian nationalism and discourses of gender and sexuality, along with its relevance for both. In this sense, my approach to furladies is not only about 'retracing' and following women's footprints in the fur trade, but also about analysing how the specific articulation between women, fur and nation embraces a broader context of signification than the one limited to the materiality and the visibility of the fabric.

Agents and beavers

One of the most evocative images to emerge from my research on fur concerns the intimate and complex links that define the bodily texture of fur ladies. The ways fur and skin are forged within the nation raises issues of agency, resistance, reproduction, sexuality and race in the materiality of fur and beaver. How do women negotiate their multiple positionalities? Whether as national wombs, skin bearers or anti-fur movement advocates, how do women impinge on the culture of the nation? In most recent studies on women, sexuality and nation conducted by Western feminist scholars,[6] the locus of analysis is too often reduced to graphic representations and texts in which the national element is gendered through imagery and commodification of women's bodies. In other words, fur and women are understood as fetishes, hardly as subjects. For example, Julia Emberley in her study on fur as cultural artefact, *The Cultural Politics of Fur* (1998), argues that codes of exchange are principally tied to a network of 'textual libidinal economies' with no consideration of existing distinctions between text, image, politics and the libidinal exchanges that define the material girl. As instructive and as remarkable as Emberley's work is at the aesthetic level, it does not allow for an adequate response to my questions concerning how sexuality, women and fur mingle to constitute the very centre of a national stock exchange, within which skin and fur together are valued. Countering such a fixed portrait, I argue that fur per se has no value without the raw materiality of the skin; it is the infinite points of contact between fur and skin that create the sexual economy of the nation. In other words, fur as the fabric of the nation owes its exchange value to the constant rearticulation and negotiation between skin and pelts.

Against interpretations that construct the female body as a static matter, I wish to introduce movement and displacement as an essential dimension of the understanding of the female subject as 'national agent'. Without a context of representation production, and consumption of the skin as a 'good', there is little room for analysing the body beyond its surface. A critical approach to women as both surface and interface allows us to frame women as both bearers and producers of the nation. The gesture of apprehending the fur ladies beyond the frozen glimpse of the fur coat speaks to my desire to embrace a more productive yet sensitive approach to the cultural economy of fur and nation. It implies, for example, a consideration of agency in its double articulation to power: as a means of resistance to the postcolonial/national order and as a means of reproduction and consolidation of national enterprise. In so doing, I critique a postcolonial representation that maintains, first, that national identity is a masculine cultural practice, and second, that sexuality is a marginal space for confronting the culture of economies involved in the debates on national identity and postcolonial subject formation.

Traditionally, women have been framed as bearers, guardians, and even cultural producers of the resources of the colony and the nation (Lewis 1996). However, an approach that frames women not only as agents, but also as economic producers, allows for the positioning of the furladies as a necessary link to understand how specific cultural events and economic activities coalesce within a sexualised, gendered and racialised organisation of domestic space. From that perspective, the nation is not only a commodity spectacle, as McClintock (1995) argues, but also a sexual stock exchange within which femininity and fur act as the prime trading values. The furladies embody the ways the cultures of national production and reproduction are encompassed in the agency of the subject. By analysing the fur trade as a sexual economy, we confront the antagonistic yet complementary dimension of female agency and production. I wish now to turn to a late 1950s fur trading post, the *My Fur Lady* theatrical revue, in order to offer a critical analysis of a domestic/urban beaver tale that addresses the interactions between furladies and popular culture, along with its resonance in a postcolonial context. Still considered today as one of the most popular theatrical revues ever produced in Canada, *My Fur Lady* offers a layered location in which national subjectivities are channelled through dynamics of imperialist and colonialist culture and practices of substituting skin for fur. A medley of political revue, fancy dress ball, post-war *Nanook of the North*[7] and commodification of colonial history, the beaver politics of *My Fur Lady* are clearly forged into master narratives of sexuality and nation. If Canada was really made of beaver, *My Fur Lady* would be the queen.

My Fur Lady: An 'Eskimo' tale

Even in my wildest dream about discovering a virgin female terrain on my *flâneur reverie* on the beaver trail, I could not imagine a more extravagant fur post to explore than *My Fur Lady* (Plate 11.2). When I first expressed my excitement about McGill's 1957 theatre revue, most of my friends and colleagues heard that I was interested in My *Fair* Lady, which they thought was a peculiar way to hail the '[savoir] faire' of the fur ladies. The initial confusion became an inspiring pun for fair fur as well as a subjective tactic to move between the different layers of skin narratives. Most of us are familiar with George Cukor's 1964 screen adaptation of the Broadway show, starring a dashing Audrey Hepburn in a gigantic hat, speaking and touting perfect English for the sake of British culture. The ultimate embodiment of Victorian fair culture, Hepburn also stands as the quintessential image of the colonised female body. Like the land, a rude, rough, wild Hepburn undergoes the different phases of progress and development: she is tamed, groomed, scrubbed, revamped, domesticated, ready to be displayed to British elite society, half-debutante, half-species exhibited before the eyes of the British court.

Figure 11.2 My Fur Lady poster, Fringe Festival, Stratford Theatre Festival, Stratford, Ontario, 22 July 1957

Reproduced courtesy McGill University Archives

Not only does a furless Hepburn get her language right, she also gets her skin clean and silky, honouring the deeds of a fair and square deal. Her body and tongue are exchanged for clean dress; a skin for a skin's worth. The grand finale of the film celebrates the new Fair Lady as the greatest achievement and discovery of civilised taste: the stunning trophy of the Great British Explorer (Rex Harrison). Completely revamped under the expertise of the Great Explorer, the Fair Lady trades her still virgin body for the respectability of marriage.

The Hollywood adaptation of Pygmalion obviously was not available to the five creators of *My Fur Lady*, the Quince 'Brothers' ('Princes'), when they wrote this amateur-turning-professional revue.[8] But the Broadway adaptation, the tale of a groomed beaver who learns to speak 'proper English' was definitely the talk of the town, inspiring the all-male Anglophone writing team of McGill's Red and White Annual Revue. As one of the creators confesses, '[the] cheeky gesture . . . [of] . . . misappropriat[ing] . . . the name of Broadway's reigning hit' (McDonald *et al.* 1975: 124) led to the national popularity of *My Fur Lady*, fur being the most Canadian way indeed to address this satire on 'domestic' politics and national affairs.

The musical, which began its professional career on 23 May 1957, was originally conceived as a college production to be produced by and for students of McGill University. Featuring non-professional actors, the production enjoyed wannabe all-star professional artistic direction, lead by composers James de B. Domville and Galt MacDermott[9] and directed, staged and choreographed by Brian and Olivia McDonald.[10] *My Fur Lady* premiered on 7 February 1957 at McGill University for the annual student Red and White Revue. Intended as a Canadian version of the Grace Kelly–Prince Rainier romance that saved Monaco from absorption into France, the storyline revolves around an *immigrant* (sic!) Inuit Princess, Aurora, performed by a Snow White amateur actress (Ann Golden) masquerading as a fancy Eskimo Pie. Aurora goes south to find a young White Canadian to marry in order to save her people, the community of Muklukko, since, failing dynasty succession, her principality reverts to Canada. 'Two acts, twelve scenes, fifteen songs and a thousand rewrites later' (McDonald *et al.* 1975: 124), Aurora finally weds the representative of the Queen in Dominion Canada, the Governor General, and, as a nuptial gift, she cedes to Canada both her body and her land. In this sheared beaver and tabloid twist on the famous Broadway musical, the Quince Brothers manage in less than three hours to tour more than three hundred years of colonial legacy, harbouring representations of national identity conveniently cleansed of any trace of Native female subjectivities. In order to proclaim a homogeneous national space, the review advocates a commodification of the others – the Eskimo female resource – as essential to preserving and expanding Canadian unity. Through the furry Aurora tale in the south, the play recasts a nostalgic narravativisation of the country wives' economy so prominent and essential in the early centuries of the fur trade.

Ironically, neither the media (that covered the show extensively) nor the creators revealed how this discourse about domestic politics and national affairs became a post-war revival of beaver trade culture, in which the survival of an

Eskimo community depends upon the trading value of the jewel of that community: Princess Aurora. Thirty years after Robert J. Flaherty, sponsored by the French fur company Révillon Frères, went north to create *Nanook of the North* (1922), it is Aurora's turn to come south in order to be discovered by the genius of the White man. Like *Nanook*, *My Fur Lady* was a vehicle for the fur trade, but the musical was also a promotional trading medium of corporate nationalism, in which fur industrialists and governmental agencies used the skin of the furladies to defend a strong vision of the Canadian nation, a vision that was totally inspired by the colonial enterprise. Aurora acts as the most vocal daughter of Britannia, eagerly plunging into the residues of British colonial culture, such as the debutante ball, and learning to perform the role of the perfect diplomatic wife. In *My Fur Lady*, the myth of the good savage is mediated through that of colonial femininity. Aurora embodies the multiple images of white women's femininity defined by Vron Ware, being at once, a responsible mother, a missionary, a pioneer and companion, but also 'a defenceless piece of property' (1992: 120). In other words, Aurora is the re-articulation – through the Eskimo woman's body – of the white European woman traveller in the colony, recalling endless references to historical representations of women and the nation. Like Les Filles du Roy who were sent by the King of France in the seventeenth century to people the colony, Aurora leaves Muklukko to become a Fille of the Queen, in order to preserve the survival of her own Inuit colony. Aurora's journey to the south would find its essence in the marriage to the ultimate colonial authority: 'GG', the governor-general.

The travelling Nordic princess revisits the beaver trail, only this time north–south, bearing to the white community the value of her skin. As Caren Kaplan argues:

> When the freedom to travel is held to be a sign of liberation for European-American women, it is inevitable that the terms and histories of modes of transportation, the production of 'difference' for tourist consumption, and the social construction of class, race, and nation become mystified.
>
> (Kaplan 1995: 47)

Reversing the traditional narrative of the fur adventurers/voyageurs leaving the civilised world to venture into the wilderness, it is the furlady who this time departs from her remote/outskirts world to marvel at the bliss of the civilised world, a world full of domesticity that actually reveals her true worth. Both merchandise and subject of her deal, Aurora carries with her the conditions of a 'square deal' with the dominant country: a skin (hers) for a skin's worth (the independence of her northern community). Moreover, as a performed and masqueraded Inuit princess, Aurora is like a ranched mink: a pristine, perfect, virgin representation of northern female exposure. On the national unity stock exchange her Eskimo skin is priceless, hence the yearning to have the Princess embrace the benefits of confederation. While Hepburn's ladylikeness was based upon her ability to 'pass' as a bourgeoise, Aurora's ladylikeness was a matter of passing as a white who is passing as an Eskimo who is now passing as white. The skin that Aurora willingly trades is actually a perfect locus for transracial sexuality: the big white bear has eaten the little beaver. Transformed into the emblem of unity, little Beaver Aurora can proudly sing 'I'm For Love' and 'I'm into a New World', two of the show's musical numbers.[11]

Offering a powerful and symbiotic illustration of skin-trading for national survival, the musical asserts both the triumph of colonial enterprise and the commercialism of identity as part of the national project. This element is even more disturbing given that the play was written and produced as a response to the debates surrounding the Massey Commission (1951). Briefly, the Massey Commission addressed the perceived necessities of establishing a better under-standing of the two settling communities in Canada, that is, the Anglophones and the Francophones, as well as giving Canadians the cultural means to show proudly to the world a unique cultural identity, from the quest for a flag to the creation of major Canadian cultural agencies. Hence the following clear message to Native Peoples: tradition (the survival of an 'Eskimo' community) and progress (the unity of the nation) are necessarily tied to the preservation of the colonial institution and the creation of national agencies. The production, circulation and marketing of *My Fur Lady* was designed to echo the Massey Commission discourse on Canadian nationalism in the 1950s, in which 'culture' meant unity and fidelity to the Queen of England and the triumph of the British legacy in the definition of the new dominion.

Quince's tale and the fur business

In the spirit of the Massey report on Canadian national identity/unity, and the most recent visit of the Queen to Canada, the satirical musical not only offered a Mondo Canuck version of current affairs, but quickly became the site of inter-mingling between the different political and diplomatic issues involved in the three-way marriage between English-Canada, French-Quebec and, of course, Britannia. In the light of the centennial fight about what constituted Canadian identity and the Canadian nation, the 'Princes' of Quince Productions developed a storyline that chronicled in various tableaux the immigrant Eskimo princess's discovery of the national identity crisis that afflicts maple leaf country and, more specifically, the national capital. In line with this 'creative' effort to reclaim the Canadian flavour and spirit of fur trade ancestors that dominated McGill cul-ture,[12] the class issue so prominent in the Fair Lady transmogrifies into a racial and ethnic issue in the furlady.

However, ethnicity and race were also punctually transposed in the play through the issue of language. The Canadian nationalist trope structured primar-ily around the question of French/English, is then rearticulated through Aurora as a metaphor for the French minority. The fact that Aurora becomes 'assimilated' in the end speaks with little ambiguity to the political situation of Quebec in relation to the rest of Canada, and does so through a dismissal of the Native and Inuit communities' specific racial and ethnic politics. Constructed as an 'inside story' with a series of intrigues unfolded before the eyes of the naive 'other', *My Fur Lady* manages to mock the paradoxes of the linguistic and constitutional political situation while implicitly praising the strong royalist tradition of one nation under one flag. By teaching Aurora about the peculiarly Canadian way to be Canadian, that is, to give up any desire for independence, the governor-general and his followers convince themselves of the beauty of being Canadian for the thus far independent community of Muklukko.

In addition to being a political seller, the play distinguished and marketed itself through its close links with the fur business. One of the major fur retailers in Canada, Swears and Wells, graciously provided all the furs for the production. *My Fur Lady* acted as a promotional window for local and national fur retailers who proudly advertised their participation in an all-Canadian beaver story – including the Hudson's Bay Company.[13] Because the producers printed a new programme for each new venue, local retailers were able to have their name tied to the musical in an early version of fur product placement. Although Montreal-based, the production nevertheless played the regional/local card extremely well, emphasising all the more the national, unitary aspect of the storyline.

The conjunctural nature of *My Fur Lady* in relation to the blooming of the fur industry in Canada in the 1950s was also timely and certainly enhanced the visibility of the revue. In the 1950s, the fur industry in Canada and around the world was literally exploding – lead by fashion designer kings like Christian Dior. The fur district in Montreal was at the core of the North American fur business, and the HBC fur houses welcomed the most important fur auctions in the world, second only to London. The cultural and political references that informed the *My Fur Lady* project/product reveal the transnational and postcolonial nature of the play. If the local references first appealed to its domestic/national popularity, what was actually praised was the incredible strength of a pro-colonial/dominion discourse in the representation of the nation and its different 'constituencies'.

The interlinked political, economic and sexual values of *My Fur Lady* in relation to post-war domestic consumerism and transnational export were even more central to the ways that the fur ladies were asked to mediate the necessary exchange between nation and fur as national spectacle. Like Buffalo Bill and his Wild West Show featuring 'Indians' playing 'Indians', the five male creators of the show toured the ladies and the Inuit Princess nationally. Embracing the postcolonial subalternity of Native women and the agency of White women in the sexual system of exchange in the development of the fur trade, *My Fur Lady* hinges on the commercialism of fur and skin in the promotion of national discourse inspired by colonial nostalgia. *My Fur Lady*, with its unique way of framing the success of national business in terms of a marriage between the 'immigrant' and the coloniser, ironically constituted a clear reference to the legitimised interracial pillow talk that dominated the first centuries of the trade, in which the intimate bonds between White trappers and Native women were seen as a vital element for the economic prosperity of the fur business. As Heather Menzies argues, 'without that legitimized interracial pillow talk, the transnational fur exchange that led to the development of an industrialised Canadian nation wouldn't have happened quite the same'.[14] *My Fur Lady* is not only about the many tender ties existing between an Inuit woman and a white man, to echo Sylvia Van Kirk's (1980) ironic yet vivid description of 'country marriages' during the golden years of the fur trade (seventeenth to nineteenth centuries), nor is it only about the whitening of the Inuit people, it is also about the exchange value of female skin in the context of a male nation-state in search of its true identity. *My Fur Lady* illustrates the importance of re-enacting over and over again – despite racial, sexual and linguistic differences – the integrationist model of imperial order. The fact that the revue was in English, mostly embracing British and colonial references, made explicitly clear that the cultural identity crisis could be solved, not through the recognition of differences, but through the recognition of the British legacy for the future of the nation-state. Mukluko becomes annexed to Canada ('qui prend mari prend pays') as Aurora, the Eskimo 'immigrant' princess, sings at the top of her lungs: 'Teach me how to think Canadian'. What is interesting in this context is that we are very far from the country wives: Aurora belongs to royalty, and that is enough to resolve the class distinction. No matter that Aurora is Eskimo, she is a true princess after all, just enough to allow a royal/national settlement. In light of such ethnocentrism and racialism, the nation cannot be threatened and is in fact secured by an immigrant Eskimo princess in search of a White husband to save her little remote northern community.

The fabric of the nation

An in-depth search through the McGill University archives revealed that behind the spooky national farce, *My Fur Lady* was actually an extremely well-structured cultural industry backed by different governmental and private interests. As participants and agents for the national unity and identity business, the actresses attached to the show were ceaselessly invited to perform as the fur pin-ups of the nation and the fur industry. The collusion between the different levels of government (national and local) and cultural agencies to make *My Fur Lady* an all-Canadian national promotional vehicle was clearly built on the model of Hollywood stars praising the war effort. As an important volume of documents – visual and printed – testified, the furgirls were quite literally campaigning for a Canadian identity strongly tied to and defined through the display of fur. The female cast became the centre of commercial and official promotional campaigns, embodying the Canadian furladies as a form of Canadian travelling Heritage show. In the tradition of the Eaton fur travelling shows that toured Canada with 400 models for 400 coats to celebrate the vitality of the fur industry in the 1940s,[15] *My Fur Lady* managed with her fur babes and bear boys through its 402 shows to re-enact the crucial relations between sexuality, nation and gender in the corporate economy. An authentic cultural industry, *My Fur Lady* played the political line all around, as the men of the production became the official spokespersons of Canadian unity, while the furladies adopted the dislocated posture of the diplomatic wives touring the nation, the naval ships, the city halls and prime minister's offices to promote the glamour of ladies in furs for the national industry.

The media representations of the furladies – from mothers of the land, caring ladies for sick children and charities, industrial and national pin-ups for the National Defense Department, to hot fur fashion beauties at the beach (as epitomised by an amazing photograph of the fur girls fancying bathing suits and fur coats *à la* Jane Mansfield, in Vancouver during a heat wave during July 1958)[16] – show the extent to which fur was valued through the display of skin. If fur stars on stage, skin triumphs offstage to ensure that the furladies were Canada's best commercial goods, the most performative trans/national geographics, and the most spectacular tourist 'features' of the nation.

In so many ways, the most Canadian of musicals owes its popularity and glory to its use of the stage and the trade as a site of identity performance that *incorporates* the racial and sexual issues intimately tied to the debate on the post-war Canadian nation. With just enough Eskimo fur references to garner fur retailer sponsorships for the 400 shows of the play, *My Fur Lady* successfully reconciled the materiality, physicality and sexuality of furladies for the nation. Hailed as 'Canada's Most Popular Gal' (Rowe 1958: 5), *My Fur Lady* represents a spectacular aspect of national sexual economy, where the true fetish-spectacle of the nation translates into the skinning of the Eskimo/exotic babe. *My Fur Lady* recreated a commercial and corporate representation of the relations between fur, nation and sexuality in the postcolonial context of the nationalist debates hitting the Canadian political scene in the 1950s. Its unique way of framing the success of national business in terms of a marriage between the 'Immigrant' and the Coloniser's representative, was ironically a clear reference to the legitimised interracial pillow talk that dominated the first centuries of the trade, in which the intimate bonds between White trappers and Native women were seen as a sign of economic prosperity and political stability for the fur business. This furry tale asserts the centrality of sexuality in the processes of postcolonial enterprise and the survival of the nation-state (albeit a diminished one). Aurora trades both her skin – her people – and her fur (sexual and nuptial) in the preservation of the nation. But what Aurora trades in fact is the power to represent her own identity as already constructed through the production of a corporate culture massively mapped out by the presence of the British colonisers through the Hudson's Bay Company. The practices of Inuit community governmentality and the allegory of independence were all subsumed to the one institution of white federalism.

Presented as 'a child of her time' by the five male creators of the revue, *My Fur Lady* stands today as a fascinating and wild expression of national 'taxidermy', taxidermy being after all about '. . . seek[ing] to make that which is dead look as if it were still living' (Tobing Rony 1996: 101). What still lives through the sexual economy of *My Fur Lady* is the manner in which beaver fur is entrenched in a double assumption of romantic popular national commodity and site of political reproduction. Far from being obsolete in the contemporary cultural moment, Aurora and the fur and skin tale can be said to be undergoing a new visibility, this time more than ever in the double mode of national vignette and producer of a culture of beaver fur. One cannot help but think of Aurora and her masqueraded skin when witnessing the most recent aggressive fur campaigns led by the Fur

Council of Canada featuring Native and White women designers as the new spokespersons of the renaissance of the fabric of the nation. While Aurora's serenade tells us, 'It's a great big wonderful [beaver] country!', a strange feeling of familiarity, sensuality and warm domesticity colours the 1990s' sexual economy of fur, in which a kaleidoscope of Auroras redeploy the natural links between skin and fur.

Notes

1 University of Toronto Press re-edited in 1999 Innis's seminal reference. This re-editing is timely as the Canadian fur industry is definitely back as an important national economic vehicle after practically two decades spent in the dog house.

2 Beaver hats so in vogue in the seventeenth and eighteenth centuries weren't made of fur but felt: 'The true beaver hat was made not from the glossy long-haired pelt but from the fine thick underhair, shaved and sheared from the skin' (Newman 1998: 41).

3 The slogan 'Fur: the fabric of a nation', was imagined and launched by the Fur Council of Canada in 1987 as part of a new marketing plan to promote the renaissance of the Canadian fur industry at national and international levels.

4 *Canadian Fur Review*, 1950–51, Vol. IV, p. 86. This event was actually the first full-fledged convention in the entire history of the fur industry to unite all the major furriers, exhibitors and manufacturers in Canada at the same time. Two fashion shows were put together under the supervision of Mrs Kate Aitken, 'unquestionably Canada's busiest woman' (1950: 83).

5 My take on the fur nation is indissociable from that of the corporate nation, strongly informed by the legacy and the politics and economics of colonial development sealed by the Hudson's Bay Company (HBC) in Canada. The Company was created in 1670 to favour the exploration and expansion of British colonial interests in America.

6 See Lewis 1996; McClintock 1995; Solomon-Godeau 1996; Yuval-Davis 1997. I am not trying to diminish the incredible and insightful contribution of these texts, but rather to point out the peripheral dimension of the economy of the female subject in their approach.

7 Quintessential representation of the interplay between fur, race and so-called Eskimo culture, *Nanook of the North* (dir. R. Flaherty, 1922) is a powerful example of a corporate production funded by the Révillon Brothers, another fur business. This staged documentary is still today considered to be the epitome of ethnographic colonialism.

8 Quince Productions consisted of five McGill Graduates: Brian McDonald, James de B. Domville, Erik Wang, Donald MacSween and Timothy Portheous.

9 For one, Galt MacDermot pursued his career in the US and became a successful musical composer. His Broadway 'creations' count among others, the 1960 musical, *Hair*.

10 Olivia McDonald's participation in MFL, while it got full credits in the programme, was always shadowed by her husband's profile as producer and star-director of the play, maintaining in fact a strong gendered division between performance (by the ladies of the play) and creation/production (by the boys). The double directorship of the McDonalds constitutes an interesting contrast between display/performance and production of the nation along the line of gendered agency. Olivia, a professional ballerina, died tragically in a car accident in 1959. Brian McDonald is still directing today.

11 *My Fur Lady: An Original Musical Comedy* ©1957 Quince Productions.

12 McGill University was founded in 1821 through fur trade. The first president and donor of McGill University was Sir James McGill, one of the most powerful and wealthy fur traders of the Northwest Company, the most serious competitor of HBC in the eighteenth century, before the merging of the companies.

13 My favourite advertisement by the HBC, which appeared in numerous programmes, featured a model wrapped in a mink cape, with the following caption (for women only): 'You'll be a "Fur Lady" on your own merits and steal the show in stunning mink!'.
14 See H. Menzies, 'Technological Systems and Canadian Development: The Case of the Fur Trade', in *Canada: The Global Village* (course packet, Carleton University, Canada).
15 This was a radio ad for the retail store Eaton to promote the 1947 Eaton's Fur travelling collection. Broadcast in October 1947 on the CBC radio show *Women's Digest*, the announcer reminds the ladies that the travelling fur exhibit now in Edmonton will be on display until 21 October, closing his blurb with 'The traveling fur style show: 400 models for 400 coats'. National Archives, Ottawa, CAVA/AVCA: 1979-0019. Eaton, for decades a rival of The Bay (HBC's retail store), was one of the largest and most culturally influential retailers in Canada. Important too, Eaton was a 100 per cent Canadian corporation, in contrast to The Bay.
16 The picture, probably shot by one of crew members, immortalised four furladies on Vancouver's beach with their furs and swimming apparel: Joan Stewart, Anne Collings, Carol Morley and Margaret Walter. McGill's Archives, Montreal, 1958/07, b/w, PR038200.

References

Emberley, J. (1998) *The Cultural Politics of Fur*, Montreal: McGill-Queen's University Press.
Innis, H. A. (1956) *The Fur Trade in Canada: An Introduction to Canadian Economic History*, Toronto: University of Toronto Press.
Kaplan, C. (1995). '"A World without Boundaries": The Body Shop's Trans/National Geographics', *Social Text*, 43: 45–66.
Lewis, R. (1996) *Gendering Orientalism: Race, Femininity and Representation*, London: Routledge.
McClintock, A. (1995) *Imperial Leather: Race, Gender and Sexuality in the Colonial Context*, London: Routledge.
McDonald, B., Domville, B., Wang, E. and Porteous, T. (1975) 'The Triumph of My Fur Lady' in E. A. Collard (ed.) *The McGill You Knew: An Anthology of Memories 1920–1960*, Don Mills, Ontario: Longman Canada Limited.
Mackay, D. (1948) *The Honourable Company: A History of the Hudson's Bay Company*, Toronto: McClelland and Stewart.
Newman, P. C. (1985) *The Company of Adventurers*, Marham, Ontario: Viking.
—— (1987) *Caesars of Wilderness*, Marham, Ontario: Viking.
—— (1998) *Empire of the Bay: The Company of Adventurers that Seized a Continent*, Toronto: Penguin.
Rowe, K. (1958) 'Canada's Most Popular Gal? "My Fur Lady" Of Course!', *Brandon Daily*, 4 June.
Solomon-Godeau, A. (1996) 'The Other Side of Venus: The Visual Economy of Feminine Display' in V. de Grazia with E. Furlough (eds), *The Sex of Things*, Berkeley: University of California Press.
Tobing Rony, F. (1996) *The Third Eye: Race, Cinema, and Ethnographic Spectacle*, Durham NC and London: Duke University Press.
Van Kirk, S. (1980) *Many Tender Ties: Women in Fur-Trade Society in Western Canada, 1670–1870*, Winnipeg: Watson and Dwyer.
Ware, V. (1992) 'Britannia Other's Daughters' in *Beyond the Pale: White Women, Racism and History*, London: Verso.
Yuval-Davis, N. (1997) *Gender and Nation*, London: Sage.

12 'That is my Star of David'

Skin, abjection and hybridity

Shirley Tate

That is my Star of David. I can't take it off right?

(Sarah)

Sarah's words evoke a truism about being Black in contemporary Britain: skin signifies. It is a mark of ethnicity, status, identity, self-hood. Her words speak of the continuation of the 'racial epidermal schema' highlighted by Frantz Fanon in *Black Skin White Masks* (1986: 112). In the colonial context, he argues, Black others bear, 'the burden of that corporeal malediction' provided by, 'the white man, who had woven [him] out of a thousand details, anecdotes, stories' (Fanon 1986: 111). Through the discursive construction of difference that emanates from the dominant culture, Black women and men continue to be placed as other: as Black others imprisoned by discourses of skin.

This chapter explores talk as a process through which Black identities are negotiated in conversations. Drawing on material gathered for a larger research project,[1] I offer an analysis of the tensions and contradictions between dominant discourses of Blackness and more oppositional discourses as they are depicted in interactants' everyday talk. I am concerned to highlight the processes by which speakers push at the limits of what they see as a dominant discourse of Blackness in order to construct an alternative version of Black identity. What I shall show is that in everyday conversation speakers engage with dominant discourses in order to reject, replace or rework them as they negotiate identities for themselves in talk. This relates to the question of skin because I ask: How are the identity positionings of Black skin within dominant discourses translated by speakers? How are these discourses of Black skin rejected in talk? How does negotiating discourses of Black skin lead to alternative identity positionings? And what does all this tell us about hybridity? Let us begin by looking at what speakers reveal about dominant identity discourses of Black skin as stereotype.

Black skin as stereotype

I have already suggested that Black women and men are imprisoned by discourses of skin which construct them as a Black other. In the following extract, Kevin shows what this imprisonment by skin means for him as a Black man who is faced with a double bind of trying to create his own Blackness whilst living with racist stereotypes.

> It's this whole struggle of living Black. I've got this Blackness I've got to walk with. And I'm trying to create my own Blackness because I'm constantly walking with a legacy of others and always will do. When people see me they see a legacy. Whether it be the derogatory things which another person has done but when they see me they see all of those things. If they see a pop star they see me. You know, they don't really . . . they never . . . do they ever really see me? You know I can speak to Black people without that problem. I am not walking with you look the same as that mugger up there and you're that pop star there or you look like the sort who's a womaniser. All these other bullshit things which has to be attached to you by people.

Here, Kevin translates the dominant white discourses of racialised skin as meaning that he lives with a legacy of derogatory things, which he later defines as the stereotype of the pop star, mugger, womaniser. He reflexively rejects this legacy by commenting on his invisibility to whiteness,[2] because he is visible only through the always already known of the stereotype. After this rejection of himself as a stereotype he places himself within a community of Black people in which 'all these other bullshit things which has been attached to you by people' does not apply.

As Black women and men, we also exist in another world to which Kevin alludes. In this world, as Kevin claims, it is possible to move beyond the otherness that is constructed through the normalisation of whiteness. This is the world of Blackness as a politics, a life and a culture. But here too skin signifies racialised homogeneity. This homogeneity must not be transgressed if a 'Black same' is to be maintained. In the next extract, John speaks about the impact of homogeneity when he translates a particular discourse of Black identity. This discourse means that, as Black people, we stereotype ourselves to the extent that we must not like classical music and must speak in a certain way, in order to be seen as authentically Black. John then rejects this positioning when he says that alongside this, 'we want to be accepted as diverse because we can be doctors, we can be researchers, collectors. We can be anything'. John moves to a position in which he sees Blackness as being more than a skin colour, but as being reduced to skin because of the policing of the borders of Blackness by individuals operating within essentialist notions of who is Black. These essentialist ideas emerge at the level of stereotype (food, speech, musical choice and dancing style) and are used to judge whether one is Black enough. His claim is that we are more than a skin colour, a position which demonstrates the double consciousness from which he views the world. It also shows something else: the possibility for the emergence of identity positions that are outside of the dominant discourse of the 'Black same':

> The problem with the Black identity is that not only do a certain amount of Black people stereotype ourselves. So do white people as well. So you know

what I mean how can you break that? I mean when on the one hand we're saying that they are stereotyping us right? But if a person says that they like classical music a lot they are not seen as really Black. Because they couldn't speak a certain way they spoke [they wouldn't be accepted]. And yet at the same time we want to be accepted as diverse you know what I mean? Because we can be doctors, we can be researchers, collectors. We can be anything. On the other hand, if a Black person isn't seen as Black enough because of the food they eat, the way they speak, the way they dance, what kind of music they like. Then it makes you think that even though its more than a skin colour yet in a sense it is simply skin colour right? That is how we differentiate.

The dominant discourses of the Black same/other based on skin as stereotype and skin as 'race', culture and community are being negotiated in the examples above. These dominant discursive positions emanating from both Black and white communities constitute the particular double consciousness of skin within which, and against which, Black speakers construct identity positionings in talk.[3]

A double consciousness of skin

In his book *The Black Atlantic: Modernity and Double Consciousness*, Paul Gilroy (1993) describes double consciousness as a double vision. Double vision allows people to be in two places at once and maintain a double perspective on reality. This perspective permeates Black diaspora consciousness and leads to identifications existing outside of, and standing in opposition to, the political forms and codes of modern citizenship because of the experiential rift between the place of residence and that of belonging (Gilroy 1997: 329). Gilroy's account is an alluring one because of its insistence that, as Black people, we share something 'at the level of the structure of feeling' (Friedman 1997: 74). But while being opposed to Afrocentricity as an identity discourse because of its essentialism, Gilroy is at the same time positing some sort of shared Black consciousness. In doing this, he shows us the continuing centrality of commonality in any account of Black identity. For my purposes here, he shows the necessity for a double consciousness of skin in any such account.

Gilroy's concept of double consciousness needs to be expanded though to include the possibility for agency in the construction of identities in talk. It is in talk that individuals make known what is 'conflictually other' in terms of the identity positioning they want to construct. The conflictually other – the voice of the other within – is made known from their position of double consciousness. For example, for Kevin, the conflictually other is articulated through the stereotypes with which he has to live; for John, it is expressed through the ideas of Black authenticity. They both also indicate the possibility for difference from the dominant subject positions which are part of their lived experience. Through the externalisation of the conflictually other and the marking of their difference from this in talk, Kevin and John erect borders between the selves of dominant discourses and the Black self they are trying to construct. Gilroy's double consciousness does not fully account then for two possibilities. First, that in talk individuals construct alternative versions of the Black self in opposition to dominant identity discourses; and second, that in such an agency, skin is salient in the construction of an-other positioning through the expulsion of the voice of the other within.

The struggle with, and expulsion of, the voice of the other within is shown next by Sheryl. She talks about her experience of being on a bus with a driver who had deliberately nearly trapped her in the doors as she got on and refused to apologise, making her even more angry. Her recollection of the event here begins at the point at which she asks the bus driver for his number

> He looked and said what? [I said] What's your number? Before he got to stop but instead of breaking gently like he did, he put the brakes on really hard so that everyone went lurching forwards right, including me. He did it on purpose obviously, so I said to him what's your number? He said oh go suck on a banana you nigger. He said it low but I could hear him clear enough. I was just so angry. Before I would have thought no I'll just report this. I should have done that but I couldn't. I just slapped him. I just punched him in his face. Two years ago this big old woman. I went buff[4] and just got off the bus.

Here we see how the stereotype 'nigger' exerts white supremacy by making a Black woman feel all of its power to know her. The driver equates Black skin with the jungle and inferiority when he tells her to go suck on a banana. At an individual level, he becomes the locus of the power/knowledge of white racist supremacy by making Sheryl other through naming. The position denoted by 'nigger' is the voice of the other within which she tells us she would not in the past have acted directly against, she would have just reported the incident at a later stage. However, at that point in her life she acts immediately against this voice of othering. First, by asking for his number so that she could complain about being nearly trapped in the door, and second, by punching him in the face when he didn't do this and called her 'nigger'. In constructing herself as a subject in talk and not a 'nigger other', she transgresses the boundaries prescribed for her by racist ideology.

In this narration of the self, Sheryl highlights for us the difficulty of being Black within a racialised context. As Craig Calhoun argues:

> It is not just that others fail to see us for who we are sure we really are. . . . We face problems of recognition because socially sustained discourses about who it is possible or appropriate or valuable to be inevitably shape the way we look at and constitute ourselves with varying degrees of agonism and tension.
>
> (Calhoun 1994: 120–1)

In this story, Sheryl narrates herself as embodying opposition to whiteness through her Black skin. Her skin is significant in her struggle to become a subject:

in her talk she shows it to be a site of socially constructed oppression, but also as a site of movement away from such oppression by creating an-other position, as is also the case for Kevin and John above.

In Iris Marion Young's view, members of oppressed groups live within a particular double consciousness (1990: 148). In the process of assuming the position of subjects within the dominant culture, oppressed people experience members of their own groups abjectly. Indeed, even when there is not a wholehearted acceptance of the dominant subject position, there is an internalisation of the fear and loathing of their group by the dominant culture. This leads oppressed people to assume the position of the dominant subjectivity towards themselves and the group with which they identify. On the other hand, Black women and men also live identities different from the dominant subject position which are based on their positive identification with Blackness. As Young puts it:

> The dialectic between these two subjectivities – the point of view of the dominant culture which defines them as ugly and fearsome, and the point of view of the oppressed who experience themselves as ordinary, companionate, and humorous – represents [. .] double consciousness. In this respect culturally imperialized groups live a subjectivity different from that lived by privileged groups, an experience of themselves as split, divided, of their subjectivity as fragile and plural.
>
> (Young 1990: 147)

Although Gilroy's focus is on vernacular culture and diaspora rather than aversive bodies, he also emphasises the dialectic aspect of the experience of oppression and, in common with Young, he sees experiencing oneself as split and plural as a way out of culturally defined racism. However, this is also the way out of the discourse of Black authenticity through the double consciousness of skin, which emerges in talk concerning lived experience. John's view of Blackness and authenticity that I examined earlier is important in understanding what I mean here. Both Gilroy's and Young's formulations of double consciousness deal with facing 'two ways at once': towards the subject position of the dominant culture and the counter discourses of the vernacular culture (Gilroy 1993: 3). John's talk shows us the possibility for difference within the subjugated knowledge of vernacular culture so that a double consciousness of skin need not necessitate a homogeneity of Black identity positionings. Indeed, what we have are *counter discourses* of the dominant discourse of Blackness represented by John so that a double consciousness of skin leads to a multiplicity of subject positions. The voice of the other within – the dominant culture's[5] version of the self – must be rejected in order to become a Black subject. Double consciousness though still continues to exist even while it is continually being reworked. This continuation amid rejection of the dominant culture's version of the self brings to mind Kristeva's (1982) view of the abject.

Abjection and becoming a subject

The abject for Julia Kristeva is an object which is radically excluded but which still challenges 'its master' (1982: 2). Although it is rejected, it does not become excluded totally from the self, but continues to disturb borders, positions, rules as the in-between, the ambiguous. Abjection is a 'danger to identity that comes from within' (Kristeva 1982: 71), a 'threat issued from the prohibitions that found the inner and outer borders in which and through which the speaking subject is constituted' (1982: 69). It 'does not produce a subject in relation to objects – an ego – but rather *the moment of separation, the border between the "I" and the "other" before an "I" is formed*, that makes possible the relation between the ego and its objects' (Young 1990: 143; emphasis added.)

Although for Kristeva, 'abjection arises from the primal repression in which the infant struggles to separate from the mother's body that nourishes and feeds it' (Young 1990: 143), Young relates the abject to Joel Kovel's (1970) account of aversive racism. Here Black women and men are made the loathsome and fearful others of white supremacy and racism is articulated through avoidance and separation (Young 1990). We can see this, for example, in Kevin's account above in which he says that he is only seen as a womaniser, a pop star and a mugger not as himself. For John the abject also has relevance as there is a clear separation between what is Black and what is not, according to the discourse of Black authenticity. Both Kevin and John show us that, 'the subject is constituted through the force of exclusion and abjection, one which produces a constitutive outside to the subject, an abjected outside, which is after all, "inside" the subject as its own founding repudiation' (Butler 1993: 3). This is how the double consciousness of skin with its competing voices of the other within and the Black subject is played out in talk. In these examples we can trace Kristeva's intra-psychic model of abjection as a more intersubjective one in which the construction of the 'border between the I and the other' takes place in the talk.

The moment of separation (the border between the 'I' and the 'other' before a subject is formed) is significant for an understanding of the place of the exclusion of the voice of the other within talk. Speakers establish the border between themselves and the dominant discourses, which they construct as 'the outside'. In this context, abjection does not simply involve revulsion/fear/creeping flesh, as for Kristeva, but rather it involves a constant and repeated process of self-othering, in which certain others become seen as revolting, fearful and as 'creeping flesh', in order to establish the border between the 'I' and the other. In talk, individuals ceaselessly confront their own, 'otherness, a burden both repellant and repelled, a deep well of memory that is unapproachable and intimate: the abject' (Kristeva 1982: 6). At the same time, 'the abject as distinct from the object, does not stand opposed to the subject, at a distance, definable. The abject is other than the subject but is only just the other side of the border' (Young 1990: 144). The process of separation from dominant discourses through talk restores the border between self and other and 'makes signification possible by creating a being capable of dividing, repeating, separating' (Young 1990: 144). Indeed, Black skin becomes the border, which is both formed and re-formed in talk.

What is of interest to me here is an understanding of abjection as that which 'disturbs identity, system, order; that which does not respect borders, positions, rules; the in-between, the ambiguous' (Kristeva 1982: 4). Young argues that the abject must be expelled in order to keep the borders of the self in place (1990: 144). So, for example, if Blackness is being claimed then whiteness would disturb such an identity, so the voice of whiteness within must be excluded. It is therefore, through verbal communication, the word, that the abject is disclosed (Kristeva 1982: 23). In other words, in order to narrate myself as Black:

> I expel *myself*, I spit *myself* out, I abject *myself* within the same motion through which 'I' claim to establish *myself* [. . .] it is that that *they* see that 'I' am in the process of becoming an other at the expense of my own death,
>
> (Kristeva, 1982: 3; emphasis in original and added on 'they')

Kristeva speaks here about the nausea produced by the skin on warmed milk and the separation from the mother and father who desire her to have it. I would like to read this as a separation from the voice of the other within so that the abject self of the dominant stereotype is replaced in talk in order for an-other 'I' to emerge.

We have seen above in Kevin's account that he is the object of the discursive positioning of skin, which seeks to position him as abject. In turn, he translates and rejects this otherness in the moment of separation at the border of the 'I' and the Black other. This is shown by what he says after he talks about the stereotypes that he has to live with and the fact that they mean that he is never really seen. He says that he can talk to another Black person without having to negotiate these stereotypes of the Black man and he will be seen for who he really is. Through these words, he rejects the Black subject position constructed within white discourse. Sheryl also goes a step further in that she proclaims what her 'I' is, in opposition to the discursive positioning of otherness. It is to be recognised as an equal, as a 'big old woman' who deserves respect. In proclaiming themselves as subjects outside of the dominant discourse, both Sheryl and Kevin make known their separation from and critique of the position 'nigger'. They show 'who' they are in talk using skin as their one certainty. Indeed, for John, skin 'is how we differentiate'. They are able to show who they are because cultural resources are indelibly marked by social position. It is therefore possible for speakers to remake the conditions of their lives in talk as they reject some subject positions and assert others (Holland *et al.* 1998).

In Iris Marion Young's (1990) view, however, abjection does not presume that Black women and men construct whites as abjected others.[6] This is borne out if we focus only on constructions of abjection as occurring within dominant discourses. However, it is important to bear in mind that identifications also emerge from Black subjugated knowledges, which ensure that there is another position from which critique can arise. Zizek writes about this in terms of ideology: 'An individual subjected to ideology can never say to himself "I am in ideology", he always requires *another* corpus of doxa in order to distinguish his own "true" position from it' (1995: 19–20; emphasis in original).

Foucault's view is that resistance or counter-discourses arise at the very points where power relations are at their most rigid and intense (McNay 1994). So Iris Marion Young's viewpoint needs to be re-read from a position which sees all power relations as potentially reversible and unstable. Indeed, at the level of talk about lived experience, we need to look at 'the abject' differently from Kristeva and see it in interpersonal interaction as that which is radically excluded by critique, rejection, and marginalisation. That which is abject becomes now that which is made 'other' through talk.

Charlene makes whiteness 'other' in the next example. Before this extract, she had been talking about why English is not a label she would apply to herself. She goes on in the conversation to claim Antigua, the Caribbean and a connectedness to the African diaspora and 'other . . . Black people as well' as being more relevant to her. This is the case as she wants 'to distance [her]self from what [she] see[s] as white British people', part of this distancing is a refusal 'to use British' or to use it 'very reluctantly'. In this way she narrates herself as rooted in a Black diasporic same because of skin whilst also making whiteness other.

> Its not just that I see myself as Antiguan. I see myself very much connected to people who are of Caribbean origins and to people of African descent glob- ally and other you know Black people as well. I just feel I don't know. British is just . . . I suppose in a sense mainly because I do want to distance myself from what I see as white British people I refuse to use British you know and I don't really. I don't know. But I use it very reluctantly.

What enables her to recognise her position is a discourse of Blackness, which has been and is a continuing counter-production of and from a Black politics of resistance in Britain. Through this subjugated knowledge, white supremacy as a discourse and a practice is translated in talk. Its resulting transparency means that white supremacy loses some of its effects in terms of the positioning of the Black other because, 'the very logic of legitimizing the relation of domination must remain concealed if it is to be effective' (Zizek 1995: 8). Charlene's talk returns us to a point made earlier: that culturally imperialised groups experience themselves as split, divided, their subjectivity as plural (Young 1990: 148). This process of splitting in the production of multiplicity is one that necessitates a consideration of addressivity and double consciousness because of the negotiation of self/other in dialogic exchange that we have seen in the quotations above.

Addressivity and double consciousness

The extract from Charlene reminds us that in becoming subjects through the expulsion of otherness, individuals are involved in a process of translating and reflexively locating themselves as both objects and subjects within discourses of

Blackness, as they construct identity positionings in talk. Such translation and reflexive application to their own positions is what I call 'translation as reflexivity' and is used in talk to constitute the border, that is, to show the separation of the 'I' and the other. Translation as reflexivity is how I would conceptualise the process of separation and othering – that is, abjection – at the level of interpersonal interaction. As such, translation as reflexivity is central to Black subject positions being produced in talk. Translation as reflexivity also implies a notion of 'existence as dialogue' (Holquist 1991: 14).

According to Bakhtinian dialogics, consciousness is based on a sense of otherness (Holquist 1991: 18). The self is dialogic, in so far as there is a dialogue between self and other in which there is a relation of simultaneity within space and time. As Michael Holquist sums up, being is simultaneous: 'it is always co-being' (1991: 25). He goes on to suggest that '[c]onceiving being dialogically means that reality is always experienced not just perceived, and that it is experienced from a particular position' (Holquist 1991: 21). One event can be experienced differently because we regard the world and each other from different centres in cognitive time/space. Furthermore, in order to see ourselves, we must use the vision of others in order to author ourselves (Holquist 1991: 28). This is significant given the earlier insistence that double consciousness continues and Kristeva's argument that the abject is never totally excluded. Such an understanding of the production of subjectivity has implications for Black subjects because the question that it begs is: how can we author ourselves given that the materials available for identities are always provided by the other? Michael Holquist speaks of this issue when he asks:

> If my 'I' is so ineluctably a product of the particular values dominating my community at the particular point in its history when I co-exist with it, the question must arise, where is there any space, and what would the time be like, in which I might define myself against an otherness that is other from that which has been 'given' to me?
>
> (Holquist 1991: 38)

The speakers quoted above show us a time and space where such a radical otherness[7] can arise as they become subjects in talk by using translation as reflexivity to reject identity discourses of the Black other. In this struggle to become a subject through radical otherness, addressivity assumes importance, since it is through this that we constantly respond to utterances from the different worlds we negotiate (Holquist 1991: 48). This means that we constantly have to translate and reflexively apply or reject these utterances, as Charlene did above when she spoke about being Black, but not being British. However, it is not just subject positions emanating from whiteness which must be rejected, as John made obvious in talking about the critical gaze of Black authenticity. Lorna takes up the theme of this gaze in the next extract when she speaks about shade as a marker of Black identity:

I always wear a head-wrap. I was walking through town and I met a Black girl who I used to go to school with we were friends for years. She's Mike's godmother and I'm godmother to her son. But she's totally submerged in white culture. And that's why I get annoyed when some Black people say to me I've just found my Blackness. Because people Black like that and they're coconuts, you know what I mean? So don't attribute it to the shade of my Blackness. I'm Black. It's not down to how much melanin I've got.

In her talk, Lorna is critical of an essentialist vision of Black identity, in which the global discourse of 'how to be Black', an ethics of Blackness, uses shade of skin as a marker of authenticity. It is this she acts against to become a subject as she constructs herself as 'more Black' irrespective of the difference produced by the shade of her skin. Lorna's claim to being more Black is based on a discourse of Blackness as consciousness. Lorna begins by placing the woman that she is criticising as submerged in white culture and then claims that she is positioned by people like her – 'coconuts' – as someone who has just found her Blackness. Her viewpoint on 'darker skinned people as "coconuts"' is where translation as reflexivity occurs in her talk because of the critique of the term 'coconuts', and her consequent separation of herself from that term. She then goes on to reposition herself as Black irrespective of shade with 'so don't attribute it to the shade of my Blackness. I'm Black. It's not down to how much melanin I've got.' She refuses the place of an addressee who has just found her Blackness and instead asserts a new address as someone who is Black irrespective of shade.

We have seen from the examples that we are preceded by a Blackness that is 'always already there' in discourse, whilst it is also in the process of being constructed. Black skin becomes dialogic as interlocutors construct a space of radical otherness by negotiating competing notions of the meaning of skin. These competing meanings require that skin itself is capable of setting up different addressivities, the most basic of which is exclusion or inclusion. In the negotiations of identity positionings, there is a movement from the address of the Black other emanating from the dominant discourse – the voice of the other within – to a Black self. The new address of the Black self arises in talk through the subjugated knowledge of Black skin as 'culture', 'race', 'community', 'consciousness' and 'politics'. As speakers use translation as reflexivity to reject the voice of the other within they become 'radically other'. Such radical otherness though also includes the vantage-point of that which is rejected because double consciousness continues: we must use the vision of others to author ourselves.[8] New addressivities and radical otherness are significant therefore in accounting for hybrid identity positionings in talk.

Hybridity and radical otherness

The rejection of the position of other and assertion of an-other position of subject shown by the speakers can be seen to be a conflictual interaction of different points of view on the world and is reminiscent of Mikhail Bakhtin's view of the interconnectedness of double consciousness and hybridity. For him:

> the hybrid is not only double-voiced and double accented . . . but is also double-languaged; for in it there are not only . . . two individual conscious-nesses, two voices, two accents as there are [doublings of] consciousnesses, two epochs . . . that come together and consciously fight it out. . . . It is the collision between differing points of view on the world that are embedded in these forms.
>
> (Bakhtin 1981: 380)

This collision is shown in the process of translation as reflexivity in talk and the rejection of the position of Black other that is a part of Black radical otherness. Radical otherness questions the boundaries of 'the Black same'. As speakers construct themselves as radically other, they translate and reflexively reject and apply discursive identity positionings in order to become subjects. This interaction reminds us of the dialogic nature of hybridity as exemplified in Robert Young's view that:

> Hybridity . . . makes difference into sameness, and sameness into difference, but in a way that makes the same no longer different. In that sense it operates . . . [as] a breaking and a joining at the same time, in the same place: differ-ence and sameness in an impossible simultaneity.
>
> (Young 1995: 26)

Lorna's talk above shows difference and sameness as an impossible simultaneity. She is constructed as different because of shade but constructs herself as the same irrespective of melanin.

Homi Bhabha takes up the theme of the simultaneity of same and different in identity positionings when he describes hybridity as 'the third space', and as:

> *not so much identity as identification . . . . as a process of identifying with and through another object, an object of otherness at which point the agency of identification – the subject – is itself always ambivalent, because of the intervention of that otherness . . .* but the importance of hybridity is that it bears the traces of those feelings and practices which inform it, just like a translation, so that hybridity puts together the traces of certain other meanings and discourses.
>
> (Bhabha 1990: 211; emphasis added)

Bhabha's model of hybridity allows for an emphasis on the movement out of domination, which is possible in talk as speakers narrate themselves as split and multiple. The abjection of otherness from the dominant culture is engaged with, but is separated from, through translation as reflexivity before an-other position-ing emerges in talk. The 'third space' of hybridity is located within talk as speakers engage in a process of showing their positioning as 'other'; separating themselves from this otherness and creating a new position which remains within a double consciousness of skin.

Bhabha's 'third space' has some boundaries of its own created by the feelings and practices which inform it, since it is based on opposition to its own others (Friedman 1997: 78). So, even though Bhabha refuses essentialism in the language of liminality and in-betweenness that organises hybridity, he also relies on such an essentialism, given the way in which the 'third space' requires an other which does not inhabit it. The skin could be thought of as the boundary that allows this hybridised third space to be formed. Although Bhabha will only allow for traces of feelings and practices, this does not deny the intervention of skin into 'the third space'. The significance of skin for Black identity positionings is striking in the extracts above. A hybridity produced by Black women and men in talk then is not raceless chaos as suggested by Robert Young (1995: 25).[9] Rather it is a hybridity that is inseparable from the skin which is already marked by 'race'.

What Kevin and Sheryl perform as they exclude whiteness in their talk is a continual critique of whiteness as a possible point of identification. As such whiteness is itself reproduced as essentialist; it is a racialised position of domination. Their critique of whiteness involves the use of skin to build a version of the self in which one becomes radically other, through establishing one's own Black particularity that is both within the skin and outside of it. A Black particularity for John and Lorna is multiple, inclusive of differences of, for example, skin shade and lifestyles and based on a consciousness that resists assimilation to whiteness. Radical otherness as a subject position means that we can stand outside of the discourses in which we would be named because of skin and instead, to name its subjects and make them other. As bell hooks argues:

> I am located in the margin. I make a definite distinction between that marginality which is imposed by oppressive structures and that marginality one chooses as a site of resistance [. . . .] This site of resistance is continually formed in that segregated culture of opposition that is our critical response to domination [. . .] we make radical creative space [. . .] which gives us a new location from which to articulate our sense of the world.
>
> (hooks 1991: 153)

A hybridity-of-the-everyday arises through the negotiation of the discursive positionings of racialised skin in talk. The 'third space' is produced as speakers engage in a process of showing their positioning as 'other', separating themselves from this, and creating an-other position. A double consciousness of skin is therefore part of hybridity. Within a double consciousness of skin, speakers enter into dialogue with the voice of the other within. Discursive positions of the Black other are abjected through the critique made possible by Black subjugated knowledges. These knowledges allow for the separation between the 'I' and the 'other' through translation as reflexivity. This separation shows us that a double consciousness of skin leads to a multiplicity of subject positions through the construction of radical otherness. The new addressivity of radical otherness has been taken above to be a hybrid positioning.

A hybridity-of-the-everyday in which skin continues to be salient is significant for hybridity theorising. It makes us aware of the dialogical nature of hybridity as speakers translate whiteness and Blackness as partial hegemonies that can be resisted. Abjection then becomes a dialogical analysis, a critique and exclusion of discourses of the same/other produced through translation as reflexivity. In new addressivities, speakers construct difference whilst using discourses of fixed 'racial' identities in this process. A double consciousness of skin maintains sameness, but this cannot be taken for granted, as hybrid identities are dialogical, relational and dependent on the relationship with the other to come into being. Skin, as a signifier of the same and different, of Blackness as 'race', 'politics', 'consciousness', 'community', and 'culture' cannot be excluded from hybridity theorising.

Notes

1   The research on which this is based was conducted during 1996–1998 as part of a Ph.D. project. The respondents were Black British of Caribbean ancestry aged between 16 and 38 and spoke about their lives in conversations with their friends, family members and colleagues.

2   Richard Dyer speaks about whiteness thus: 'For those in power in the West, as long as whiteness is felt to be the human condition, then it alone both defines normality and fully inhabits it . . . the equation of being white with being human secures a position of power. White people have power and believe that they think, feel and act like and for all people; white people, unable to see their particularity, cannot take account of other people's; white people create the dominant images of the world and don't quite see that they construct the world in their own image; white people set standards of humanity by which they are bound to succeed and others bound to fail. Most of this is not done deliberately and maliciously [. . .] White power [. . .] reproduces itself regardless of intention, power differences and goodwill, [. . .] because it is not seen as whiteness, but as normal' (1997: 9–10).

3   Stuart Hall sees identities as positions that are constantly being transformed and are never complete, as ideas, world views and material forces interact with each other and are reworked. Identity is, 'never fixed, it's always hybrid. But . . . because it comes out of specific histories and cultural repertoires of enunciation, . . . it can constitute a "positionality", which we call provisionally, identity. . . . So each of these identity-stories is inscribed in the positions we take up and identify with' (1996: 502).

4   Buff relates to the punch she gave to the bus driver.

5   Here, I mean both Black and white culture.

6   Young states that this is an impossibility because the subject point of view for any subject, whatever their group membership, is identified with that of privileged groups under imperialism (1990: 147).

7   Here I mean an otherness that is other than that which has been given to us.

8   This is significant because, 'the Other . . . has a perspective on the subject that enables him both to see the external body that constitutes the subject's vantage point on the world, and also to see that body as part of that world. This is a perspective that is at once radically different from that of the subject, yet also serves to complete it' (Jefferson 1989: 154).

9   Robert Young uses this term to refer to the restless interstitial notion of hybridity which has been theorised in British Cultural Studies.

References

Bakhtin, M. (1981) 'Discourse in the Novel' in *The Dialogic Imagination*, Austin: University of Texas Press.

Bhabha, H. (1990) 'The Third Space – Interview with Homi Bhabha' in J. Rutherford (ed.) *Identity, Community, Culture, Difference*, London: Lawrence and Wishart.

Butler, J. (1993) *Bodies That Matter: On The Discursive Limits of 'Sex'*, London: Routledge.

Calhoun, C. (1994) 'Social Theory and the Politics of Identity' in C. Calhoun (ed.) *Social Theory and the Politics of Identity*, Oxford: Blackwell.

Dyer, R. (1997) *White*, London: Routledge.

Fanon, F. (1986) *Black Skin, White Masks*, London: Pluto Press.

Friedman, J. (1997) 'Global Crises, the Struggle for Cultural Identity and Intellectual Porkbarrelling: Cosmopolitans versus Locals, Ethnics and Nationals in an Era of Dehegemonisation' in P. Werbner and T. Modood (eds) *Debating Cultural Hybridity, Multi-Cultural Identities and the Politics of Anti-Racism*, London: Zed Books.

Gilroy, P. (1993) *The Black Atlantic: Modernity and Double Consciousness*, London: Verso.

—— (1997) 'Diaspora and the Detours of Identity' in K. Woodward (ed.) *Identity and Difference*, London: Sage Publications.

Hall, S. (1996) 'The Formation of a Diasporic Intellectual: An Interview with Stuart Hall by Kuan-Hsing Chen' in D. Morley and K. H. Chen (eds) *Stuart Hall: Critical Dialogues in Cultural Studies*, London: Routledge.

Holland, D., Lachicotte W., Jr., Skinner, D. and Cain C. (1998) *Identity and Agency in Cultural Worlds*, London: Harvard University Press.

Holquist, M. (1991) *Dialogism: Bakhtin and his World*, London: Routledge.

hooks, b. (1991) 'Choosing the Margin as a Space of Radical Openness' in *Yearning: Race, Gender and Cultural Politics*, London: Turnaround.

Jefferson, A. (1989) 'Bodymatters: Self and Other in Bakhtin, Sartre and Barthes' in K. Hirschop and D. Shepherd (eds) *Bakhtin and Cultural Theory*, Manchester: Manchester University Press.

Kovel, J. (1970) *White Racism: A Psychohistory*, New York: Pantheon Books.

Kristeva, J. (1982) *Powers of Horror: An Essay on Abjection*, trans. L. S. Roudiez, Chicester: Colombia University Press.

McNay, L. (1994) *Foucault. A Critical Introduction*, Cambridge: Polity Press.

Young, I. M. (1990) *Justice and the Politics of Difference*, Princeton: Princeton University Press.

Young, R. (1995) *Colonial Desire – Hybridity in Theory, Culture and Race*, London: Routledge.

Zizek, S. (1995) 'Introduction: The Spectre of Ideology' in S. Zizek (ed.) *Mapping Ideology*, London: Verso.

13 Robotic skin

The future of touch?

Claudia Castañeda

Can robots have skin? To ask this question about skin in relation to robots is also to raise the issue of the human, or rather the human-ness of skin, and the nature of its touch. The apparent givenness of human nature and its materialisation in bodies have been topics of sustained feminist inquiry. More specifically, feminists, as well as other critical theorists, have stressed the importance of interrogating the human as that which grounds inequalities of gender, as well as race class, and sexuality in materialised form, that is, *in the flesh* (see Martin 1995; Butler 1993; Haraway 1991). Feminists working in science and technology studies in particular have also begun to ask whether the human continues to be as singularly powerful under contemporary conditions of techno-social change as it may once have been (Hayles 1996; Halberstam and Livingston 1995; Haraway 1991). Human nature as it is investigated, generated and lived, is said to be undergoing a transformation that explicitly breaches the human/non-human divide. The term 'cyborg', which refers to human-animal or human-machine hybrids, has come to displace 'human' as the sign of this transformation. To ask whether robots have skin, then, is to ask about 'our' post-human nature and its embodiment as it is being re-imagined in technoscientific domains.

The term 'cyborg', short for cybernetic organism, signifies entities that combine human and non-human elements. As Donna Haraway (1991) has noted, cyborgs are the 'illegitimate offspring', of the military-industrial complex and its deadly projects. From this point of view, robots (as cyborgs) can be seen only to reproduce an existing technoscientific order of things in which old hierarchies of race, gender, class, sexuality and normalcy (to name only some of the dominant vectors of bodily differentiation) are simply re-embodied. But, as Haraway goes on to suggest, cyborgs can also be 'exceedingly unfaithful to their origins' (1991: 151). In their less conventional incarnations, cyborgs become particularly useful for re-theorising embodiment in feminist terms precisely because they provide alternative re-figurations of the body that do not simply rework old hierarchies of embodiment (Haraway 1991: 154). An unfaithful cyborg might well provide a powerful alternative form of embodiment, one that challenges the hierarchies of embodiment through which 'the human' – as well as some forms of the 'post-human' – have been constituted.

Cyborgs generated in and through technoscience clearly cannot simply be celebrated for their breaching of boundaries; boundary-crossing does not in itself constitute an effective politics, and can, in fact, enact violent erasures and re-embody longstanding forms of inequality, including those around issues of race, class, gender and sexuality (Ahmed 1998; Lowe 1996; Gonzalez 1995). Cyborgs must therefore be considered in terms of how and to what effect their boundary-crossing takes place. Indeed, thinking through the cyborg cannot simply entail the use of the generic category 'cyborg' or the concept of embodied boundary-crossing. Instead, cyborgs must be considered in terms of their particular material-semiotic embodiment (Haraway 1991). That is, they must be thought of in terms of how a particular body's matter and meaning work in and through each other: how the stuff of this body generates meanings, and how its meanings come to be materially embodied.

The cyborgs I want to consider here are created in the interdisciplinary field of artificial intelligence, or AI. Not all AI cyborgs have skins, or even bodies. These robots are interesting with regard to the skin because they are being created in more or less explicit relation to the human, and to human intelligence in particular. Traditionally the highest and most complex form of intelligence known to science, human intelligence, constitutes the limit beyond or around which AI robots are designed, built and evaluated. As it turns out, these robots do have skins. But by the very fact of not being (strictly) human, robotic skin makes it both possible and necessary to ask questions of the body and its boundaries that do not assume their 'nature', in every sense of the word. If the skin is a bodily envelope that constitutes the material limits of the human body, for example, what is the cyborg skin? Rather than assuming the skin as a bodily border or limit, I want to ask instead how robot bodies are made, and made to cohere as bodies. Cyborg skin becomes important here as part of a material-semiotic body whose limits and borders must be investigated rather than assumed. What, then, is the difference between human and cyborg skin? If 'we' (former humans) are already cyborgs, then how might a focus on skin enable both the difference between cyborgs, and the nature of their encounter, to be thought?

AI embodiments

The term 'AI' covers a number of approaches to the problem of intelligence and 'life' that coincide in their vision of a future in which the boundary between the natural and the artificial ceases to hold any power or meaning (Hayles 1996: 157). This multiplicity of approaches is paralleled by AI's cross-disciplinary borrowings, from psychology, to neurology, engineering and computing. Beyond these basic commonalities, however, AI projects do not share any single perspective on the means or aims of their work. Most importantly, they disagree on what counts as an intelligent life form. AI imaginings are consequently materialised in a variety of ways, including computer-based virtual worlds and simulations, as well as robot prototypes. In some cases, text on a screen is considered sufficient evidence of intelligent life when, for example, it can exhibit the capacity to evolve. In other cases, intelligence takes the form of language, also displayed as text on a screen, or as shapes (circles, triangles and so on) that 'eat', 'reproduce', 'compete', and 'die', These forms, together with the specific capacities they are seen to exhibit, are the materialisation of different commitments to embodiment as a feature or aspect of intelligence.

AI projects can be divided into two main categories with regard to embodiment. Two-dimensional forms projected on a computer screen constitute a different kind of embodied intelligence than do three-dimensional life forms (robots). Squares and circles interacting on a computer screen, for example, are constituted in part through the boundary that is established between the computer screen and the viewer. The squares and circles do not have the capacity to move in the world on this side of the screen. The interface between 'us' and AI's bodies is restricted, furthermore, to this limited and limiting boundary.

Much more interesting and challenging for my discussion of cyborg skin and embodiment are the three-dimensional bodies invented in AI. Here robots, rather than computerised animations, play a central role. While robots do not behave as intelligently, by some standards, as two-dimensional intelligent life forms, AI researchers interested in three-dimensional embodiments offer a vision in which the not-yet intelligent robots of today may eventually participate effectively in 'our' everyday worlds as two-dimensional forms of AI embodiment cannot do. Two of the better known robots to emerge from AI are Hans Moravec's 'robot bush' and the Massachusetts Institute of Technology (MIT)'s 'Cog'. 'Robot bush' is Moravec's name for a robot design based on existing AI principles, while Cog is an actual robot first built in 1993. I consider these two robots here in terms of the embodied post-human futures that are imagined through them, and the differences their robotic skins might make to feminist theories of embodiment. In what ways, in other words, are these robotic bodies faithful cyborgs, and in what ways are they unfaithful? To what extent does their particular form of skin and its quality of touch suggest alternative forms of embodiment and relationality between bodies that might be useful for feminism as it seeks to challenge the making and remaking of embodied relations of inequality?

Hans Moravec is one of the most famous proponents of post-human AI futures. *Mind Children*, the first of three books written by Moravec for a non-specialist audience, includes in its futuristic speculations the idea for a robot that would not simply emulate humans but entirely replace them. Noting both the power and the limitations of human hands, Moravec invents his robot bush as an extraordinarily dexterous entity. He moves from a general account of the robot's capacities to an 'actual design', describing the robot's structure as a 'large branch that splits into four smaller ones, each half the scale' (Moravec 1988: 104). This branching and splitting extends to twenty levels, from an initial meter-long trunk that is ten centimeters in diameter. The aptly named 'bush' ends in a trillion tiny 'leaves' (Moravec 1988: 104). Each of the leaves is a millionth of a meter (a micron) long, with a diameter ten times as small. The robot's dexterity is enabled, in this design, not only by its myriad fine and jointed branchings, but also through their movement. Not only are the leaves tiny, but they are also quick, able to vibrate at a million times per second. The joints also make the bush almost infinitely flexible, able to fold itself up in various ways to provide strength and stability, to unfold itself for more intricate tasks, and even to fragment into a 'co-ordinated swarm of smaller bushes' for still other purposes (Moravec 1988: 104).

While Moravec makes little mention of other kinds of bodily features, touch emerges as the robot bush's most important sensing mode, where skin is its critical medium. In order to understand Moravec's materialisation of robotic touch *in and through skin*, it is important to know about the sensing mechanisms that have been imported into AI from industrial robotics. Since at least the 1980s, industry has commissioned the design of robotic devices, mostly arm- and hand-like computerised machines, to execute specific repetitive tasks that involve the grasping and manipulation of objects. Questions of 'skin' and 'touch' as part of robotic tactility appear in the relevant literature on tactile sensors. Tactile sensors are devices attached in various ways to robotic grippers, to aid in the grasping and manipulation of objects. These sensors are specifically designed to calibrate accurately the force of the robotic device's grasp so that, for example, the machine uses enough force to pick up and move an object without crushing it in the process (Pugh 1986). As compared to simple gripping, tactile sensing involves detecting force at different points simultaneously, and changes in force across time. This way of conceptualising touch is derived from scientific understandings of the skin. One research team describes the resulting metonymic relation between tactile sensors and human skin as follows: 'tactile sensing can . . . be considered as an approximation to skin-like properties since areas of force-sensitive surfaces are capable of generating continuous signals as well as parallel touching' (Jayawant *et al.* 1986: 199). This skin-likeness is obtained not only at the level of function (skin-like properties), but also at the level of materiality (force-sensitive surfaces). In fact, function (tactility) and materiality are inextricably linked in this understanding of touch, so that sensing requires a skin-like materiality to enable a skin-like quality of touch. Furthermore, materiality has become inextricably linked to tactility in industrial robotic bodies, such that an adequate sense of touch has come to be a requirement for efficient manipulation in industrial assembly (see, for example, Checinski and Agrawal 1986).

In designing his robot, Moravec uses this basic understanding of sensors. While he does not refer to skin or skin-like qualities directly, his description of the robot's capabilities for touch suggest an implicit acceptance of the need for skin-like qualities that is built into industrial sensors. In contrast to its industrial counterparts, however, the robot bush (and robotic AI more generally) requires more from touch than the capacity to carry out specific, narrowly defined tasks. Moravec endows his robot with sensors; but as part of the robot bush's elaborate physical structure they enable a qualitatively different kind of touch as compared to either humans or industrial robots. As Moravec puts it:

> If each joint can measure the forces and motions applied to it, we have a remarkable sensor. There are a trillion leaf fingers, each able to sense a movement of perhaps a tenth of a micron and a force of a few micrograms, at speeds up to a million changes per second.
>
> (Moravec 1988: 104–5)

Like industrial robots, the robot bush touches by detecting changes in force over space and time. But the robot bush's distinctive and extraordinary capacity lies in the numbers of joints available for sensing and the speed and precision with which its body accomplishes it.

Moravec makes the comparison between the human and the robot explicit when he notes that a human eye has vastly less sensory capacity than even one leaf finger (1988: 105). In fact, as a form of vision, touch is one of the robot's distinctively superior features as compared to the human. In addition to feeling the world through touch, the robot bush would also 'see' through touch. Moravec describes how this could be possible in vivid detail:

> If our bush puts its fingers on a photograph, it will 'see' the image in immense detail simply by feeling the height variations of the developed silver on the paper. It could watch a movie by walking its fingers along the film as it screened by at high speed.
>
> (Moravec 1988: 105)

Whatever else can be said about the limits of this scenario, it fundamentally alters what it might mean for us to 'see', both physically and phenomenologically. Vision, here, becomes a matter of contact between the robotic fingers and a visual medium, such as photographic or cinematic film. In transferring the medium of vision from the eye to the robot bush's sensitive fingers, Moravec re-materialises vision as well as touch.

In addition to 'feeling' images, the robot fingers could 'be sensitive to light and temperature' as well as 'other electromagnetic effects' (Moravec 1988: 105). Moving further away from the sensation of touch in the form of direct contact between the robot's body and an object, Moravec suggests that the fingers could 'see' not just by feeling, but by becoming a kind of eye:

> The bush could form an eye by holding up a lens and putting up a few million of its fingers in the focal plane behind it. It may even be able to get by without the lens by holding a bunch of its fingers in a carefully spaced diffraction pattern, thus forming a holographic lens.
>
> (Moravec 1988: 105)

In the first part of this description, the fingers become like a retina, which registers the light as it passes through the human eye's lens. In the second part, the fingers themselves form a lens that, unlike the human lens, produces holographic images. In fact, this rather fantastically imagined robot's touch would be so powerful, Moravec concludes, that its 'superior touch sense' would 'totally substitute for vision' (1988: 105).

Significantly, the robot's visual sensing capacity comes into being only through the technological re-materialisation of the (human) body into a superhuman form. This re-materialisation is significant with regard to the human/non-human boundary, not only because of its links with technology and artifice, but because the robot bush is more than just a prototype for some arbitrary additional life form. For Moravec, AI is nothing less than the next evolutionary step for humanity, a kind of leap beyond biology into a post-human future.

In this future, humans will have out-designed themselves and their kind, to be succeeded by their own creations. Human bodies will necessarily become extinct through this process, in Moravec's vision. However, he also imagines that a robot with extraordinary touching capabilities could be enlisted to 'download' human minds into robotic bodies. Moravec's scenario for this process begins with a robot surgeon touching a patient's exposed brain in its anaesthetised skull. Together with the still-conscious patient, the robot examines a simulated version of the person gleaned from the brain and 'downloaded' into a robotic body. Once the simulated test has been checked for accuracy, the surgeon extracts the necessary information from successive layers of brain tissue for transfer, excising cell layers one after the other. As the surgeon evacuates the skull of its contents, the mind is transferred from the human brain's now superfluous cells to the computerised robot. Again, Moravec describes this transformation in vivid detail, relying in part on his interpellation of 'you', the reader:

> Eventually your skull is empty, and the surgeon's hand rests deep in your brainstem . . . In a final, disorienting step the surgeon lifts out his hand. Your suddenly abandoned body goes into spasm and dies.
>
> (Moravec 1988: 148)

In this passage, Moravec directly addresses the reader as the subject of the robot's operation. The active agent of transformation is not the reader, however, but the surgeon's hand, whose powerful touch maintains consciousness, life and death. So, while the robot surgeon maintains its existence in embodied form throughout, the human is subject to a series of transformations. It moves from embodied consciousness through embodiment without consciousness to disembodiment. And the human is positioned in such a way that it is possible to watch the 'abandoned' body die from a detached distance.

It is not too difficult to see that this scenario's intelligibility depends on mind–body dualism. Only in this way would it be possible to retain a mind while discarding the brain bit by bit. The 'self' is materialised here only as data residing in, but not dependent on, brain cells. This fully informatic notion of the person simultaneously makes it possible for the split between mind and body to be temporary, for the mind to be re-embodied. And it is the surgeon's touch, ironically, which re-materialises the self in its new robotic body.

Moravec continues his account with a vivid description of the self's transformation, all the more compelling because he identifies this self with the reader, 'you':

> For a moment you experience quiet and dark. Then, once again, you can open your eyes. Your perspective has shifted. The computer simulation has been disconnected from the cable leading to the surgeon's hand and recon-

nected to a shiny new body of the style, material and color of your choice. Your metamorphosis is complete.

(Moravec 1988: 148)

The feel of the surgeon's hand in the brain, as well as 'our' shift in perspective, is unmistakably sensual in these passages, which invite us to experience this transformative re-embodiment along with Moravec. For me, the power of this description suggests not only a fascination with technology itself, but also a desire and even longing for this kind of technological re-embodiment. It is as if the perspectival shift Moravec imagines could only be accomplished through such a fantastically complex technological means.

I will return to this questionable identification with technology and invention later on. For now it is important to note that in the act of locating touch at the centre of his transformative vision, Moravec also neatly solves the messy problem of human mortality (Hayles 1996) by implicitly linking a new, vastly more complex and elaborate sense of touch to a yearning for the post-human as an alternative to the limits of human life and death. The surgeon's touch becomes the agent of the post-human transformations that enables this escape. So, the robot-as-surgeon itself materialises a repudiation of the human body (or even a prior cyborg one) in favor of a newer, more powerful model made in its own image: the robot is a materialised form of this repudiation. This robot simultaneously materialises a hierarchy in which the human is located below the robot in a narrative of progressive embodiment. At the same time, there is no effective difference between the human as an 'imaginary morphology' (Butler 1993) and the cyborg. Both establish a hierarchy of embodiment that simultaneously requires and forgets its 'others'.

While the robot bush poses numerous problems as a resource for a feminist theory of embodiment, I am still compelled by its suggestiveness. Moravec's imagined robot bush can touch molecules and is capable of feeling, not just millions of parts of a machine, but also the relations between them. What would it be like to touch the visual in the way the robot bush can, feeling the image of the still photograph or sensing the moving image of film as it speeds past one's touch? The robot bush is an effective cyborg in so far as it challenges the separation of human from non-human, and does so *through* its specifically *sensory* embodiment. Furthermore, this robot suggests the lack of any absolute distinction between vision and touch, which in turn troubles the very ground of objectivity, again *in* and *through* embodied touch. That is, it refuses any strict distinction between distanced (objective) vision and the subjective, embodied contact.

A closer look at the enduring associations between vision and objectivity suggests more precisely why the robot bush might be useful for re-theorising embodiment. In a critique of the assumed isomorphism of vision and objectivity that draws in part on Merleau-Ponty, Cathryn Vasseleu (1998) argues that vision acts as the ground of objectivity only when it is assumed to establish a relation of distance between subject and object. It is possible, therefore, to think vision in different terms, specifically as a form of touch.

Touch, for Vasseleu, is not contingent on direct contact between the body – the skin – and an object. Instead, she understands the body as an entity that actively experiences the world, such that experience is always embodied, and the nature of touch is constituted through the encounter between the body and the world. From this perspective, touch is a relational *quality* that arises out of embodied inter-action. Touch constitutes an experience of the world that cannot be detached from its embodiment, but is also not reducible to the body itself.

Vasseleu extends this notion of touch to the eye in elaborating an alternative theory of vision, in which vision is not always already structured as a particular relation in advance of an encounter. Instead, the nature of the relation between the seer and the seen establish the nature of vision. For Vasseleu, then, vision can entail an embodied interaction with the world, rather than necessarily taking the form of an objectifying gaze.

Moravec's robot-surgeon is a literal embodiment of Vasseleu's theory, in the sense that the robot re-materialises vision as touch in a variety of ways. While Vasseleu herself rejects materiality as a necessary feature of her theoretical re-formulation, materiality may be essential to any sufficiently effective feminist reformulation of embodied interaction. Is it enough, in other words, to re-formulate vision in experiential terms without re-formulating the material stuff, the body, through which that vision is experienced? If so, how should the body and its skin be re-thought? If not, what is the relationship between the materiality of touch and its relational quality? How, in other words, might the skin come to matter in cyborg worlds?

Skinning touch

The MIT media lab's 'Cog' robot offers some additional resources for addressing these questions. Short for 'cognition', Cog was generated out of a different approach to robotic AI from Moravec's. For Cog's makers, the goal is to create a kind of intelligence that does not depend on consciousness in the sense of self-presence or internal mental states, but rather on a kind of interactive capacity. As Daniel Dennett, a member of Cog's team of builders, has put it:

> The aim of this project is not to make a conscious robot, but to make a robot that can interact with human beings in a robust and versatile manner in real time, take care of itself, and tell its designers things about itself that would otherwise be extremely difficult if not impossible to determine by examination.
>
> (Dennett 1994: 146)

Attempting to put aside the problem of making 'a robot that is conscious in just the way human beings are', Dennett and his team ask what kind of intelligence can be produced in robotic form. They set about in a trial-and-error process of designing and building Cog that involves various kinds of 'compromise', such as eyes with off-centre foveas (Dennett 1994: 139). In spite of their difference from centered human foveas, the team concludes, this model should still endow the robot with good-enough visual capacity to accomplish complex tasks.

Clearly, human likeness remains a point of comparison and departure for this project. In fact, Cog is more akin in some ways to a human body than is the robot bush. It has a head, eyes, arms and a torso (legs are part of its future design at this writing). Cog is also designed to undergo a developmental period of experiential and embodied learning. Given that development is a progressive and linear form of change through which the human has been constituted (Castañeda 1996), Dennett's description of Cog's design process as an 'extended period of artificial infancy' reinforces the importance of human likeness as a benchmark for the project. Making the comparison between Cog and the human explicit, Dennett describes the robot in its initial developmental phase:

> Like a human infant, [Cog] will need a great deal of protection at the outset, in spite of the fact that it will be equipped with many of the most crucial safety-systems of a living being. It has limit switches, heat sensors, current sensors, strain gauges, and alarm signals in all the right places to prevent it from destroying its many motors and joints.
>
> (Dennett 1994: 146)

While Cog appears to resemble the robot bush in its use of sensors, the comparison between Cog and its human counterpart is more explicitly linked to the skin, in that a skin-like covering turns out to be the solution of choice for protecting the infantile robot. Despite being bolted to a stand at hip-level, this early version of Cog could suffer from injuries to its especially large 'funny bones', as 'motors stick out from its elbows in a risky way'. Not surprisingly, from this point of view, skin and touch turn out to play a central role in this process of artificial development. Rather than resorting to 'heavy armour', Cog's team propose that the robot will be endowed with 'patches of exquisitely sensitive piezo-electric membrane "skin"'. Like its many sensors (described above), this skin will act as a warning device, 'trigger[ing] alarms when they make contact with anything' (Dennett 1994: 139).

A piezo-electric membrane is made of a crystalline substance that converts applied pressure into an electric charge. As described above, the piezo-electric membrane would emit an electric charge when 'touched' (where touch equals pressure) that would in turn be interpreted by the computer program running Cog. The reduction of 'skin' to an alarm system here should be temporary, its creators suggest, since Cog is supposed to learn how to protect its funny bones from any harmful contact. But the piezo-electric membrane will also serve as a more versatile material, providing sensitivity to different parts of the body including fingertips. Its 'exquisite' sensitivity here will enable it to feel everything from 'a gentle touch' to 'sharp pain' (Dennett, 1994: 139).

But, like the robot bush, Cog relies on industrial robotics and its borrowings. Dennett and his team use neurophysiological understandings of touch, also used in industrial robotics, to generate Cog's. In its neurophysiological guise, touch is divided into three main components: pain, temperature and pressure. According to this system, touch is reducible to pressure, for example, in the form of a single unit that varies in intensity but not in kind. The resulting variation in pressure is one critical aspect of the sensation neurophysiologists call touch.

As Dennett, notes, this version of touch can be represented as an 'information packet' such that variations in touch are quantitatively rather than qualitatively different from one another (1994: 140). In organic bodies, tactile nerves generate the different quantities of information, according to the neurophysiological view. The central nervous system then integrates them and interprets them as different kinds of touch. In a parallel system, Cog's piezo-electric 'skin' will send signals through wires to the central control system, which in turn interprets the signals in the form of sensation or touch (Dennett 1994: 139). Thus, Cog's capacity for touch is human-like in so far as human touch is already scientifically defined as an information packet travelling through a circuit.

Cog's sense of touch, and its materiality, or 'skin', is not imagined in exactly the same way as the robot bush's. It does not have the robot bush's extraordinary dexterity, nor its extended tactile sensitivity that includes visual capacities in its repertoire. But Cog's design may have even more potential for redefining embodied touch, because Cog is not imagined as a static information-processing system. Instead, Cog is designed as a changeable system, so that the robot 'is itself infinitely revisable'. The agent of change, furthermore, can be either 'Cog's own experience' or 'the tinkering of Cog's artificers' (Dennett 1994: 140). So while Cog's skin and its capacity for touch might be rather limited in its early incarnations, the robot's embodiment – including its skin – is designed to change in response to its interactions with the world. Cog's skin might remain a kind of alarm system that protects the body from harm as a result of these interactions, but it might also be entirely redesigned and re-materialised in ways that have yet to be determined. So it is the particular relationship that Cog and its environment (including the design team) generate between them that will in turn generate subsequent versions of Cog. The material requirements of Cog's touch, and the kind of skin that its touch requires, will be generated by way of this relation as well.

Conceptualised from the outset as neither human nor anti-human, but other-than-human, Cog is already an alternative kind of body. As the embodied effect of a relation between an entity and its environment, Cog has been imagined outside an economy of the same. That is, this robotic body is designed to regenerate itself in forms that are potentially quite different from any we know at present. Through its changeable design, this robotic body has the capacity to become a body generated in and through alterity. That is, Cog does not necessarily reproduce itself, but may instead produce new versions of the body. At its best, Cog's design offers the possibility that bodies might not be reproductions that inhabit the single category 'human', but are rather always already forms of embodiment generated in and through their alterity.

The future of touch: feminist robotics?

Neither Cog nor the robot bush is unproblematic, however, in its conceptualisation or materialisation. Ultimately, the limit for both robots lies in the imperative of functionality through which their 'skins' and corresponding 'touch' have been designed and generated. To the extent that the robots' functionality is *in* their skins and the quality of their touch, neither can escape this limit.

Still, the robots' cyborg embodiment is also compellingly suggestive, particularly the embodiment of touch as a way of experiencing in the world. Rather than being grounded in the flesh of human embodiment, these robots' touch is generated through a different combination of materials and qualities: leaf fingers, myriad joints, sensors, exquisite sensitivity, visual touch, piezo-electric membranes, changeability. This robotic re-embodiment of touch suggests that bodies must indeed be both material and semiotic, but that they do not need to conform to the 'imaginary morphology' (Butler 1993) of the human, with all the internal hierarchies and absolute differentiation from the non-human this entails.

Merleau-Ponty's phenomenological understanding of bodily sensation can be useful here, because it insists on the imbrication of the body and the world in perception. For Merleau-Ponty, the nature of perception is constituted through the sensory apparatus (hearing, touch, vision) of the body and the particular way each sensory apparatus apprehends the world. Writing about vision and touch in particular, Merleau-Ponty uses the example of patients whose sight has been restored through cataract removal to describe this intimate relation:

> The blind man's world differs from the normal person's not only through the quantity of material at his disposal, but through the *structure* of the whole. A blind man knows quite precisely through his sense of touch what branches and leaves, or an arm and fingers, are. After the operation he marvels that there should be 'such a difference' between a tree and a human body. It is clear that sight has not only added fresh details to his knowledge of the tree. What we are dealing with is a mode of presentation and a type of synthesis which are new and which transfigure the object.
>
> (Merleau-Ponty 1996/1962: 224; emphasis in original)

It is not necessary to repeat Merleau-Ponty's reproduction of the normal and the pathological to take up the idea that particular bodily materialities are constitutive of particular experiences and knowledges of the world. Thus, a body with the sensory capacity for vision and touch knows the world differently from one that has the sensory capacity for touch without vision. As Merleau-Ponty carefully points out, it is not that the latter person has no sense of space, but rather that this person's sense of space is tactile rather than tactile *and* visual. So too, the nature of a formerly blind person's sense of touch is fundamentally altered with the acquisition of vision. Specific differences in bodily materiality render equally specific capacities for experiencing and knowing the world. Differently

materialised bodies must also therefore experience the 'same' object or phenomenon differently.

From this point of view, touch cannot be understood in general abstract
terms. Instead, it must be conceptualised as the site of possible encounters
between bodies and worlds, in which the quality of the encounter is established
through the material-semiotic nature of the body in relation to the touch of one
body against or with another entity. Touch does not have to involve direct physical contact, in this formulation, but it does require some form of embodiment,
or 'skin'. This skin cannot be a border in the abstract sense, nor is it automatically a site of communication or mutuality. Instead, the skin becomes a site of
possibility in which the nature of the encounter is established through the process of 'touching', one body *in relation* to another. The quality of the encounter,
its 'feeling', is not established by the toucher or the touched alone, and so cannot be judged in these terms. One body's pleasure cannot exist in the face of
another's experience of violation, and pleasure in the encounter is in no way
guaranteed.

To imagine the skin as a site of possible embodied encounters is not only to
imagine the inequality and potential violence of such encounters. Cog and the
robot bush do not help much in going beyond this point, as both embody unequal
encounters. For example, Cog may undergo transformative bodily changes, but
the research team does not; they 'tinker' with Cog, but Cog does not tinker with
them. Conversely, the robot-as-surgeon consumes its creator's consciousness
through touch, but the process of re-embodiment is based on a repudiation of
human embodiment as inferior.

Missing from both scenarios is the possibility of mutual pleasure *in* the particular material-semiotic embodiments that constitute encounters, a pleasure that is
precisely not about fetishising, consuming or 'eating' the other (hooks 1992).
Instead, it is about a quality of touch that in the act of 'feeling' the other's
particularity, establishes a relation in and through alterity. This relation cannot be
reduced either to sameness or to the free-floating play of difference. Understood
as the medium of embodied encounters, the skin does not guarantee such relations, but grounds their possibility in and through bodies configured in terms of
alterity.

Of course, such imaginings are projections of what we can imagine as possibilities from the present. But I have used robots as cyborg embodiments that offer
a point of departure different from the human in suggestive ways, not because
they alone make an alternative, not-human conception of the body and its skin
possible. Cyborgs do not render the human obsolete, as Halberstam and Livingston have noted, but rather 'participate in re-distributions of difference and
identity' (1995: 10). In fact, the reference to human *likeness* in both robots suggests
an ongoing negotiation with the human in which the skin, as well as other aspects
of the body, remain both human and not human. Paraphrasing Sara Ahmed's
critique of hybridity in a different context, I would argue that the cyborg's hybridity undoes the human/not-human binary, but it can also recuperate the human as
an origin and truth against which the robot's value is always measured (1999:

96–8). In addition to using AI robots as resources for rethinking the skin in terms of an encounter, it can be useful to rethink the body and its skin through more traditionally recognisable 'human' bodies as well.

The notion of the skin as both a materiality and the site of relationality makes it possible, finally, to describe bodies more generally outside of the 'human' and its hierarchies of difference – race, class, sexuality, age, and so on. The fact that these hierarchies are established in and through bodies suggests the necessity of such a project. Cog and the robot bush provide a notion of the other-than-human, and the possibility of touch imagined in different terms. As I have argued, this possibility is not lodged in the robots themselves, but rather in the potential relationality that becomes evident through their different and very particular embodiment. The difference between the 'human' and embodied alterity is not the difference between fleshy skin and piezo-electric membranes, or between organic and hybrid bodies. Rather, it is the notion of touch as the relation between materialities (skins) that enables embodied alterity. The resulting bodies are other-than-human *and* other-than-cyborg in and through their skins.

References

Ahmed, S. (1998) *Differences that Matter: Feminist Theory and Postmodernism*, Cambridge: Cambridge University Press.

—— (1999) '"She'll Wake up One of These Days and Find She's Turned into a Nigger": Passing Through Hybridity' *Theory, Culture and Society* 16, 2: 87–106.

Butler, J. (1993) *Bodies that Matter: On the Discursive Limits of 'Sex'*, New York: Routledge.

Castañeda, C. (1996) 'Worlds in the Making: The Child-Body in the Production of Difference', Ph.D. Dissertation, University of California at Santa Cruz.

Checinksi, S. S. and Agrawal, A. K. (1986) 'Magnetoelastic Tactile Sensors' in R. Pugh (ed.) *Robot Sensors*, Vol. 2, Bedford: IFS (Publications).

Dennett, D. (1994) 'The Practical Requirements for Making a Conscious Robot', *Philosophical Transactions of the Royal Society of London*, A 349: 133–46.

Duden, B. (1993) *Disembodying Women: Perspectives on Pregnancy and the Unborn*. Cambridge, MA: Harvard University Press.

Gonzalez, J. (1995) 'Envisioning Cyborg Bodies: Notes from Current Research' in C. H. Gray, S. Mentor and H. J. Figueroa-Sarriera (eds) *The Cyborg Handbook*, New York: Routledge.

Halberstam, J. and Livingston, I. (eds) (1995) *Posthuman Bodies*, Indianapolis: University of Indiana Press.

Haraway, D. (1991) *Simians, Cyborgs, and Women: The Reinvention of Nature*, New York: Routledge.

Hayles, K. N. (1996) 'Narratives of Artificial Life' in G. Robertson, M. Mash, L. Tickner, J. Bird (eds.) *FutureNatural: Nature, Science, Culture*, New York: Routledge.

Helmreich, S. (1998) *Silicon Second Nature*, Berkeley: University of California Press.

hooks, b. (1992) *Black Looks: Race and Representation*, Boston, MA.: South End Press.

Jayawant, B. V., Onori, M. A. and McWatson, J. D. (1986) 'Robot Tactile Sensing: A New Array Sensor' in R. Pugh (ed.) *Robot Sensors*, Bedford: IFS (Publications).

Lowe, L. (1996) *Immigrant Acts: On Asian American Cultural Politics*, Durham, NC: Duke University Press.

Martin, E. (1995) *Flexible Bodies: Tracking Immunity in American Culture from the Days of Polio to the Age of AIDS*, Boston, MA: Beacon Press.

Merleau-Ponty, M. (1996/1962) *Phenomenology of Perception*, trans. C. Smith, New York: Routledge.

Moravec, H. (1988) *Mind Children*, Cambridge, MA.: Harvard University Press.

Pugh, A. (1986) *Robot Sensors*, vol. 2. Bedford: IFS Publications Ltd.

Vasseleu, C. (1998) *Textures of Light: Vision and Touch in Irigaray, Levinas, and Merleau-Ponty*, New York: Routledge.

Index